The Indian Foreign Policy Bureaucracy

Westview Replica Editions

The concept of Westview Replica Editions is a response to the continuing crisis in academic and informational publishing. Library budgets for books have been severely curtailed. Ever larger portions of general library budgets are being diverted from the purchase of books and used for data banks, computers, micromedia, and other methods of information retrieval. Interlibrary loan structures further reduce the edition sizes required to satisfy the needs of the scholarly community. Economic pressures on the university presses and the few private scholarly publishing companies have severely limited the capacity of the industry to properly serve the academic and research communities. As a result, many manuscripts dealing with important subjects, often representing the highest level of scholarship, are no longer economically viable publishing projects--or, if accepted for publication, are typically subject to lead times ranging from one to three years.

Westview Replica Editions are our practical solution to the problem. We accept a manuscript in camera-ready form, typed according to our specifications, and move it immediately into the production process. As always, the selection criteria include the importance of the subject, the work's contribution to scholarship, and its insight, originality of thought, and excellence of exposition. The responsibility for editing and proofreading lies with the author or sponsoring institution. We prepare chapter headings and display pages, file for copyright, and obtain Library of Congress Cataloging in Publication Data. A detailed manual contains simple instructions for preparing the final typescript, and our editorial staff is always available to answer questions.

The end result is a book printed on acid-free paper and bound in sturdy library-quality soft covers. We manufacture these books ourselves using equipment that does not require a lengthy make-ready process and that allows us to publish first editions of 300 to 600 copies and to reprint even smaller quantities as needed. Thus, we can produce Replica Editions quickly and can keep even very specialized books in print as long as there is a demand for them.

About the Book and Author

In this book, Jeffrey Benner traces the history of the Indian foreign policy bureaucracy from the British period to the present, focusing on the bureaucracy's role in shaping policy. Because the bureaucracy has become an active agent in the policy process, its implementation of policy has often differed significantly from the original policy formulated by top leadership. The book includes a description of the foreign service cadre and a systematic breakdown of the functional and administrative structure of the Ministry of External Affairs, as well as the larger bureaucracy.

Jeffrey Benner is a Ph.D. candidate in political science at the University of Chicago.

To
my mother and father
for their love and support

The Indian Foreign Policy Bureaucracy

Jeffrey Benner

Westview Press / Boulder and London

A Westview Replica Edition

All rights reserved. No part of this publication may be reproduced or transmitted in any form or by any means, electronic or mechanical, including photocopy, recording, or any information storage and retrieval system, without permission in writing from the publisher.

Copyright © 1985 by Westview Press, Inc.

Published in 1985 in the United States of America by Westview Press, Inc., 5500 Central Avenue, Boulder, Colorado 80301; Frederick A. Praeger, Publisher

Library of Congress Cataloging in Publication Data
Benner, Jeffrey.
   The Indian foreign policy bureaucracy.
   (Westview replica edition)
   1. India--Diplomatic and consular service. 2. India--Foreign relations administration. I. Title. II. Series.
JX1840.B46 1985   354.540089   84-19569
ISBN 0-86531-875-1

Printed and bound in the United States of America

10 9 8 7 6 5 4 3 2 1

Contents

List of Tables xi
Preface xiii

Chapter I: FOREIGN POLICY BUREAUCRATIC ANALYSIS . . 1

Chapter II: THE BRITISH INDIAN FOREIGN POLICY
              BUREAUCRACY 9

  SEVENTEENTH AND EARLY EIGHTEENTH CENTURIES . . . 9
  AFTER 1763 11
  THE NINETEENTH CENTURY 16
  THE TWENTIETH CENTURY 20
  AFTER 1940 30
  INDEPENDENCE 34
  THE BRITISH AGENT 36
  THE FOREIGN AND POLITICAL SERVICE 37
      Service Composition 37
      Indianization 39

Chapter III: THE INDIAN FOREIGN SERVICE 43

  THE SEED CADRE 45
  CONTEMPORARY SERVICE STRUCTURE 48
  TRAINING 52
  SOCIALIZATION 55
  RECRUITMENT, INDUCTION, PROMOTION 57
  DISSENT 60

Chapter IV: THE PROCEDURAL HIERARCHY 62

  QUASI-CENTRAL EXECUTIVE 65
      The Prime Minister 66
      The Independent Foreign Minister 67
      The Minister of State 74
      The Deputy Minister 75
      The Junior Minister 76
  OPERATIONAL BUREAUCRATIC LEADERSHIP 77
      The Secretary 77
      The Additional Secretary 89
      The Joint Secretary 90
      Junior Officers 93
  PROCEDURAL "THEORY" 94

Chapter V: BASIC ADMINISTRATION 96

    ADMINISTRATIVE METHOD 108
    THE PILLAI COMMITTEE 112
    COMMUNITY COORDINATION 114

Chapter VI: RESEARCH, INTELLIGENCE AND THE
            FOREIGN POLICY BUREAUCRACY 120

    RESEARCH AFTER NEHRU 124
    RESEARCH AFTER 1971 130
    RESEARCH: 1982 134
    CADRE AND ACADEMIA 138
    INTELLIGENCE AND INDIAN FOREIGN POLICY 141
        Military Intelligence 144
        The Cabinet Bodies 147
        Community Fission 149

Chapter VII: ECONOMIC AND POLITICAL-MILITARY
             POLICIES 153

    POLITICAL-MILITARY POLICY 158

Chapter VIII: PARTICIPATION IN INTERNATIONAL
              ORGANIZATIONS 163

    INTERNATIONAL LAW 166

Chapter IX: INTERNATIONAL AND DOMESTIC SERVICES . 167

    INFORMATIONAL SERVICES 167
    PUBLIC RELATIONS 175
    CULTURAL RELATIONS 176
    PROTOCOL 181
    CONSULAR, PASSPORT AND VISA DIVISION 183

Chapter X: MODERN LEADERSHIP AND THE BUREAUCRACY . 185

    NEHRU AND THE BUREAUCRACY 185
    AFTER NEHRU 204
    JANATA AND THE BUREAUCRACY 213
    AFTER JANATA 216

Appendix A: NEO-REDUCTIONISM 221

List of Abbreviations	227
Bibliography	229
Index	281

Tables

2.1	Foreign Department staffing: 1861-1905	21
2.2	Duty allocation: 1905	22
2.3	Branches of Foreign Department: 1905-28	41
2.4	Foreign and Political Department officers: 1919-35	42
3.1	IFS: the first eighteen years	46
3.2	Combined cadre strength: 1981-82	50
3.3	Distribution of IFS officers according to parent's profession: 1966	57
4.1	MEA administrative hierarchy	64
4.2	Hierarchy composition: 1952-55	65
4.3	Secretarial jurisdiction: September 1982	86
4.4	Secretarial jurisdiction: 1951-55	87
4.5	Additional secretarial jurisdiction: September 1982	88
4.6	Joint secretarial jurisdiction: 1953-54	89
5.1	MEA divisions: 1955	103
5.2	MEA divisions: 1970	104
5.3	MEA divisions: 1982	105
5.4	Expansion in headquarters staffing: 1948-66	106
5.5	Total staff strength: 1957, 1969	106
5.6	MEA revenue expenditures: 1981-82	107

5.7	Indian foreign policy community	113
6.1	Functional divisions: 1963	121
6.2	PPRC membership	127
6.3	PPRD structure: 1982	135
6.4	Indian intelligence community	143
6.5	JIC, JIC Steering Committee membership	144
9.1	ICCR structure	180
10.1	Regional Indian diplomatic representation	219
10.2	A chronology of political control	220

Preface

This study is one of the administration of Indian foreign policy, but it is something more than that. I have suggested in various places that an analysis of bureaucratic functions can shed some light on Indian foreign policy. However, my early intention to make this chiefly a study of the causality between bureaucratic politics and foreign policy seems now a little ambitious, and so the study as the reader finds it has been scaled down considerably. I hope that the reader forgives me both for not attaining those earlier goals, and for letting the old ambitions remain in several places in the text. This is only a preliminary study, and will be followed by a much more comprehensive treatment of the topic to be published in mid-1988. Then I hope to shift this discussion to a somewhat higher conceptual level, a necessary step if this sort of study is to become useful to the student of foreign policy and not just to the student of administration. This study is a complete revision of my Indian-published book, *Structure of Decision*.[1]

This study had many contributors, people who went to great troubles to help make this study work. This manuscript was supervised in various stages of its completion by Henry Hart, Bhabani Sen Gupta, and Bernard Cohen. Dr. Sen Gupta especially went far out of his way to help me in my research and the publication of an early draft of this book in India. He exerted a strong conceptual influence on the manuscript's evolution. Neil Richardson aided my research establishment in New Delhi. Joseph Elder gave me much encouragement in the pursuit of the topic and has helped me in the evolution of the final analytic product. Finally, Lloyd Rudolph assisted me in the history of the Office of the Prime Minister. In the final stages of this manuscript's production these men's assistance has helped turn an assemblage of facts and half-baked ideas into a readable, credible work.

When my research was under way another large group of scholars were with great benefit involved. Marcus Franda and his wife, Vonnie Franda, were indispensable

---

[1] Jeffrey Benner, *Structure of Decision: The Indian Foreign Policy Bureaucracy* (New Delhi: South Asian Publishers, 1984)

allies in breaking interview ground. I.J. Bahadur Singh, K.P. Misra, Bimal Prasad, Satish Kumar and S.D. Muni were all very helpful in explaining how different aspects of bureaucratic process contribute to final policy. Kuldeep Mathur helped me to locate some research materials that threw much light on the darker corners of the bureaucracy. K. Subrahmanyam consented to a very interesting interview on the subject of political-military coordination. Most of the information on the current bureaucratic environment presented in this study came from interviews with bureaucrats functioning in various positions both within the Ministry of External Affairs and elsewhere in Indian government. Their contribution to this manuscript is quite visible, but they are not mentioned by name to spare them any difficulties.

Others helped in various guises. N. Parameswaran Nair's PhD. dissertation is used heavily in the second chapter of this book, and his work has made much of the historical bent of this study possible. I was unable to contact Dr. Nair about his twenty-year-old research, and hope that he approves the wider propagation (presently only one copy of his work is known to exist) of parts of his very valuable work. J. Bandyopadhyaya and Shashi Tharoor were other scholars of great influence upon this study. Though I have been critical of some of their data and analysis, their excellent studies inspired this author and this book. I express my deep gratitude as well to the staffs of the Indian Council of World Affairs library, Jawaharlal Nehru University library, Benares Hindu University's Centre for the Study of Nepal and the University of Wisconsin's Memorial Library for their excellent research facilities. I also thank the University of Chicago's Computation Center for the use of their text editing and formatting **SUPERWYLBUR SCRIPT GML** facility. Despite the assistance of the above, errors in fact, of omission, or in interpretation are entirely the responsibility of the author.

My parents, David and Linda Benner, went along with me at every stage of the study's development without complaint (though they had ample cause at times for such). I can hardly begin to express my thanks to them for the help they rendered to me. My personal thanks go also to Rajender Lal Kuthiala and my friend R.C. of San Jose, the former a good friend and the latter an important inspirational support in this study.

Jeffrey Benner
Chicago, Illinois
October 1, 1984

I
Foreign Policy Bureaucratic Analysis

In the study of India's position in the world community we may look at a variety of objects to different benefit. Many such studies have been about the content of Indian foreign policy, or more precisely, of the position that the Indian government has taken on the many issues to have developed in post-World War II global politics. Of particular interest is the mechanical formulation of foreign policy. Equipped with such knowledge we may be able not only to better interpret Indian foreign policy but perhaps will be able to anticipate future shifts in policy, and to prescribe changes which may lead to improvements in the way policy is formed (once values are defined). Two possible approaches to the study of policy formulation lie in the study of policy flows or the chain of decision-making, and in the study of structures provided for policy formulation. The first is dynamic and the latter static, but together they would give us a very good idea of how policy is developed. The first dynamic approach would demand a specific, temporally-bounded (historically defined) inquiry into a foreign policy decision to lay bare its policy-making antecedents. Such studies, primarily of crisis decision-making, have been made of the 1962 Cuban missile crisis which transpired between the United States and the Soviet Union. Such studies have been conducted for India, but the area remains largely unexplored.[1]

---

[1] For studies of the missile crisis, see Graham T. Allison, *Essence of Decision* (Boston: Little, Brown and Company, 1971) or Elie Abel, *The Missile Crisis* (New York: Bantam, 1966). Two case studies of Indian decision-making are Ashok Kapur's *India's Nuclear Option: Atomic Diplomacy and Decision Making* (New York: Praeger Publishers, 1976), and Arun Kumar Banerji's "Role of the Diplomat in the Decision-Making Pro-

Also mostly unexplored is the static, structural context of Indian foreign policy formulation, the study of bureaucratic and central executive structures. This study is primarily one of the Indian foreign policy bureaucracy, not only of the Ministry of External Affairs but of the surrounding foreign policy "community." It is not primarily an administrative study, though I deal with some purely administrative topics in an effort to show areas in which the machinery works well and not so well. This study has a secondary purpose in outlining the relationship of the top leadership, the "central executive," to the lower career leadership. I also deal with the historical development of the bureaucracy and of the bureaucracy--central executive relationship.

This approach to the study of bureaucracy as a determinant in foreign policy has a privileged position within the larger science of international relations. International relations, the study of human society on the largest possible magnitude of organization, is generally subdivided into a number of smaller issue-areas for simplicity (as economics may be subdivided into micro- and macroeconomics). Different solutions to the "level of analysis problem" have been proposed on an ad hoc basis, subdividing international relations theory into two to five separate levels. I have moved from ad hoc typologies to the development of a jurisdictional methodology labeled "neo-reductionism" (see Appendix A). Within the context of neo-reductionism, bureaucratic influences are assumed to be dominant within certain classes of international relations behavior. Organizational studies are not new to social science, but the application of organizational research to foreign policy problems was initiated in the 1960s, roughly at the time of the Kennedy administration, to deal with the new Washington bureau labyrinth. As a neo-reductionist submethodology, the bureaucratic level-of-analysis was most junior and therefore methodologically least developed.

The importance of the bureaucratic level-of-analysis, though, is not disputed; it is just not known yet how important the bureaucratic level-of-analysis will be as part of the total analysis.[2] The initial

---

cess: Some Case Studies," *India Quarterly,* April-June 1979, pp. 207-22. The author suggests that a good subject for a future study would be one of the decision-making that led to the Indian policy stance on the 1979 invasion of Afghanistan by the Soviet Union.

[2] For a critical view, read Robert J. Art, "Bureaucratic Politics and American Foreign Policy: A

observation behind the bureaucratic level-of-analysis is that policy does not emerge like the Platonic Idea from a void, but comes about through the operation of processes which may not be entirely concerned with the formulation of policy. A bureaucrat, for example, is not just a government official but a man or woman with family responsibilities, who may be concerned for the sake of his or her family that taking a certain policy stance might jeopardize his career goals. He may then not take the position, even if it makes for "good" policy. In the political decision-making process distortions of various types, for a variety of reasons, may occur. The scientist using this level-of-analysis thinks not only of what the "good" policy may be, but imagines himself inside the bureaucracy and asks: what type of policy is likely to emerge, given these formulative conditions? It is plausible even without looking into actual events that errors of different kinds might occur in a large organization's production and implementation of policy, but there are many documented cases of bureaucratic "interference" in policy. For example, during the October 1962 missile crisis President Kennedy ordered a blockade of Cuba in such a way as to minimize the chances of a reckless Soviet response, but the actual blockade was carried out according to very inappropriate standard blockade procedures, simply because that was the way that the Navy had always done things.[3]

Several like examples can be drawn from recent Indian history. We begin with an issue in military planning, the purchase of Gnat aircraft. In the early 1950s India's need for a good fighter jet was acute. By way of finding a solution the British statesman Mountbatten recommended the purchase of the low-altitude Gnat fighter from Follands Company of Great Britain. Nehru and defence minister Vellodi both liked the Gnat's capability rating and recommended its deployment, as it was a much less expensive plane than anything else of its calibre on the market.[4] The Air Force, however, preferred the French Ouregon, due to the Ouregon's greater technical sophistication, and stalled for over a year and a half before Nehru finally was able to pressure the air force to accept the purchase.[5]

Critique," *Policy Sciences* 4 (1973), pp. 467-90.

[3] Abel, pp. 169-71.

[4] "Defence," of course, is King's English rather than the American spelling.

A second example of Indian bureaucratic politics lies in the clash between the External Publicity Division in the Ministry of External Affairs (MEA) and the related services of the Ministry of Information and Broadcasting. Immediately after 1947 a long quarrel had begun over who should represent Indian information abroad. Foreign service and information service officers would frequently not speak with each other in Indian missions abroad, and there was much duplication of efforts between the two bodies. A 1948 Cabinet decision on the quarrel was not carried out by either External Publicity Division or the Ministry of Information and Broadcasting (the Cabinet recommended bimonthly coordination meetings between the Secretaries of MEA and the Ministry of Information and Broadcasting. Contrary to this advice only two meetings were held 1948-58[6]). This is a picture not of a perfectly rational implementation of policy, but of a community with strong internal conflicts of interest; in short, a political bureaucracy. Bureaucratic politics can also be seen in the April 1965 decision by Shastri to create a Committee of Secretaries "for the coordination of political, economic, cultural, and other activities abroad." It was speculated that Shastri had created the Committee in an attempt to bypass the left-of-center MEA in formulating certain pro-Western policies, and this is certainly plausible, if not the only possibility. Obviously, the Indian bureaucracy does have an element of internal conflict, making a political approach necessary.

Possible evidence that the study of diplomatic and foreign policy organization may allow the prediction of international behavior may be found in the interest shown by some government bodies. O'Leary and Coplin report that of uses of political quantitative data by the Department of State's Bureau of Intelligence and Research (INR), "[n]umber of diplomats or diplomatic missions" is mentioned more than any other political data but "[t]roop and arms strength."[7] Though this is

---

[5] B.N. Mullik, *My Years With Nehru*: -16 (New Delhi: Allied Publishers, 1972), pp. 125-31. According to Mullik, Gnats were used very successfully in the October 1965 war with Pakistan, as well as in the 1971 Bangladeshi Indian air operations. In the 1971 war they beat the performance of the Soviet MiG-25s utilized by the Pakistanis.

[6] Werner Levi, "Foreign Policy: The Shastri Era," in K.P. Misra, ed., *Studies in Indian Foreign Policy* (New Delhi: Vikas, 1969), p. 194.

probably due in part to the familiarity of such data to State Department analysts rather than because of the usefulness of the information, strength of diplomatic representation has considerable conditional utility as an index of international relationships. It is a corollary of this observation that the secretariat of those embassies and representations abroad, the foreign policy bureaucracy, would be regarded by these analysts as an important source of information about the international relationship. If, for example, information from a particular nation or region is regarded as especially valuable, we would expect special care to be taken to ensure proper handling and analysis of the information. Perhaps we would find a larger proportion of senior analysts in the section of the bureaucracy in communication with the diplomatic representation of that region. We might thereby discover the value of an international relation to an elite through the study of the bureaucracy.

The organizational response to the international environment will differ by nation and by period. United States leadership has at different times vested confidence in the use of staffs, a special Assistant to the President, and in the Secretary of State in attempting to manage the bureaucracy. In Great Britain, leadership has handled the problem by the use of unofficial agents, by relying heavily on the Cabinet Office and through the frequent mergers of departments. In India, with its powerful Prime Ministership, its responsibilities and constraints as a developing nation and the strong legitimizing influence of foreign affairs for Indian leadership, we can expect a significantly different organization to develop, despite the British organizational precedent in South Asia.

How does it develop? It is a common myth held by administrators and students of administration that development occurs when the administrator grasps through a problem-solving process that a problem exists, and sets up a new or modifies an existing division to handle the problem. Then, the officers of the new division come in at ten, do their jobs, and go home at five. This myth treats any type of administration as a machine in which one feeds a certain input, and receives a measured output (political scientists of the

---

[7] Of all uses of quantitative data by the INR in the given sample, political, economic or social, "[n]umber of diplomats or diplomatic missions" ranked only fourth among twenty-two categories. Michael K. O'Leary, William D. Coplin, *Quantitative Techniques in Foreign Policy Analysis and Forecasting* (New York: Praeger, 1975), p. 6.

structuralist school may be said to treat national political life in a similar fashion). The national leadership needs only to crank the lever, and the government will faithfully do its duty. It is an organic view, treating the bureaucracy as an organism in which the various "cells" of the body work together in harmony by their very nature. Organizational malaise (dissent, inefficiency, corruption) is a rare aberration which can be quickly corrected by proper administration. It is not usually granted that organizational equilibria may be dysfunctional relative to leadership. The only internally completely cooperative subset of any social system, however, is the unit subset of the human being (and even here it is doubtful that internal tradeoffs resulting from internal conflict do not occur). Above the level of the individual, political, conflictual behavior to some extent determines outcomes rather than mechanistic, formally determinate systems. We need, therefore, to transcend the perspective that informal, political behavior is somehow countersystemic and illegitimate. Such behavior may in some cases not serve the interests of leadership, but this should not arrest research within such a nonnormative framework as the author assumes. It is equally true, though, that bureaucratic politics is frequently played out to the advantage of national political leadership.

For all this, we need not consider the bureaucracy a Hobbesian wonderland, but simply acknowledge its indeterminacy or superdeterminacy. In the United States examples of the operation of bureaucratic politics can easily be found. During the Johnson administration, biological weapons were increasingly seen as a political liability, being of little use to American defense efforts, and attempts were made to abandon the weaponry. However, because the Secretary of Defense and the Joint Chiefs of Staff were in disagreement on many other issues, the Secretary decided to support the biological weapons program in return for the army chief of staff's support on other issues.[8]

This study will define bureaucracy rather broadly. We consider those entities the bureaucracy which fullfill the following three conditions:[9]

---

[8] The biological weaponry program was not abolished until the Nixon administration and the end of the Vietnam War. See I.M. Destler, *Presidents, Bureaucrats and Foreign Policy* (Princeton: Princeton University Press, 1974), p. 60.

[9] One might also call the set of all such entities the foreign policy establishment, but the label of establishment would include a set of perceptual modes,

1. They are involved in the formulation of foreign policy, or in implementation of the generated policy. Most groupings considered under this subdefinition would be involved in both formulation and implementation. Indira Gandhi's primary role is of a policy formulator, but when she represents India at international conferences she is acting as implementor. The MEA implements policy, but, as we shall see, it also plays a very important part in the formulation of policy. In this study, that group with the most comprehensive veto in the formulation of policy will be referred to as the *central executive,* while those individuals most responsible for the implementation will be termed *operational*.

2. They may be either individuals, small groups such as committees, or large organizations. This is perhaps not a standard administrative definition, but foreign affairs administration is not a standard case. The foreign policy process does not take place within a single ministry predominately, as does domestic security policy (which is left to the Home Ministry), or as in the regulation of Indian banking, which is conducted by the Ministry of Finance. Foreign policy and operations are probably potentially more identifiable with certain individuals, small groups and committees than other areas of government activity. Some entities which we may consider under this definition may not be easily classified in terms of the individual, group or organization. When the foreign minister speaks on some matter, does he speak as a powerful individual, at his own behest, or as a representative of the MEA? Or is he instead voicing the general sentiments of the cabinet?

3. They are either government or government-affiliated individuals or bodies. This will not be a study of the effect of public opinion or of lobby groups on foreign policy formulation (the domestic level-of-analysis' jurisdiction), though these may play a role in the policy process. With this last subdefinition, we have widened our

---

as well as a static organization within its effective designation. I do not in this study wish to detail organizational ethos and operational codes, but only the structure of relationships.

understanding of the bureaucracy as something beyond the MEA, but remaining within the constraints of the Indian government community.

II
The British Indian Foreign Policy Bureaucracy

We invoke Clio, the muse of history, in this chapter. It only may be useful but is certainly interesting to trace the early history of the bureaucracy, just as we trace the nexus of events which have led to our present strategic balance.

Indian independence was achieved in 1947, but the interim government was operational for some time previous to independence. That interim period had deep foundations in the British Indian administration. Our study will be concerned mainly with the modern period, but by virtue of a British rule in India more than a century and three-quarters old at the time of independence, there was an extant foreign affairs organization with traditions and bureaucratic precedents. In India, the transition to the administrative forms of a modern state were not so dramatic nor turbulent as in certain African and Asian states in which the entire administrative staff was shipped out when colonial rule was broken. Not only was there previous to independence an induction and indoctrination of a small but well-trained cadre of Indians into the Indian Civil Service (ICS), but the British constitutional genius was also carefully infused into emergent Indian governmental codes, resulting in continuity, not historical fracture, between the administrative ways of the British and those of the independent Indian leadership.

2.1   SEVENTEENTH AND EARLY EIGHTEENTH CENTURIES

Long before a bureaucracy had been developed to administer British expansion in India, the forms of Western diplomacy had been introduced to the subcontinent. English missionaries in the seventeenth century served as emissaries of the British to the Moghul court.[1] These men, the heads of various orders of agencies, were diplomatic agents outside of the European diplomatic system. We see in this early period other manifestations of a developing subcontinent diplomacy. In 1723, the British East India Company signed its first treaty with an Indian state, an event which marked the beginning of the most important of British Indian diplomacy's roles, that of managing relations with the Indian states. That treaty first signed was the Treaty of Anjengo, with the Raja of Travancore. As many similar treaties followed Anjengo, the task of dealing with the Indian states became rapidly more complex. The confusion was not just that of numbers (there were over 640 Indian states) but also resulted from a deep British involvement in the affairs of each of these states after the acceptance of paramountcy in the states' internal affairs (post-1857). Complexity of coordination was not only horizontal but vertical as well. In the acquiescence to paramountcy the states retained their internal autonomy, while relinquishing to the British the powers of communication, defense and foreign relations. British control of the states' external relations eventually became quite complete, and N. Parameswaran Nair writes that the states

> . . . could not receive even a commercial agent of a foreign power at his title. Commercial treaties were arranged for them by the Paramount power. They were not allowed to accept titles or honors from any foreign country or body. Their subjects were issued British passports and were given protection as British citizens in foreign countries.

As the affairs of the states began to be the subject of more British thought, terminology was devised by the close of the eighteenth century to describe these responsibilities. Work with the princely states came to be known as "political" as opposed to work in the North-East Frontier Agency (NEFA), in the North-West Frontier Province (NWFP), or virtually any other part of the eastern world, which was designated as "foreign." This distinction was to remain an important influence on British administration throughout the era.

---

[1] One of the best known of such men was Sir Thomas Roe, who served in the Moghul court (1615-19).

British Indian Bureaucracy   11

The functions of the "foreign" sector of the bureaucracy would also rapidly grow, considering the rate of British imperialist adventurism after 1600. As Nair describes, the 1600 East India Charter

> . . . had defined the jurisdiction of the Company not only over the whole of India, but also over the whole of the east. Numerous examples can be given of such territorial acquisitions by the Central and Local Governments during these years, like the acquisition of Ceylon in the first decades of the 19th century, the possession of St. Helena from 1658 to 1671 and again from 1673 to 1834, Lord Wellesley's projects about Mauritius and Batavia and the despatch of Indian forces to Cairo in 1800, the acquisition of Singapore in 1819 and the direct administration of the Straits Settlements till 1867 and the like. Active foreign relations were maintained with states and chieftains in Arabia, the Persian Gulf Area, Aden, Persia, Afghanistan, Tibet, Western China and Siam. In short, a very wide conception was 'entertained by the Governors-General of Indian responsibilities and foreign interests.'[2]

2.2   AFTER 1763

Somewhat previous to the establishment of a formal organization for external relations a general government for British expansion was established. As Nair writes,

> On 3 November 1763 J. Graham, Secretary in the Public Department proposed to the Board a plan 'for the better regulating of transacting the business of Council at the Presidency of Fort William' and to 'remedy the present blended and irregular Method of Conducting the Business'. He suggested the division of the work into two Departments-- 'the one to be termed the Publick and the other the

---

[2] N. Parameswaran Nair, *The Administration of Foreign Affairs in India with Comparative Reference to Britain* (New Delhi: School of International Studies [dissertation], 1963), pp. 6, 10, 12.

Secret Department'. The former was to deal with 'all Affairs relating to shipping, Revenues, Fortifications, Accounts, Appointment of Servants', etc. The Secret Department was to conduct 'all Military Plans and Operations, the country correspondence and all Transactions with the Country Government'.

The designations of Public and Secret seem roughly to correspond to the modern division of public policy into low, domestic policy matters and high, foreign "power" policy. That even such a basic division of labor had not been necessary before 1763 is evidence of the small scale of East India Company's activities. The Secret handled a very wide range of activities in the early years after 1763, its records dealing with the battle of Buxar, the expedition against Cooch Behar, the cession of Kora and Allahabad to the Nawab Vazir, the Rohilla war, the British mission to Bhutan and Tibet, and clashes with French factories in Bengal, to name a few. The East India Company's early expansion had low administrative costs, with a staff of only a secretary and assistant secretary for both the Public and Secret Departments, one sub-secretary exclusively for Secret Department administration, and under him seven assistants. The secretary at that time received an annual salary of Rs. 4000.[3]

In 1774, four years before Cornwallis surrendered at Yorktown, the British had already established a large and well-administered government in India. It was divided into three departments, Public, Secret and Revenue, each of which was headed by a secretary, the highest career officer in the East India Company's government. We see in the secretary's preeminence one of the oldest surviving conventions of the British period, the present bureaucracy's most important link with the past. The second oldest surviving British Indian foreign policy convention, that of a government external affairs body, was effected in 1783 with the establishment of a Foreign Department.[4] This Foreign Department was separate from the three older divisions, but was headed by the secretary of the Secret Department. It thus did not enjoy a completely autonomous existence, but was granted powers as part of the Secret

---

[3] Nair, pp. 41-43.

[4] The Foreign Department was not, as Dutt relates, set up in 1842. Subimal Dutt, *With Nehru in the Foreign Office* (Calcutta: Minerva Publications, 1977), p. 20.

Department, which itself was fully separated from Public in 1783 and given a separate secretary. The responsibilities of the first Foreign Department are seen in the Government of India declaration that

> [t]he Secret Department properly comprises all subjects of a Political Nature, all the correspondence with the Presidents and Select Committees at the other Presidencies, also with the Councils there on Political Affairs. All the correspondence with Residents at Foreign Courts and at Benares all Transactions with Foreign Nations and Powers and every Military Operation or Movement of Troops which is either Ordered or undertaken.[5]

With its new organization the Secret Department had a secretary, sub-secretary, head assistant, nine assistants, two examiners, one register, and a ministerial staff of thirteen, for a staff total of twenty-eight (two years later this was trimmed a bit for "economy," a bureaucratic measure that would prove of timeless value).

That a fourth department was established to handle foreign relations in an eighteenth century colonial possession seems curious. Indian political relations with nations besides Great Britain should properly have been handled through London, but there were practical considerations which argued against this kind of centralization. Technology, or the lack of it, was the reason for a foreign policy center in India. From its seventeenth century emergence as a European convention until certain developments in the late nineteenth, the embassy was a formidable policy force for the country that it represented, concerning the nation that it was accredited to. This power flowed from the long interval taken by the round-trip passage of a letter or human emissary. Because of this, the agent or ambassador had to have broad powers to interpret his country's policies over the seasonal periods required to obtain formal clarification. When the telegraph came into common usage, and especially when the first undersea cables were laid, the central tendency of policy power began to change. The advent of the cable as a means of bureaucratic communication removed the rationale behind the policy centralization of embassies and agencies. Communication between London and any part of India took

---

[5] Home Department/Public Branch/OC, September 23, 1783, No. 16.

from six months to a year, making the direct management of the empire from its metropolitan center impossible. London remained in full control of those broad policies which took a fairly long time to create and enact.⁶ Calcutta remained in careful mastery of the daily operations of the government bureaucracy, and could through control of the movement of the machine often influence even broad policy by presenting London with *fait accompli* (this being typical during the expansion phase, when the governor-general on his own initiative could and did start a number of regional wars).

The period of greatest Calcutta-bureau autonomy had been 1600-1765, the trading period, and in this interval the ". . . autonomy was greater in the conduct of . . . relations with the Indian powers-- the Mughal Emperor at Delhi and the nawabs and chieftains in other parts of India."⁷ During this period, the power of the Indian bureaucracy was not prescribed but rather expedient. As soon as Whitehall had access to the requisite political structure (emerging in 1858), they wasted no time in centralizing to the degree possible. The author suggests however that the British might have wanted to maintain a decentralized decision-making rather than allow the bureaucratic art to imitate life, as happened with the advent of new communications technology. Another factor which encouraged greater decentralization was political expedience. Great Britain had an empire, but also a democracy whose politicians had to answer to the British parliament and people. The farther that imperial decision-makers were located from London's legislative halls and the inquisitive British press, the better for empire. News of the East India Company's (and later the British government's) activities in the east might yet make its way to Britain, but any political effects would be lessened by the time and distance that such news would take to leak out.⁸ Despite the apparent benefits of this kind of

---

⁶ We are assuming the identity of East India Company and British government policies even before the 1858 takeover. Previously, had there been any doubt of this coincidence of interests Whitehall would not have hesitated to take control of East India's operations. The question, however, requires a deeper look than this study can take into the London-Calcutta relationship.

⁷ Nair, p. 22.

⁸ Perhaps this decentralization of imperial decision-making was a factor contributing to the long life of British *samraj hakumet*, suggesting that divide-and-rule policy was applied not only to subject peoples

decentralization, there were dangers in allotting policy powers between London and Calcutta. Later, in 1812, two envoys were simultaneously appointed to Teheran by the authorities in the two policy capitals.

> While the London envoy went on conducting peaceful negotiations for a treaty, a military expedition was on the move to Teheran on orders from Calcutta. The confusion was settled only when a third envoy with greater powers than the earlier two arrived from London and concluded a definite treaty.[9]

In 1784, the first attempt was made to effect a superdepartmental control of foreign policy management. The Pitt's India Act of that year provided for a secret committee of the Court of Directors, consisting operationally for most matters of the chairman and deputy chairman, but made up of a larger group of decision-makers on the full range of topics. This group might be judged similar to the Cabinet Committee on Political Affairs of the modern Gandhi regime, both in the "height" of policy conducted by the committees and in the aggregate power of membership. The secret committee was though, unlike the present cabinet committee, a decision-making body. In 1786, the Secret Department was divided into four distinct branches: the Secret and Political, Secret and Military, Secret and Foreign, and Secret and Reform. The Secret Department at that time ceased to have a separate life, and these four branches were each made a distinct entity. The Secret and Political Department dealt with the Indian states. One important function of this department was state-oriented espionage toward the control of state elites and other intrastate groups. It maintained an internal intelligence network (the modern Indian Intelligence Bureau, while having very different responsibilities, inherits much of its breadth of powers from the old Secret and Political Department).

The Secret and Foreign Department dealt with the tribals in the western and eastern North; with Nepal, Tibet and Afghanistan, and with British possessions in the Persian Gulf. As remarked upon earlier, it also handled foreign relations for the Indian states. The

---

but, in the logic of empire, to one's own administration. Soviet administration seems increasingly to follow a similar philosophy.

[9] Nair, pp. 25-26.

Secret and Military Department was the British border, expeditionary and internal police force. The Secret Department as a single bureau was again revived in 1790, only four years after it was disappeared as such, and conducted Calcutta's military planning and all transactions with the metropolitan center ("country government"). The Foreign and Political wings of the previous Secret setup were separated from and given equal administrative rank to Secret. They were then, with Secret, placed under one secretary. By the turn of the century there were four secretaries heading the British government in India, one in charge of the Public (including commercial) Department, a second heading the Secret, Political and Foreign Department, and one heading the Military Department. In 1799 the four departments were put in the general charge of a fourth chief secretary, with each department headed by secretaries instead of sub-secretaries (sub-secretaries had been in charge since 1796).

2.3 THE NINETEENTH CENTURY

The activities of the Foreign Department underwent massive expansion in the nineteenth century, when in 1827 the diplomatic expenditures of the government of India amounted to nearly 500,000 pounds sterling, ". . . greater than the then diplomatic and consular charges, pensions included, of Great Britain, by far the largest of any nation in Europe."[10] No important changes in structure occurred until 1833, when under the Charter Act of that year the Military and Secret Departments as well as legal consultation became the exclusive concerns of the government of India, with the same secretary taking over the Secret, Political, Revenue and Judicial Departments. This came about as a joint secretariat between the government of Bengal and the government of India was founded. Before that, all of India was administered, through the offices of the East India Company, under the government of Bengal. The Secret, Political and Foreign Department was redesignated in 1842 as the Foreign Department, under the governor-generalship of Lord Ellenborough. Its internal work continued to be divided into secret, political and foreign jurisdictions, or:

- *Secret*. All government transactions connected with wars, negotiations and missions.

---

[10] Nair, p. 50.

- *Political.* Correspondence with residents and agents in ". . . Native Territory, managed Territory and Non-Regulation Provinces."

- *Foreign.* Transactions between the government of India and "Foreign European Powers."[11]

Later that year the government's practice of recording political and foreign proceedings separately was stopped, and the two were combined into one file series. At that time, then, there were only two branches in the Foreign Department.

The newly-merged Government of India secretariat had in 1843 four secretaries (each earning a salary of Rs. 52,000), heading the Home, Foreign, Finance and Military Departments. This somewhat more homogeneous and sturdy bureau structure matched the more politically stable superstructure provided by the assumption of direct British government control in 1858. Calcutta was made the seat of the new government, the climax of a gradual shift since 1765 from Bombay and Madras (which had enjoyed some early authority) toward Bengal and Calcutta. A momentous event for India's political future, assumption of power by the Crown did not immediately cause any changes in the bureaucracy, though it did cause some alterations in the policy process. A Secretary of State for India was created by the 1858 Government of India Act. The secretary of state was now in charge of India's foreign relations. He was vested with all the powers and duties exercised formerly by the president of the East India Company's Board of Control and the Secret Committee of the Court of Directors. The ability of outsiders to affect the conduct of foreign relations was effectively negated by the classification of all relevant communications as secret. These documents might be shared with a member of the new council only at the secretary of state's discretion. The great power of the secretary of state created a contradiction, in that London of a few decades later would be promoting the idea of an India with quasi-international status--at the same time having foreign relations run by a secretary of state directly responsible to the British government, not to the government of India.[12] It could not, though, have been a worse contradiction than that of a governor-general who represented the British government as the viceroy as well as the government of India as the governor-general. The governor-general had, in any case, the

---

[11] Nair, p. 50.

[12] Nair, p. 36.

final say on foreign affairs. The secretary of state was only the administrative head.

During Lord Canning's governor-generalship, in 1861, all the departments but one were put under the charge of members of the executive council of the governor-general of India. This was the bureau-historical basis of the Indian portfolio system. The early portfolio system, as established by the Indian Councils Act of 1861, changed the system which government leadership adopted in conflict resolution. Previously, the secretary of the Foreign Department would circulate papers on various topics to members of the council in order of seniority (beginning, of course, with the governor-general). A member would record his opinion on the paper, differences of opinion would be clarified by discussion, and in this way policy was created. The secretaries merely implemented policy established by the council in this fashion. Under this early system, the governor-general was in foreign policy not only the seniormost member but had also a veto of sorts on the policy process itself. This power was established partly by the Charter Act of 1793, and partly by tradition or the legitimization of practice. Lord Dalhousie (Governor-General 1848-56) was particularly well-versed in this tradition. Dalhousie had papers sent not to the seniormost member under him, but to the member whose expertise concerned the topic of the paper. Dalhousie on his own initiative was able to upset the process, but only temporarily, through the power granted him by the 1793 act.

Lord Canning's system changed the old policy process, in which each member was put in charge of a particular department and dealt on his own judgement with the issues brought up by that department. Only issues of broader impact were referred to the council, and this at the member's own discretion. These reforms, generally known as the portfolio reforms because of the system's resemblance to the constitutional portfolio system but not known as such to the men who used it, remained in effect until 1947. They were effective and long-lived because they helped the council to deal with the government's expanding workload without forfeiting policy powers to agencies outside the council. The new system lost the holistic effect that the previous system had, of having all members agree on each topic presented before the council. It was, however, scarcely avoidable, as the volume of paper passing through the council's departments made engineered unanimity on single issues impossible.

The Foreign Department, interestingly, was the direct charge of the governor-general and had no niche in the portfolio system. In 1861, then, two important steps in the formation of India's future government were taken: (a) the establishment of the portfolio structure; (b) the establishment of the dominance or policy-monopoly of the executive in the control of the Foreign Office. Nehru's assumption of the foreign portfolio in the interim government and thereafter becomes in this light not an original personal initiative, the unique product of Nehru's personality, but the simple assertion of the Indian head of government's traditional prerogative to the foreign portfolio. During the British period this was a prerogative of the viceroy, and later became that of Nehru.

At the time of the portfolio reforms the Foreign Department was headed by a secretary, assisted by deputy and assistant secretaries. By the Foreign Department's entry into the twentieth century, a distinct set of foreign responsibilities had developed, namely:

1. External policies.

2. Relations with foreign states beyond the subcontinent (i.e., non-Indian states).

3. Diplomatic recognition of consuls.

4. Passport grants.

5. Control of relations with tribal powers and the administration of police and militia employed in connection with the northern tribal powers.

6. The Indian Political Service (or before 1937, Foreign and Political cadre) and the Berar Commission.

7. Relations with the Indian states and intra-Indian quasi-state powers (such as the minute estates).

8. The imperial service troops.

9. Control of the administration of the Hyderabad-assigned districts, Ajmere-Merwara, and British Baluchistan, other than business specially allotted by this rule to another department.

10. Supervision of the department for the suppression of thuggi and dacoitri in the Indian states.

11. Extradition proceedings and extraterritoriality.

12. Political prisoners.

13. Political pensions.

14. Titles.

15. Ceremonials.

16. The Orders of the Star of India, Indian Empire and Crown of India.[13]

Only functions one through four and eleven are those which one might expect in a modern foreign office; five through ten are imperial functions, and thirteen through sixteen are purely ceremonial and oriented toward the officers' welfare.

2.4 THE TWENTIETH CENTURY

In 1878 the Red Sea telegraphic cable was laid, connecting London and Bombay and closing the gap between the decision-makers permanently.[14] Now it would be possible for Whitehall to exert continuous pressure on the daily operation of the bureaucracy, though a great deal would continue not to be reported by cable. The early system was unable to absorb anything more than a modest flow of information in either direction.

Before the laying of the cable, Calcutta had both an active and passive influence on Whitehall. The active influence was, as noted, that Calcutta had a great deal of autonomy in formulating her own policy due to the long interval between communications. On the other hand, despite the inability of Calcutta to communicate directly, or perhaps because of that, Calcutta's image in the mind of London passively influenced imperial leadership. London leadership had in their solitary planning to anticipate the response of Calcutta, forcing them to factor in an implicit or passive Calcutta presence. This no longer being the case after the laying of the Red Sea cable,

---

[13] Adapted from Nair, p. 58.

[14] Previous to the undersea cable, some message traffic was conveyed, less efficiently, by overland cables running part of the way through Persia. This was one of the ways in which Persia became vital to the control of India, in a very immediate international security sense. British Imperial War Cabinet, Eastern Committee, Cab 27/24, December 19, 1918, quoted in Robert Axelrod, ed., *Structure of Decision: The Cognitive Maps of Political Elites* (Princeton: Princeton University Press, 1976), p. 90.

> [b]y the latter half of the nineteenth century . . . control of foreign relations had passed completely into the hands of the Secretary of State for India, and of the British Foreign Office in London. This was conclusively proved during the Viceroyalty of Lord Curzon. On the question of Tibet, Afghanistan, Persian Gulf etc. the Government of India could act with little freedom and the policies carried out were invariably those formulated in London.[15]

Table 2.1: Foreign Department staffing: 1861-1905

1861	one secretary, one under-secretary, one assistant (or junior) under-secretary
1871	assistant abolished, two attachés for secretariat training were added.
1875	assistant secretaryship recreated.
1881	junior under-secretary added.
1894	additional assistant secretary (concerned with NWFP) created.
1905	additional deputy secretary created.

source: Nair, pp. 56-57.

The Foreign Department during this period handled several chores normally in the jurisdiction of the Home Department, such as the administration of non-regulation territories and the management of telegraphic communications. But as Home developed the ability to manage these duties, these responsibilities also were transferred to Home. Of its external responsibilities, Foreign had to handle relations with Afghanistan, Ava, Muscat and Zanzibar, in all of which agencies were established. The non-regulation territories were considered domestic responsibilities. To administer this blend of permanent foreign and temporary domestic functions, the Foreign Department was divided into six parts: judicial, revenue, finance, military, political and general. The first three are generally not expected of a Foreign Department, but concerned the

---

[15] Nair, p. 30.

Table 2.2: Duty allocation: 1905

deputy secretary	External Section A	Baluchistan, Persia, Persian Gulf, Turkish Arabia

staff: one superintendent, eight clerks

special assistant secretary	External Section B[a]	Aden, Assam, Bhutan, Burma, China, Egypt Nepal, Red Sea and Somali Coast, Siam Sikkim, Tibet, pilgrim traffic

staff: one superintendent, eight clerks

deputy secretary	Frontier Sections A and B	Afghanistan, Central Asia (excluding Kashgar), frontier, Frontier Corps, Kashmir, Khyber, Khorassam and Seistan, North-West Frontier petitions

staff: one superintendent, nine clerks

[a] On temporary loan from Foreign Office, London.
source: Nair, p. 62.

non-regulation territories. The judicial branch handled thuggi and dacoitri cases, and the revenue branch collected land tax (the branch growth of the department is shown in Table 2.1).

The distinction in this period between foreign and political topics became more complicated. Generally, relations with Asian (Asiatic, in the British imperial lexicon) states were designated political and those with European states, foreign. But in some cases the Asian states enjoyed a degree of independence from British rule comparable to that of the European powers. Relations with Afghanistan, Iran and Ceylon, as well as work done by the British in non-regulated or tribal territories, thus constituted foreign relations. Relations with the Indian states were overshadowed by paramountcy, so that such became political relations. Relations with Nepal were alternately classified as both foreign and political.[16]

Under Lord Curzon, steps were taken to improve coordination between the London and the Indian offices, steps taken because of the increasing instability or flux of the European system. British policy makers were by then especially concerned with India's vulnerability to European moves, and particularly the Indian and Iranian vulnerability to the Russian giant. Colonial imperialism had turned from a positive-sum to a zero-sum game. As Curzon wrote in 1903,

> [t]he first result of this . . . has been that the foreign policy of the Government of India is brought into increasing connection with the Foreign Office in London, and that questions have to be considered and decided not exclusively from the point of view of their bearing upon Indian interests, but from their relation to the policies of the Empire at Large.[17]

In order to strengthen the ties between London and India, Lord Curzon obtained the transfer on a temporary basis of a member of the Foreign Office to India as an additional assistant secretary.[18] The officer had over ten years of experience in the Foreign Office's Asian Department and was thus very helpful in clarifying the views of London for an Indian Foreign Department which had over the years developed a very independent organizational viewpoint. Curzon also attempted to obtain the transfer of some Foreign Department officers to Whitehall, but despite the utility of such a transfer for training purposes the Foreign Office rejected this proposal.

The main tasks of the Foreign Department in 1905 were handled by two deputy secretaries and a special assistant secretary (of equal status to the additional assistant secretary, which position was at that time occupied by the transfer from the London Foreign

---

[16] Nair, pp. 54-56.

[17] Despatch from the Governor-General in Council to the Secretary of State No. 62, May 14, 1903, *Foreign Department-General-A Proceedings,* June 1903, Nos. 4-12, pp. 13-14.

[18] Nair, p. 61.

Office) supervised by the secretary of the department. Their responsibilities in 1905 are described in Table 2.2. The special assistant secretary had clearly a heavy workload, and it was hoped in fact that the appointment of a special assistant secretary would ease the duties of the two deputy secretaries, as well as lighten the burden of drafting taken up by the viceroy and secretary. To adopt drafting responsibilities would have made the special assistant secretary a far more powerful officer than the assistant secretary. But it was probably unrealistic to expect any man, even one with long experience in the Foreign Office, to take up such a large workload, and throughout his term (the standard one of three years) the special assistant secretary assumed no drafting work.[19] This attempt to ease top leadership's work burden was not successful, but the effort was not a very serious one. The central and most important result of the officer transfer from London was the injection of a measure of Foreign Office perspectives into the Indian apparatus.

It was important, though, as a first attempt at reducing a growing workload. The Foreign Department's responsibilities and paperwork after 1900 grew rapidly, following the topical expansion of British policy. As a Foreign Office Proceedings for 1906 states,

> [s]omething must be done to relieve the Foreign Department. The political work proper has increased enormously of late years, owing partly to a more active policy in developing and improving the administration in the Native States of India, but mainly to the nearer advance of Foreign Powers to India and the necessity for greater care in conducting the external relations of India.[20]

The heavier duty load of the department was the result of basic changes in British Indian policy, but the greater volume of work might have later forced some changes in that policy, as a type of feedback spiral. The organizational burdens having been recognized, it led the British to liberalize many political policies, such as the removal of Baroda, Sikkim and Bhutan from Indian government control, greater reliance upon local authorities and the greater decentralization of

---

[19] Nair, p. 63.

[20] *Foreign Department, General-B Proceedings,* May 1906, p. 313.

control. The consequence was that on January 1, 1914 a Foreign and Political Department replaced the earlier Foreign Department.

Responsibilities in the Foreign and Political Department were split between the foreign secretary and the political secretary, with the foreign secretary running three sections, F, N and X. F Section dealt with NWFP, Afghanistan and Nepal; N Section with the Near-East, and X Section dealt with all those parts of the world not handled by F or N Sections. The Foreign and Political Department, despite its having resources which could have served as such, was not a foreign office or a miniature replica of the Whitehall bureaucracy. It was an extension of Whitehall, but did not have the policy breadth that the Foreign Office had. It had only certain highly particular functions, and its powers were carefully circumscribed. As K.P.S. Menon writes of his experience of being in charge of X Section,

> [w]hile dealing with the whole world . . . I realized how little the Government of India under British rule was concerned with the world. It took no interest in south-east Asia except when there was some question connected with the treatment of Indian immigrants--and that was the concern of E.H. and L. [the Department of Education, Health and Lands]. It did not take much interest in the Middle East, except in those Arab sheikdoms which were British Protectorates. It interested itself in the Persian Gulf rather than Persia. As for the U.S.A., its main concern was that American opinion should not be misled by Congress agitators into thinking that India was ripe for independence. The Soviet Union was a closed book to us. Russia and China were seething with events but the Government of India did not bother about them. China, it was thought, had been a happy hunting-ground for warlords from time immemorial and would continue to remain so forever. The Indian Government's interest in Russia was even less than that of Baldwin, who, when Prime Minister, sent a note to the Foreign Office, saying "People are always asking me what is happening in Russia. Please let me have a note. Not more than half a page.'

The size of the department of external affairs in 1935 [it was in fact called the

> Foreign and Political Department] . . . reflects . . . the size of its responsibilities then . . . In 1935 it consisted of a single Secretary and two Deputy Secretaries, namely Olaf Caroe and myself.[21]

The adoption of two secretaries followed from the larger departmental workload; either another secretary or another department for political affairs would have been needed. Managing relations with the small local rulers of India now had little to do with foreign work, and the complexity of filing and communications was no longer amenable to the controlling influence of one secretary. After 1914, the foreign secretary's duties were cut down to a group of eleven tasks, namely:

1. External policies;

2. Relations with non-princely nation-states;

3. Consular appointments;

4. Passports;

5. Indian overseas in all A-mandated territories, in those administered by a foreign power under a B or C mandate, in Egypt, and outside the empire except in Surinam;

6. The control of relations with trans-border tribes and of the administration of frontier constabulary and militia employed in connection with such tribes and of the administration of tribal territory in so far as it is administered;

7. The control of the administration of Baluchistan;

8. Petitions in jirga cases in NWFP and adjoining tribal territories;

9. Political prisoners, e.g. Afghan refugees;

10. Extradition and extraterritoriality;

11. Communications encypherment and decypherment for the government of India.[22]

---

[21] K.P.S. Menon, *Many Worlds: An Autobiography* (Bombay: Oxford University Press, 1965), p. 138.

The Foreign and Political Department was unique in having two secretaries, and was by this time probably the most prestigious and visible department in the government. While separate in functions, the foreign and political wings shared the same housing and facilities, which had by that time become quite extensive. The new status of the Foreign and Political Department led to the development of an institution, that of a strong foreign secretary, which has continued up to the present as an important influence in foreign policy formulation. World War I was probably a factor in the foreign secretary's newly-found power, due to the strengthened British awareness of the possibility of external interference in Indian affairs during that unstable period. But a large part of that power resulted from the governor-general's incidental primacy in foreign affairs.

> Due to the numerous responsibilities of the Governor-General, which naturally exceeded that of any Member of the Council, the Secretaries of this Department came to wield much greater authority and influence in the administration of their Departments than other Secretaries. Moreover, while other Departments were represented in the Legislature by the Members of the Council, the two Secretaries themselves were the principal spokesmen of their Departments in the Legislative Chambers, the Governor-General not being a Member of either chamber of the legislature. It was no wonder that the position of the two Secretaries were regarded generally as something special in the government. The Foreign Secretaryship used to be regarded as 'the blue ribbon of service.'

The foreign secretary's influence also sprang partly from the role that India was playing in the League of Nations and the International Labor Organization, as well as in tackling the growing overseas Indian communities problem.[23] Proposals, some years after 1919, were circulated in an attempt to bring the functions of the foreign secretary and political secretary together into one office (a return to the pre-1919 state of affairs), but these proposals were dropped as

---

[22] Nair, p. 67.

[23] Nair, pp. 68-70.

impractical.

The bridle of British control placed in 1858 over Indian foreign affairs was loosened a bit by the 1919 Government of India Act. By that time, Indian relations with some of the other British dominions had expanded, so that intra-Commonwealth relations had become a large part of the total Indian foreign relations picture. The 1919 Act made, for the first time, a distinction between dominion (later, more commonly known as Commonwealth) relations and external affairs.[24] External affairs, under the Act, remained under the governor-general's discretion, but the British Indian government was given in both economic and political matters more than a token degree of freedom in dealing with other dominions. The organizational response to this Act would come several years later.

In 1919 the Foreign and Political Department was a relatively large portion of an extended government of nine departments. The number of departments increased further when in 1937 the Foreign and Political Department was halved into an External Affairs Department and a Political Department, the responsibilities of both corresponding to those of the earlier Foreign and Political Department Branches. The 1935 Government of India Act was the reason for this bifurcation. Before the Act foreign and political tasks were separated on the grounds of practice, and organizational precedent, but without legal or constitutional grounds. The 1935 Act provided such a legal basis, by placing foreign responsibilities under the control of the governor-general in council and political responsibilities under the supervision of the Crown representative. Two years later, on April 1, 1937, the departments were given separate life, with the External Affairs Department under the formal leadership of the governor-general, and the Political Department now part of the British government but still headed in his capacity as Crown representative by the Governor-General. This, then, was a variation in the organization induced not by internal policy influences (as were the changes in 1919) but rather by policy initiatives from the outside.

Immediately prior to the beginning of World War II we have a department which for the first time in the foreign policy bureaucracy's history is concerned purely with foreign relations (following, however, the British definition of foreign). In ten years the External Affairs Department or its foreign policy successor would become part of a non-British Indian government, making crucial the developments in the next

---

[24] Nair, p. 17.

ten years of the bureaucracy. Before 1941 the Department of Education, Health and Lands had an Indian Overseas Section concerned with Indians residing in other dominions and other parts of the world.[25] Long before 1947 the Indian overseas community had become quite large (there being, for example, before 1935 over 800,000 Indians in Ceylon) with the Section in the late 1930s also increasing in size. The Indian Overseas Section in 1941 became the Department of Indians Overseas, now independent of the Department of Education, Health and Lands. The new department was concerned with the emigration of Indians to other parts of the Commonwealth, with the interests of Indians overseas, with pilgrimages from India to holy shrines outside India (the present-day Haj Cell is a remnant of this function of the Department of Indians Overseas), and with repatriations of Indians abroad, but the growth of the overseas community is not the only reason for the growth of the Department. The above-mentioned Government of India Act of 1919 gave India considerable freedom in dealing with other dominions, and a large chunk of inter-dominion diplomatic relations arose from the problem presented by the Indian communities resident in those countries. Therefore, not only did the problem grow, but a larger share of the total Indian community issue came to be tackled by the Indian government. In 1944 the Department was redesignated the Department of Commonwealth Relations, consonant with the Department's work-focus in Commonwealth relations policy. At even this late period the Department of Commonwealth Relations was unique in having an Indian at its head.

We see about this time an entire foreign policy community forming, with foreign policy no longer the designated task of only one department, but represented by responsibilities scattered among several such bodies. The Department of Commonwealth Relations and the External Affairs Department were, minimally, the essential members of that community. Moreover, the Labour Department handled work arising from Indian membership in the International Labor Organization, and the London Foreign Office exerted a great deal more influence in the Government of India's foreign policy after 1935 than at any previous time, especially as political stability in both Europe and India began to deteriorate and make laissez-faire an increasingly difficult governmental policy to justify. Foreign affairs had by

---

[25] Indian Institute of Public Administration, *The Organization of the Government of India* (New Delhi: Somaiya Publications, 1971), p. 35, gives the date of 1945, but Nair's account seems better researched and is certainly more detailed, so we use Nair's dating.

the mid-1930s become a far larger enterprise than could be managed by one government department acting alone.

2.5 AFTER 1940

Modern India's initiation to the conduct of international relations was paradoxically both graduated and abrupt. On the one hand, before 1947 the External Affairs Department had agencies and residencies in several countries, which were similar to standard diplomatic missions. India had enjoyed a limited representation in the League of Nations, and after 1945 took part in many of the activities of the United Nations, as well as in the process of the International Labor Organization. For over two centuries the Indian government and the East India Company had had much more freedom in the direction of foreign policy, and had developed their own traditions and ways of thinking in this realm. The Indian government had also a considerable degree of freedom in dealing with other members of the Commonwealth. All of these factors made gradual the transition from British to Indian formal control and government. On a lower level, personal and informal in character, consisting of the objective tools of government, the transition was more abrupt than gradual. The functions of the British Indian foreign policy administration were not those of a European Foreign Office but those of a control bureaucracy the reflection of an imperial relationship. This reflection carried only a faint glimmer of past and contemporary European diplomatic practice. Therefore, a large part of the apparatus was superfluous to the diplomatic and foreign policy needs of an independent India. The number of Indians who had had government top executive experience was also very low. This meant that when India achieved independence many of the intangible operational factors and assets of the bureaucracy would disappear and the cumulative benefits of many years of involvement in certain kinds of international relations would vanish with the exit of the British. The operation of a foreign relations bureaucracy within a democratic domestic environment rather than within the internal conditions of an imperial colony would make the Indian adherence to many of the practices (particularly that of extreme secrecy) of the British undesirable. The Indian government servants would therefore have to devise their own bureau procedural framework and rule-regimen.

When Nehru came to head the interim government, he had to assemble a foreign relations apparatus. That

Nehru should model his organization after the British had several grounds. First, the British during the interim were still, through their delegates and the diplomacy of Mountbatten, influencing proceedings directly. They could put forward many procedural suggestions and not have great difficulty in gaining their acceptance. Since the constitution in its draft used the British constitution as a take-off point, other elements of political theory and administrative practice tended to sneak their way in from the British. Indian leadership was somewhat free to adopt what they considered best in British political theory for application in India, or at least sufficiently free to avoid charges of perpetuating through the constitution British imperial influence. Because of the theoretical Indian liberty in constitutional draft, ideas which were de facto British came to be perceived as uniquely Indian. Another strong influence was that of the armed forces in India. The Indian army, always a predominately Indian power with no more than a cadre of British officers, was one of the biggest inheritances of the days of the British raj. The army and the railway system were the two infrastructural survivals of the British which inhibited with greatest strength a general anglophobic post-1947 political reaction. In the army was set in its entirety the British system of military administration. Having accepted this massive representation of British administration, the author hypothesizes that the rejection in other government sectors of British methods would not have been possible (following cognitive dissonance theory).[26]

Other, less formal processes came into play as means by which the British continued to exert influence. The British had trained a small army of clerks and administrators to run their machine in India. This had begun with Cornwallis, who divided the services into two groups, that which served commercial concerns and that involved in political affairs. By 1947 the commercial group had largely disappeared, while the political group had a role potentially to play in the new government. Qualified people would have to be found in the new India to fill positions opened with the departure of the British. There would be a new India, but it would be run (at least in the beginning) with the staff of the old India. Even at the time that Nehru entered the government, on September 2, 1946, the top positions in the Department of External Affairs were manned by the British.[27] Thereby an "ICS

---

[26] Leon Festinger, *A Theory of Cognitive Dissonance* (Stanford: Stanford University Press, 1957)

generation" of officers was generated, students of British Indian administration but teachers of the new bureaucrats.

Nehru's reliance on former officers of the Indian Civil Service (ICS) and Political Service was probably increased by the shock of partition. Partition was more than a demographic or a geographic and religious division of the subcontinent, but was also an administrative and political sundering. The military was divided between the two countries, and the army of political servants given the right to leave the Indian government and enter Pakistani circles. The interim Department of External Affairs was divided into Indian and Pakistani sections, and in the halls of South Block (a euphemism for the Indian foreign office) were seen in profusion both *khadi* jackets and Jinnah caps.[28] Nehru had not only to contend with depletions in British manpower but also with the Pakistani defections. The small number of Indian regular officers made it very difficult to be selective about who would stay on, and Nehru's selection standards had to be lowered. Another result of the partition was the problem among the new officers of perceived allegiance to the fledgling Indian state. Among those remaining Muslims, how many could be counted on to back India when altercations arose with Pakistan? It is true that in the interim the Muslim League was suspicious of what it saw as an attempt to build up a Congress-dominated diplomatic organization, which would be used, they thought, to broadcast anti-Pakistani propaganda internationally. It was for this reason that Vijaya Lakshmi Pandit's appointment to Moscow was postponed.[29] Because India had reason conversely to fear that it might lose control in a crisis of this powerful body of civil servants, Nehru made special efforts to give Muslim civil servants fair treatment and placement. Somewhat more concerned was Sardar Vallabhbhai Jhaverbhai Patel (1875-1950), who once called Nehru the "only nationalist Muslim" in India, voicing the suspicion of other conservative Hindus in the government that the allegiance of Muslim officers was uncertain. Conjunction of the realistic possibility of impaired allegiance and the conservative Hindu fear of Muslim subversion forced Nehru and other top leadership into a tense personnel selection situation during the first years of

---

[27] M.O. Mathai, *Reminiscences of the Nehru Age* (New Delhi: Vikas, 1978), p. 193.

[28] Dutt, p. 4.

[29] Nair, p. 126.

independence.

This unselective, unavoidable lowering of standards led to a conflict, in which that which was most needed was also least desirable. The ICS was composed of men indispensable because of their administrative experience, but who combined with their experience some undesirable traits. One of these was the expensive lifestyle of the ICS officer. As Indra Datt notes,

> . . . the British rule . . . has been damnably expensive. It has been a 'Rolls-Royce administration in a bullock-cart country'. A few comparative figures may be illustrative of the point. The per capita income in the United States [c. 1947] is more than twenty-two times than what it is in India and the cost of living in America is notoriously high . . . Yet the President of America draws a salary of Rupees 17,062 per month, as compared to the Viceroy who draws Rupees 21,333 per month. Again Poland is far richer than Bihar and its population is also very much less. The President of the Polish Republic received a salary of Rupees 1560 per month (1939), while the Governor of Bihar draws Rupees 8,333 a month. A District Magistrate and even Principals of certain Government Colleges may receive a higher salary than the President of Poland . . . Hitherto instead of demanding that the scales of salaries of the British personnel should be brought down, the Indian section of the personnel has helped to crush the taxpayer by demanding that their salaries be raised to the scale of Europeans.[30]

Other discordant elements of the ICS ethos would present Nehru and his senior officers with difficulties, making this inheritance from the British a mixed blessing.

The extent to which the British maintained an invisible presence in India despite their formal withdrawal is surprising. Former viceroy Mountbatten continued to play a role in early Indian political affairs, especially as a mediator in the Indo-Pakistani dispute and as a stabilizing figure during the

---

[30] Indra Datt, *Diplomatic Service in Free India* (Lahore: Indian Book Company, 1947), p. 53.

post-1947 communal riots.[31] The cabinet secretariat of the modern government has since 1947 been located in the recently vacated North Block-South Block complex of buildings on the end of Rajpath Road in New Delhi. The secretariat buildings, designed by Lutyens of London, were used also by the British for their secretariat. The establishment of the new government in the imperial grandeur of the central secretariat set the standards for a new government that was not going far out of its way to shed the symbols of the previous regime. The extent to which symbols were retained is shown well in Maxwell's account of the Indo-Chinese talks preceding the 1962 border war. According to Maxwell, one of the rooms in the presidential palace even in 1960 had ". . . its walls hung with life-size portraits of the last of the Viceroys and his Vicereine . . ."; it was in this room that Chou En-lai gave his April 1960 press conference on the Sino-Indian talks. As Maxwell continues, "[f]or the Chinese, it must have been incomprehensible that proud and patriotic Indians could allow such reminders of past servitude to decorate important rooms in their President's palace."[32]

Nehru, whose office was originally located in Rashtriapati Bhavan, soon moved into South Block, where the Prime Minister's office has been located ever since. And in this way, the new Indian government moved into its new responsibilities using many old administrative practices and conventions, just as an occupying army uses materièl left behind by the retreating force without alteration in the form of the materièl, only changing the side for which the materièl is utilized.

2.6 INDEPENDENCE

In 1947 the Department of Commonwealth Relations was merged with the External Affairs Department (a decade old at the time of merger) as the Department of External Affairs and Commonwealth Relations. The amalgamation between the two departments would have been accomplished earlier than mid-1947, but there was more to the merger than just linking secretariats. The different missions and representations abroad also had to be brought under one authority, and there lay a problem.

---

[31] See Alan Campbell-Johnson, *Mission with Mountbatten* (London: R. Hale, 1951)

[32] Neville Maxwell, *India's China War* (New York: Doubleday and Company, 1972), p. 167.

The Department of Commerce did not want to give up its gigantic London High Commission, without which the Commerce Department's diplomatic overseas representation and coordinative headquarters staff would shrink very noticeably in size. But it finally let go as it had to, though almost at the last possible administrative moment.

Before the merger both departments were similar in size and internal organization, despite their different origins. The Department of External Affairs was headed by a member-in-charge of external affairs, who had under him one secretary, one assistant secretary, one joint secretary, one deputy secretary, four under-secretaries and nine superintendents who themselves supervised the clerical staff. The Department of Commonwealth Relations was somewhat smaller, with one member-in-charge, one secretary, one assistant secretary, one deputy secretary, one under-secretary and five superintendents, as well as a pilgrim officer and an officer on special duty.[33] We see in these early departments all the career ranks found in the modern MEA (with the exception of attaché, director, deputy director, and several specialist officers), another inheritance from the British. Indian overseas representation before 1947 was slight. Under the External Affairs Department, there were only two agency-generals, for the U.S. and China (the agency-general was a post-1937 form of the British Indian quasi-diplomatic residency). There were also Indian representatives in the British missions to Persia, Afghanistan and Tibet, as well as External Affairs administration of the NEFA and NWFP. Under the Department of Commonwealth Relations were two high commissions in South Africa and Australia, and agents in Burma, Ceylon and Malaya. Under the Department of Commerce was the large London High Commission, as noted.[34]

On August 29, 1947 the Department of External Affairs and Commonwealth Relations, as well as the seventeen other existing departments, was redesignated as a ministry. In March 1949 the burdensome suffix "Commonwealth Relations" was dropped and the Ministry of External Affairs, at least as a title, was born.

---

[33] Datt, pp. 85-86, quoting *The Statesman's Year Book 1944-45*, p. 52.

[34] *Report of the Committee on the Indian Foreign Service* (New Delhi: Government of India, 1966), p. 1.

2.7 THE BRITISH AGENT

In this period there were a number of British Indian agents (agent is here used as a diplomatic designation) who reported directly to the External Affairs Department about events and policy in the states to which they were accredited. The agent was, as ministerial diplomat, a central British Indian external political device. In the seventeenth century developed the tradition of calling the representative of the East India Company in the Indian state the British agent, political agent or simply agent. The early agents were accredited only to the Indian states and to subcontinent powers. The titles of envoy and resident arose as representation to the Indian states increased, both appointees to larger states than those in which political agents were generally stationed. To state groupings would also be appointed agent-generals, agents or commissioners, but no title was given senior to these (Foreign and Political Department ceremonial fullfilled a similar function to that of diplomatic protocol with regard to the Indian states). The political agent served as British envoy, as a communication channel between states, and as negotiator in both internal and external matters. As Nair aptly describes,

> ... the Resident was much more of a minister than an Ambassador; he carried the subsidiary system into effect; he was the organ through which the subsidiary system functioned; he had the delicate task of 'governing those, who, from their station, should themselves be Governors.' The 'advice' of the Resident was generally an order or command, and, except in cases where he himself felt it his duty to leave the Indian rulers to themselves his authority was all-comprehensive.

The political agent was well-established in most Indian states by the time missions began to be established outside of the subcontinent. In 1798 Mehdi Ali Khan, as a representative of the British Indian government, conducted a mission to Teheran with the purpose of negotiating an initial treaty with the Shah of Iran (which was successfully concluded in 1805). This was the first time that a representative of the British Indian government sent with clearly diplomatic intent such a mission abroad. This new type of agency expanded to include representations (during World War II) at

Sinkiang, Chungking and Washington. The first Indian High Commission was set up in London in 1919.[35]

The residencies, their successor agencies, and other allied mission forms might, under certain conditions, have given Indian nationals valuable diplomatic experience. In some cases these missions certainly did serve training purposes, but due to the domination of overseas postings by British officers most Indians experienced such work only, at best, as junior officers. Only the United Nations mission (after 1945) had diplomatic ambassadorial status, and prior to the formation of the interim government only thirteen other missions existed, ". . . spread mostly over the few countries and territories immediately beyond the borders of the country."[36] So there were difficulties involved in using such a small and anglo-dominant structure as the basis for a later independent Indian diplomacy, but the benefits of having even such a small base of mission representation were indispensable. After India gained independence, most of the agencies were converted automatically into diplomatic missions of the new government, with few changes in staffing.[37]

2.8 THE FOREIGN AND POLITICAL SERVICE

The service cadre which furnished the early Foreign and Political Department's manpower was named after 1937 the Indian Political Service (IPS; previously known to British officers as "F. and P."). The IPS had within it two important dualisms. First, its membership was a composite entirely of two other services, of the ICS and the Indian army. Second, its membership was both British and Indian, or, as the annals of the time put it, European and native.

2.8.1 Service Composition

There was never a "fresh" IPS recruitee, as its entire membership was derived from the senior ranks of the older services. For this reason the IPS was sometimes described as a "service within the service;" it was a

---

[35] Nair, pp. 80, 81; Menon, p. 147.

[36] Nair, p. 91.

[37] Ram D. Sathe, foreign secretary during most of the post-Janata period, received his first commission in China this way.

highly selective personnel pool characterized by the relative intensification of the group traits of competition and bureau survival. Competition among army officers for admission was especially strong (army officers were selected largely for their proficiency in subcontinent and regional languages). Contrarily, competition within the ICS for IPS postings was poor, as there was a small pay-reduction suffered in moving between coequal grades from the ICS to the IPS (though because there was no negative movement from the IPS to the ICS, the IPS still experienced a net increase in the competitive personnel trait). Intra-ICS and intra-army competitions were separate, and a dual-cadre system existed which not only set up separate entrance requirements for army and ICS officers, but preserved those service distinctions even after these men were accepted into the IPS (which served to offset the structural effects of personnel competitiveness). Former ICS officers occupied a much larger proportion of senior positions in the IPS than their overall (junior and senior) share of the IPS, and upon joining they started at a grade equal to that from which they departed in the ICS, whereas former army officers started at the bottom of the hierarchy. Moreover, to encourage more ICS officers to enter the IPS, they were paid according to an altered and strengthened payscale rather than by the normal army inductee payscale.

In response to the army officers' pressure the dual-cadre system was in 1911 abolished.[38] Institution of fair treatment in remuneration did not, though, erase the bureau structural distinctions which separated men of remarkably different civilian and military backgrounds, background differences which could not be denied by a collective ethos. Before the abolition of the dual-cadre system in 1898 there were seventy-three cadre posts, of which approximately fifty-two were reserved for military officers and eighteen for civilians. The upper age-limit for an IPS candidate was twenty-seven; the age of the Sandhurst army recruitee was on the average nineteen to twenty years, and of the ICS recruitee twenty-four years. The military officers in non-secretariat positions were organized into nine grades; ICS civilians dominated secretariat (policy-formulative) positions. While intra-service discrimination officially ended with the 1911 reforms, officers remained in the posts which they occupied before the reforms, and the military/civilian division of labor changed much more slowly than the reform timing suggests. The preservation of a strong and distinct

---

[38] For a full description of the dual-cadre system, see Nair, pp. 95-102.

military perspective (cognitive system) and component in the IPS makes for an interesting contrast to the modern IFS, the officers of which are thoroughly civilian in outlook and training.

2.8.2 Indianization

In the early 1900s the British Indian rulers seem to have fully accepted in abstract that a much larger proportion of Indian nationals must be brought into the IPS, but there was less unanimity concerning the actual methods and timetables whereby such Indianization was to be accomplished. The ICS was the domain of British nationals, but the IPS was reserved even more easily for British officers. The general unwillingness of the ICS to take in Indians was partly service racial chauvinism, but the Indians' exclusion from the the IPS was based upon factors external to the structure of British service racial perceptions. As Menon explains,

> [t]he reason for the exclusion of Indians was that the Princes would not like their own countrymen to be Residents or representatives of the Paramount Power, and that an Indian, and especially a Hindu, would not be able to command the respect and obediance of the unruly Muslim tribes on the Frontier.

It was also objected that due to the confidential nature of work in the Foreign and Political Department, only the most politically-reliable personnel could be chosen for many of the positions, and race was assumed to determine political loyalties. It was feared that Indian nationalist fervor would undermine the loyalty of Indian IPS officers (the same problem, it will be recalled, of perceived allegiance affected Muslim recruitment into the post-1947 foreign office). Ironically, such a criterion could be applied with greater strength the closer India came to the transfer of power, to the time when Indianization was of the greatest importance (a case of destabilizing positive feedback). Another factor which slowed the induction of Indians during the 1930s was the separation of the Foreign and Political Department from direct British Indian government control, thereby reducing by one the number of departments open to Indian officers.[39]

---

[39] Menon, pp. 80, 135; Nair, pp. 116, 118.

The representation percentages were quite high, in comparison with the "native" involvement in the governments of either the South African or French Algerian colonial regimes. In 1939, the ICS was made up of 759 Europeans and 540 Indians. But the proportion of Indians in commanding positions was low. In 1921, there were in the Foreign and Political Department thirty-eight Indians and 115 Europeans in the Rs. 500-1000 monthly salary range, but above Rs. 1000 only three Indians and 193 Europeans were employed.[40] The situation was not hopeless, but far too few Indians were employed in the heavily skill-intensive administrative posts that would effectively prepare officers to stand alone, after the British left. It should be clear that the motivation for Indianization proceeded more than from the ethical right of Indians to administer the subcontinent, but also from the need for a large class of national administrators for an inevitably (given the structure of the British imperial system) independent India. Since British Indian administrators seemed aware of the need for Indianization, and seemed less tainted by racial prejudice than their British colonial counterparts elsewhere in empire (as well as in comparison with the French, German and Italian colonial systems) it seems likely that the retardation of the Indianization programs was the result of bureaucratic or organizational inhibitors (though the lack of an adequately-educated recruitment base in India also played a role).

The slow rate of Indianization made for both serious qualitative and quantitative deficiencies in post-independent manpower and the staffing of diplomatic offices. Of the thirty-six initial recruits to the future IFS, only four had any international experience, as very few of the benefactors of Indianization ever got into the IPS (most tending to remain in line ICS and army posts) and of the few who got into the IPS seventy-five percent were shuffled off into political (rather than foreign) task-oriented positions. The effects of this lack of manpower with international relations experience were exaggerated by a lack of sufficient staff for posts requiring even minimal training and experience. It was estimated that three hundred men would be required to staff the post-1947 Indian diplomatic-representative system, but in fact barely fifty Indians at the time were qualified for such work.[41]

---

[40] Menon, p. 262; Nair, p. 114.

[41] Nair, pp. 111, 125.

Table 2.3: Branches of Foreign Department: 1905-28[a]

1905	1910	1912	1928
Frontier	Frontier	Frontier	Frontier
Internal Sections {A,B}	Internal Sections {A,B}	Internal Sections {A,B}, Ceremonial	Internal
External {A,B,C}	External {A,B,C}	External {A,B,C}	External
General	General	General	General
Record Room	Record Room	Record Room	Accounts
	Establishment {A,B}	Establishment {A,B}	Establishment
	Cypher	Cypher	Cypher
			Near East
			Honors
			Reforms

[a] including its transformation into the Foreign and Political Department.
source: Nair, p. 70.

Table 2.4: Foreign and Political Department officers: 1919-35

	1919	1935
political secretary	1	1
foreign secretary	1	1
joint secretary	-	1[a]
additional secretary	-	1[a]
deputy secretary	2	2
additional deputy secretary	-	1
under-secretary	1	2[b]
assistant secretary	1	2
advisor for Far Eastern questions	1	-
registrar[c]	1	-
Total	8	11

[a] temporary
[b] one temporary
[c] rank of assistant secretary
source: *Foreign and Political Department, File No. 72(7)-E/35 of 1935*

III
The Indian Foreign Service

The levels-of-analysis are equally critical and mutually-exclusive analytic fields, neither nuclear nor indivisible. There are several sublevels-of-analysis conceivable within level-three, which share the same topical and axiomatic substance, but within which models simplify entirely different aspects of behavior (that is, they carry entirely disjoint sets of exogenous variables). In this study we distinguish three sublevels to level-three, namely the abstract, organizational and actual. The abstract analysis regards the entire bureau community as some number of operationally internally-coherent entities which interact in a competitive, political fashion to determine policy. In this simplification the foreign and defense ministries, for example, are assumed to disagree with each other, having different perceptions of their interests, but total internal policy-coherence is assumed. The second, organizational subanalysis will expose the highly complicated processes which go into the creation of supposedly coherent policy, and inquires into the heterogenous makeup of externally "single-policy" bureaux. The organizational sublevel is one of much more synchroneous internal processes than those internal to the phenomenological universe of the abstract sublevel, so that we are able to speak of precise and relatively stable informational structures and procedural patterns. The interactions between the entities on the abstract level are on the other hand apparently easier to observe, but hypotheses at the abstract sublevel are less easily subject to falsification tests, and data is less substantive or less objectively-based. Discussions of bureau process on the highest abstract sublevel can seem, unless the discussant is careful, even hyper-theoretical and undefensible. The imprecision typical of analysis at this level may be rectified by parallel work at the two lower sublevels. In this methodological framework the lowest sublevel, the actual, is *a priori* the strongest, focussing upon the transactions between individual bureaucrats, real human beings, in a bureau environment. The various case studies of foreign policy decisions take place predominately at this sublevel. Only the cognitive structure of the individual bureaucrat need be assumed here without prior knowledge, no more than is required of behavioral approaches elsewhere in the social sciences. Because the operational day-to-day activities of the foreign policy bureaucracy are within the jurisdiction of this sublevel, it may be regarded as the most objective; the two higher levels have a relatively virtual reality (using the term "virtual" as the theoretical physicist uses it; cessation of functions at the two higher sublevels will not lead to a cessation of life at the actual sublevel, but the converse is certainly true) in regulating the life at this "real-world" actual sublevel.

The power of administrative structures can easily be either underestimated or overvalued. They are boundaries which can frequently be transcended by individual bureaucrats, and there are many interactions which might occur within the limits of the bureaucracy without being prescribed by organizational guidelines. Thus, much occurs that cannot be reached by any purely administrative study. Fortunately, we are able to build up a fairly comprehensive, though very static, picture of who the men of the bureaucracy are and how they might be expected to act as individuals, rather than as dependent variables of the bureaucratic system function. As this is the basis of a static model, we do not yet show transactions between officers, or the relation of an officer to the problem-solving process. It is analogous to our taking a large number of frames from a motion-picture film, and subjecting each to analysis upon its own merits. As Von Neumann and Morgenstern write,

> . . . our theory is thoroughly static. A dynamic theory would unquestionably be more complete and therefore preferable. But there is ample evidence from other branches of science that it is futile to try to build one as long as the static side is not thoroughly understood.[1]

---

[1] Von Neumann and Morgenstern, *Theory of Games and Economic Behavior* (New York: Princeton University Press, 1944), p. 44.

3.1 THE SEED CADRE

The men at the center of the early IFS were previously of British Indian cadres, the ICS and IPS. Just as the IPS was during the British Indian bureaucratic system an elite within an elite of the ICS, those men of the early IFS with ICS and IPS backgrounds constituted an IFS intra-elite. These men (forwarded from the former Secretary of State's Services) are labeled in this study the seed cadre, due to the catalytic role which they played in the early IFS, analogous to the role which the seed plays in the chemical process of crystallization. The seed cadre were bound within a community of shared interests persisting from their days with the British leadership. K.P.S. Menon and M.C. Chagla were both classmates at Oxford and participated in the network of "Old Boy" relationships generated by membership in that institution. These ties linked Indian bureaucrats of that period and of that special cadre to each other and to former British colleagues, the latter of whom had managed to develop for themselves legitimacy among professionally-proximate Indians. K.P.S. Menon writes that he did not

> ... have that highly developed civil service consciousness which N.R. Pillai had. N.R. was imbued with the British tradition that it was the duty of a civil servant to serve the government of the day regardless of its political complexion. I knew this principle, but sometimes I was vexed by the thought that it was one thing for an Englishman to serve a government, Liberal, Labor or Conservative; another for an Indian to serve an alien government.[2]

This equanimity was politically inappropriate but may have been helpful in their later tasks as diplomats and bureaucrats to those men who held such views. No hard data yet exists on the prevalence of these attitudes, but it is clear that due to the need of skilled manpower the upper attitudinal tolerance-threshold of the larger political system was quite high. The IFS seed cadre of thirty-six officers was not for the most part selected for their diplomatic experience, because only four had prior experience in foreign relations management. These men were K.P.S. Menon, G.S. Bajpai, H.S.

---

[2] K.P.S. Menon, *Many Worlds: An Autobiography* (Bombay: Oxford University Press, 1965), pp. 57, 135.

Table 3.1: IFS: the first eighteen years

Immediate needs granted by	thirty officers, former Secretary of State's Services
	more than eighty officers from Federal Public Service Commission, and from "Special Selection Board from among officers holding Emergency Commissions."
Since then	172 officers, from 1947 to 1965, were recruited through UPSC competitive examinations.

On January 1, 1966, the IFS cadre consisted of:

	officers
permanently seconded from ICS, IPS and IA and AS	20
selected through FPSC	33
selected through Special Selection Board	33
promoted from ISI posts	5
promoted from IFS(B)	18
selected through competitive examinations	<u>162</u>
Total	271

source: *Report of the Committee*, p. 4.

Malik (who had been in British days consul-general for New York) and P.A. Menon (who had been secretary to the agent-general in Washington). Among the cadre recruits without foreign precedents were Subimal Dutt, N.R. Pillai, R.K. Nehru, C.S. Jha, Rajeshwar Dayal and T.N. Kaul.[3] The majority were not chosen for foreign experience but rather for their administrative talent. After the formation of the seed cadre axis came the recruitment of about one hundred overage candidates, in the process of which the IFS began to resemble the British IPS. The IPS and IFS shared a similar dual mixture of ICS and military officers, though only the four IFS seed cadre bureaucrats with foreign experience had gained their experience in the IPS. In this regard, the important difference between the old IPS

---

[3] Menon, p. 274; T.N. Kaul, *Diplomacy in Peace and War* (New Delhi: Vikas, 1979), p. 84.

and the early IFS was that their military-civilian composition was evolved differently. Regular recruitment channels existed for induction from the military into the IPS, whereas for the IFS induction from the military in the overage category was a stopgap measure. The overage recruitment group included some professionals as well as some members of the old Indian (princely) states.[4] Most overage candidates, however, were brought into the early IFS from either the civilian or military sectors of the British government.

The IFS of the Nehru period was not as professionally confident of its mission as it might have been, there being too much interference in the careerists' work by Nehru, Krishna Menon and other central executive members. Perhaps because of this the IFS's pace of expansion in the beginning was quite slow, with only four officers brought into the service in 1951-52. This pace continued throughout the Nehru period, with an increase in the rate of recruitment after the 1962 border conflict.[5] The increased recruitment fervor, however, was not enough to close the gap between needs and actual manpower levels. This early languor in recruitment was matched on the diplomatic level when in 1951-52 only one new mission was opened abroad. Though foreign policy has always seemed a very high Indian government priority, budgets have been limited and IFS recruitment has had difficulties. It is through the weight of years rather than rapidity of progress that the IFS has reached its present size.

---

[4] Dr. I.J. Bahadur Singh, Indian diplomat emeritus and student of the Indian overseas communities, was among the former group; K.M. Panikkar, a former advisor to the Kashmir state ruling family, was a member of the latter group. The Maharashtran ruling family also had a family member in the early IFS. Interview with S.D. Muni, Jawaharlal Nehru University.

[5] Shashi Tharoor, *Reasons of State* (New Delhi: Vikas, 1982), p. 31; Ministry of External Affairs, *Annual Report 1951-52*, p. 3; *Report of the Committee on the Indian Foreign Service* (New Delhi: Government of India, 1966), p. 84.

3.2 CONTEMPORARY SERVICE STRUCTURE

The individual officer looks to the IFS organization as guardian of his welfare and consequently of his family and his position in society, but what can be provided in bread and butter (or perhaps better put, *roti* and *chawal*) is limited by economics. The IFS is small, ". . . among the smallest and most economically run Diplomatic Services of the world."[6] As a result of this an ambassador or secretary in MEA made (in 1982 figures) only Rs. 3500 monthly, making competition with the private and foreign private sectors difficult. Though perks include free and high-quality housing and transportation, the salary is still far below what a professional might make elsewhere. The pay and perks at the top of the scale form the base which determines pay at lower rungs of the ladder. As in other administrative services the grading of posts and determination of seniority is a function of gross weekly take. The IFS is organized into a number of junior grades, above which is a senior scale with its own internal subdivisions. Above this general salary structure lie the selection posts, attained not in automatic promotion but through special high-level recommendation. The scale structure has never within the organization been a serious point of friction, though it would be surprising if there were not some dissatisfaction. Grumbling on this topic was a favorite nineteenth century ICS pastime, at a time when salaries were many times what they are today for the IFS and IAS.[7]

The hierarchy is not monolithic but more an arrangement of cadres loosely mapped onto a central salary scale. The early foreign policy bureaucracy was run by men and women who owed allegiance to a number of services; at that time there was not just one IFS, but several. As T.N. Kaul laments,

> . . . Nehru tried to weld us all together into a homogenous family, but interservice rivalries and jealousies, the class structure and composition of the service, made it into a heterogenous hotchpotch. The new entrants who came in through open competitive examinations were a fine lot and very promising, but many of them soon imbibed the mannerisms and methods of their seniors and thought of themselves as an elitist group, a cut above the

---

[6] *Report of the Committee*, p. 6.

[7] *Report of the Committee*, p. 47; Nair, p. 48.

> IAS and other services . . . Some of us tried to integrate the various branches of the Ministry into one Service. We also proposed an interchange between IFS and other All India Services, like IAS at junior levels. This would have given wider experience to the IAS and dug deeper the roots of the IFS into the soil of India, but vested interests prevented this . . .[8]

Kaul implies that the problems encountered in interservice coordination resulted from the juxtaposition of the old bureaucracy onto a radically different environment. However, the confusion seems strictly to have been between the newly-created services rather than between the new and the old. What existed in the beginning of the modern period was a community of services, the IAS, IFS, Information Service, and the {A, B} branches of the IFS, all contributing in some way to the formulation and implementation of foreign policy. Because a single service capable of handling all of the needs of early Indian foreign policy could not be set up immediately, many other participants were "brought into the action." Eventually the major digressions from IFS leadership, such as the Information Service, were assimilated into the IFS.

MEA is today, with few (but mostly Information Service) exceptions, staffed by members of the {A, B} branches of the IFS, the Interpreters' Cadre and the Research Cadre. Newest is the Interpreters' Cadre, the rules of which were only being notified (that is, the particulars of cadre organization were only finalized) in June 1978, with recruitment initiated in 1979. While MEA has at its disposal among the IFS regular careerists fluency in over twenty-three languages, this is a resource not always easy to tap. The officers are first diplomats and second translators, so extensive language work had to be specially provided for. In 1975-76 there were twenty-eight members of the Interpreters' Cadre in the ministry, and as seen in Table 3.2 their numbers have not grown considerably since the development of this special cadre.

Other than the Research Cadre the largest component outside of IFS(A) in MEA is IFS(B), formally constituted on August 1, 1956 to man posts ". . . of a ministerial character and some higher non-ministerial posts not usually held by IFS officers." The sanction to form the new cadre had been obtained from the cabinet in the period 1952-53. From 1956 recruitment

---

[8] T.N. Kaul, p. 84.

Table 3.2: Combined cadre strength: 1981-82

IFS(A)	
grade I	18[a]
grade II	21[a]
grade III	80[b]
grade IV	82
senior scale	249
junior scale	100
training reserve[c]	50
leave reserve	18
training reserve	19
deputation reserve	20
IFS(A) total	657
IFS(B)	
grade I	119
grade II/III	324
grade IV	916
grade V, VI	690
grade II cypher subcadre	195
selection grade of stenographers' subcadre (SSC)	50
grade I of SSC	75
grade II of SSC	537
grade III of SSC	120
combined research cadre[d]	45
interpreters' cadre	33
IFS(B) total	3,104
total cadre strength	3,761

[a] excluding one post temporarily upgraded from grade III.
[b] excluding one post of FA EA and three ex-cadre posts.
[c] junior scale.
[d] including isolated research posts.
source: *Report 1981-82*, p. 82.

proceeded for three years, first among those officers already in MEA, the Ministry of Commerce and the Ministry of Industry. This was followed by a recruitment drive aimed at the remaining central ministries, capped off by recruitment from some of the state governments. When foundation recruitment was ended B branch's strength was set at a "permanent" 1700 with 600 "temporary" posts, though the size of the IFS(B) has since then risen steadily. In 1975-76 IFS(B) had an overall strength of 2832 and the present strength (as seen in Table 3.1) indicates a 9.60 percent expansion, or 1.54 percent annually. An expansion of B branch has served to ease the chronic shortage of manpower in MEA, even of officers, so that IFS(B) careerists can be found in a number of under-secretary posts in the ministry. A few IFS(B) officers have been promoted even to deputy secretary posts.[9]

In 1966 there were, including clerical and stenographers' grades, 278 officers in the IFS(A) and 2400 in IFS(B). In order to more effectively regulate these rapidly growing resources at least two cadre reviews were initiated in the past seven years. The first such review was completed in 1979, included both branches of the IFS, and led to changes in the staffing of missions abroad. In 1982 a second cadre review was in progress in consultation with the Ministry of Finance and the Department of Personnel and Administrative Reforms. Part of the findings of this second review may concern the decline of the multifunctional officer in the missions abroad. The generalist IFS has long handled manpower shortages in the missions abroad by making a single officer responsible for a number of functions, but this has saddled the diplomat abroad with too much work. Since 1981 this problem has been partially rectified through the replacement of the multifunctional with single-function full-time officers, aided by supporting staff.[10] The supporting staff force is drawing mostly upon IFS(B) resources, so that the major shift in cadre emphases for the eighties has been a widening of the range of positions occupied by B branch employees. This is undoubtedly closely related to the shift of mission manpower from the prestigious capitols of the North and South Asian neighborhood (see chapter 10).

---

[9] The Research Cadre will be dealt with in chapter 6. *Report 1978-79*, pp. 67-68; *Report 1975-76*, p.129; *Report 1952-53*, p. 3; *Report of the Committee*, pp. 5, 105; also personal interview, Dr. Satish Kumar, Jawaharlal Nehru University.

[10] *Report of the Committee*, p. 84; *Report 1978-79*, p. 67; *Report 1981-82*, pp. 59-60.

3.3 TRAINING

The IFS officer's (IFS without suffix will be understood to mean IFS[A]) minimally thirty years of service (with mandatory retirement at the age of fifty-eight) is initiated with a three-year training period. The conduct and duration of this training period have long been topics of debate, with pressing manpower requirements making a less extensive training period very attractive. Though training continues to be very involved, a number of changes in priorities have transpired. The following excerpt describes the training regimen in 1953:

> The Indian Foreign Service has crossed the formative stage and new entrants are now selected on the results of an annual competitive examination which is open to university graduates within the ages of 21 and 24. Recruits on first appointment as probationers spend a few months in the Indian Administrative Service Training School in Delhi where, along with cadets of other services, they receive instruction in subjects connected with the administration of the country, and in Indian History, Economics and Hindi . . . at the end of this course this time they study international affairs, international law, history and economics, and also begin the intensive study of a foreign language. On leaving the university they spend some months in the country whose language they are studying. Thereafter, they receive about a year's training at the headquarters of the Government, in the Ministries of External Affairs, and Commerce, and Industry, to gain familiarity with some aspects of their future work. A period of service at the headquarters or in a mission abroad in the rank of an Attaché may follow. At the end of the three-year probationary period, the young officer embarks on his career as a member of the Foreign Service after crossing the final hurdle of a departmental and a language examination.[11]

---

[11] *Report 1953-54*, p. 27.

In the 1950s a large portion of the IFS probationers' academic training took place in foreign universities, this necessitated by the lack of adequate indigenous training facilities. Satisfying the language requirements of one year of study in two foreign languages was particularly difficult, as adequate linguistic training facilities inside India were for a number of years missing. Most candidates studied in Great Britain and the United States; the five IFS candidates accepted in 1951, for example, received their initial training in the U.S., Great Britain and Switzerland. In time language facilities were improved, and Allahabad and Benares Hindu Universities became major early training facilities. All diplomatic academic training now takes place at Jawaharlal Nehru University (JNU), whose growth as a diplomatic training center began in 1969. The first classes in diplomatic studies at JNU took place in 1971, eventually developing into a full departmental program. Teaching conditions at both Allahabad and Benares Hindu Universities were then stagnating, so that diplomatic instructional centralization, already a tendency, became mandatory. In 1971, the School of International Studies in New Delhi was also merged with JNU, strengthening the program and simplifying the New Delhi training regimen considerably. At present about fifty IAS/IFS candidates come annually from the portals of JNU.[12]

After JNU much of the trainees' time is spent at the Lal Bahadur Shastri Academy of Administration (in the British period known as MacCalfe House) in Mussourie. Training is continued at the Indian Institute of Foreign Trade, the Institute of Mass Communications and the Institute for Defence Studies and Analyses (IDSA) at which, respectively, the topics of administration, propaganda and security studies are covered. All this takes place in a two-year period initiated after the candidate attains a B.A. in diplomatic studies (when the candidate must be between twenty-one and twenty-eight years old). This is presently followed by one year of working experience as an under-secretary in South Block, where the trainee will stay for three or four months before transferring to another real-world post. The long period of hands-on training has British precedents, as contrasted with the American and German emphasis on academic preparation.

---

[12] *Report 1952-53*, p. 3; for these insights into academic training the author is much indebted, again, to S.D. Muni, who has done his PhD. dissertation on this and related topics.

Besides these three broad training areas of academic, special institutional and working experience, there were several, more uniquely Indian, interjections into the training process. In 1954-55 it was decided, in a very Gandhian vein, that IFS probationers should spend six months in a rural district before moving on to other tasks.[13] This was in addition to a junkey of much of India for officers with little experience of life in other parts of the country (called the *Bharat Darshan*), as well as a period spent attached to a military unit. All of this was undertaken to discourage the development of elitism in the IFS, but the training interludes have been criticized as taking too much time from the more pressing matters of practical diplomacy.

Training is under the jurisdiction of certain personnel sections within MEA's Administrative Wing. An attempt was made in the late 1960s to set up a Directorate of Training to centralize management of the instructional process, but this idea appears to have been dropped.[14] No currently available estimates of the effectiveness of Indian diplomatic training exist, but probably a less scattered curriculum would help matters considerably. A Foreign Service Institute, where the probationer might spend the entire two years of institutional training, would make instructional phasing much easier and would help trainees to see themselves as professionals with a very special and critical job. As it is, IFS officers are trained almost as if they were just overseas IAS officers. Though the diplomat and bureaucrat be combined in one person the skills drawn upon in the two roles are very different. A task distinction between bureaucratic and diplomatic skills must be made during the probationary period. A Foreign Service Institute would also help to utilize the valuable experience of the many diplomats emeritus in the instruction of new recruits, a resource which must be utilized if Indian diplomacy is to learn from its errors and improve. Finally, a point covered in the next section, the Institute would aid in the external political control of bureau socialization processes. Without such a control over socialization, a control led from the beginning of officers' bureau careers, the engineering of more effective (from the perspective of the central executive) policy structures must remain far more difficult.

---

[13] *Report 1954-55*, p. 2.

[14] *Report 1971-72*, p. 131.

3.4 SOCIALIZATION

Socializational, integrative, and elite-formative forces within the IFS community are not as strong as in the American and British foreign policy organizations. Of a total (in 1967) of 3,453 officers in the United States Foreign Service, only nineteen black, sixteen hispanic and nine Asian American officers served. In 1981, fourteen years later, members of minority groups made up only 2.5 percent of the foreign service.[15] The IFS, however, ever since Union Public Service Commission examinations began have had a strong all-India and transcaste appeal, with even in the higher pay-grades consistently over ten percent representation of the scheduled castes and tribes. Quotas are set under Scheduled Castes-Scheduled Tribes (SCST) requirements to maintain at least a twenty percent representation for members of these groups, so, despite impressive attainments, the government's SCST guidelines have not been achieved. Among Class I (the highest of the salary divisions) employees in 1978-79 only 7.3 percent were from the scheduled castes and 3.9 percent from scheduled tribes, for an 11.2 percent total. Percentages were somewhat higher for the other classes until in the lowest Group D or Group IV the twentieth SCST percentile is reached and surpassed. In order to raise SCST percentages in the three higher salary groups, in 1975-76 a special "watchdog" administrative cell was set up.[16] Part of the problem raised by increases in SCST representation is that the scheduled groups are subject to educational handicaps which make it difficult to meet quotas in some areas without lowering educational standards in government service.

Though not strong, some signs of elite formation within the foreign policy bureaucracy do exist. The IFS seed cadre had within it some officers, as already mentioned, with a very "British" outlook. They would have constituted a force, though possibly negligible, in favor of recruitment with a class bias. G.S. Bajpai was in favor of an induction system that would have allowed the selection of officers based at least in part on the social backgrounds of the candidates (to be discussed further in section 3.5). The IFS has demonstrably been a family affair for many officers, such as

---

[15] *Diplomacy for the '70's: A Program of Management Reform for the Department of State,* Department of State Publication 8551, Department and Foreign Service Series 143 (released December 1970), p. 278; *Chicago Tribune,* June 4, 1984, section 3, page 5.

[16] *Report 1978-79,* p. 114; *Report 1975-76,* p. 54.

K.P.S. Menon. In 1952, the year of his retirement as foreign secretary, Menon's son was first secretary in the London High Commission, his first daughter had married an Indian member of the UN Secretariat, and his second daughter had married the Indian consul-general in San Francisco. The present (since March 1984) ambassador to the U.S., Kayatyani Shankar Bajpai, is the son of G.S. Bajpai and has a son, Jayanti, who shortly (c. 1984) was to join the IFS.[17] These are but two cases of what seems a widespread phenomenon. As we can see from Table 3.3, about forty-seven percent of MEA officials in 1966 had fathers in various government positions (a strong urban bias is also apparent). Nehru also had a number of family members in foreign policy positions.[18] The subject deserves further study in the light that it may shed in understanding Indian foreign policy. We would expect to see stronger shared organizational cognitive structures to develop where family relationships among officers are more prevalent.

The role of women, who currently occupy about one of every eight IFS posts in MEA, has steadily and successfully expanded since early barriers to their advancement were taken down.[19] During the Nehru period a ruling that female officers who married had to resign from the IFS prejudiced the foreign service against women considerably. The rule, later found discriminatory and unconstitutional, was abolished early in the Nehru period. Now the major handicap facing prospective female probationers in the IFS arises from pre-recruitment family attitudes rather than on-the-job bias. Once the conservative family bias is overcome, the extended Indian family is much easier for the working woman to manage than the nuclear family of her American or European counterparts.

---

[17] Both K.S. Bajpai and his son had boarding school careers at St. Albans, in Washington, D.C. K.S. Bajpai, though, went on to Oxford and his son has pursued university work at Georgetown. Menon, p. 276; *New York Times*, March 20, 1984, p. 12.

[18] To be discussed further in chapter 10.

[19] According to the Congressional Caucus for Women's Issues, the percentage of women among the United States foreign service remained the same, twenty-six, in the period 1970-81. In 1981, only three percent of all the senior State Department jobs were held by women. *Chicago Tribune*, June 4, 1984, section 3, page 5.

Indian Foreign Service   57

Table 3.3: Distribution of IFS officers according to parent's profession: 1966

urban		rural	
government employees	81	landlords	12
teachers	25	laborers	2
business, professional	44	miscellaneous	1
miscellaneous	7		
total	157	total	15
percentage of urban to total recruitment		percentage of rural to total recruitment	
percentage of urban to total population		percentage of urban to total population	

source: *Report of the Committee*, p. 146.

3.5 RECRUITMENT, INDUCTION, PROMOTION

Recruitment from JNU and other preparatory academic channels is ordinarily the task of the Union Public Service Commission (UPSC), but before its establishment other methods were used. Selection of the first seed cadre and overage batch of officers was made by the Federal Public Service Commission's (FPSC) Special Selection Board. The Board had Lala Shri Ram as chairman and the foreign secretary, commonwealth secretary and commerce secretary (all of the interim government) as members. Over the objections of G.S. Bajpai the Board was dismantled immediately after the selection of the first 130 officers; M.O. Mathai claims that it was taken down under charges of nepotistic abuse.[20] After this in 1948 the first UPSC examinations were held, with the final batch of overage recruitees brought into the organization in 1949. Since that time IFS recruitment has been through the UPSC portal, with a handful

---

[20] See M.O. Mathai, *My Days with Nehru* (New Delhi: Vikas, 1979), pp. 119-21.

of high-level political appointments. The non-IFS lower grades apparently bypass the UPSC, though at which point this transition is made is not known.

In 1948-65 172 officers were brought into the IFS, thirteen of whom were women and nineteen members of SCST groups. Since then there have been serious IFS manpower shortfalls. The problem is first brought up by the *Report of the Committee on the Indian Foreign Service,* recommending the expansion through a variety of techniques of IFS cadre from 278 officers in 1966 to 550 in 1976. The techniques included:

- the conversion of temporary to permanent posts;

- increased university recruitment;

- the induction of IFS(B) personnel into IFS posts (the *Report* recommended annual induction of IFS[B] into ten to fifteen percent of A branch posts opened that year);

- additional overage recruitment;

- the "borrowing" of talent from the IAS and other services.

In charge of the transfer of manpower is the Foreign Service Board, ". . . responsible for all diplomatic, commercial and consular postings and transfers, promotions and confirmations of Foreign Service officers of the Indian Foreign Service and Grade I of the Indian Foreign Service(B)."[21] It was in 1966 headed by the foreign secretary with a membership of Secretaries East, West, Commerce and MEA's Joint Secretary of Administration Wing. Promotion, the most difficult task of the Foreign Service Board, is made strictly on merit for IFS grades I-V, and on the basis of seniority-cum-merit for the lower grades. Accelerated promotion from IFS(B) to IFS postings and from lower to higher grades is also made upon merit.[22]

Probably the most important transfer of resources inside MEA is the movement from B to A branch of IFS; it is certainly the Pillai suggestion taken most seriously by modern leadership. There has been since IFS(B)'s creation a great deal of {A,B} friction which arose from disparities in the distribution of what are known to officials as the "three P's": (a) promotions; (b) payscales; (c) perks. Promotions were not rapid

---

[21] *Report of the Committee,* pp. 2, 73, 85.

[22] *Report 1970-71,* p. 84.

enough for IFS(B) officers, and payscales and perks were regarded as inequitable for IFS(B) employees. The induction of IFS(B) officers into IFS ranks, similar to the Department of States's policy of lateral entry, is a way of easing interbranch tension while also easing the manpower problem.[23] In 1975-76 52 new posts were opened in the selection grade of Grade VI of IFS(B) and four posts with the designation of record keeper were created in Group D in order to improve the advancement opportunities for IFS(B) employees. But even with this and other induction channels open there has not been full implementation of the Pillai Committee's recommendations. An A branch strength of 550 was envisioned for 1976, but by 1975-76 only 454 officers had been recruited.[24] Because the Pillai Committee recommendations were probably forwarded on more of an intuitive than a rigorous planning base, the indicated seventeen percent shortfall in manpower goal-attainment is not conclusive in determining actual manpower deficiencies. And even if the assessed requirements were correct, the shortfall says nothing about the source of the shortfall. The shortfall may, for example, have had political (e.g., the Pillai Committee's possible failure to impress the policy elite with the accuracy of its prescription) rather than operational (e.g., the MEA's inability to train sufficient number of new recruitees in time) causation.

According to one Indian diplomat, one of the problems with modern IFS recruitment is that IFS membership does not confer the sense of tangible power and affluence that even IAS work does, not to mention its prospects in competition with the business community.[25] A young person's future career, even for one brought up in a sophisticated, Westernized family, is still largely determined by his parents. Parents can easily understand and boast about their son gaining the directorship of an agricultural program near Agra, but to say rather that he is vice-consul in the West German embassy can bring more puzzlement than praise. The opportunity for graft and corruption is also for the IFS officer somewhat restricted. Behavioral controls for the foreign service are more efficient than controls for the civil service. Gain through unlawful or immoral means is regrettably expected by many Indians of their offspring, and the perceived gain of IFS

---

[23] This is the suggestion of I.J. Bahadur Singh, personal interview.

[24] *Report 1975-76*, pp. 54, 128.

[25] Personal interview. Summer, 1982.

employment is lowered relative to the IAS by that token. The IFS has "no more glamor," and opportunities to travel are opening up within the business community and IAS (because of domestic ministries' participation in the foreign policy community). The IFS, in short, is now facing competition. This is a crucial domestic-bureaucratic/level-three--level-four relationship.

3.6 DISSENT

Rebellion against the established order inside MEA has occurred but is not common.[26] Resignation, an internationally-comparatively common channel for disagreement, is a rare occurence inside MEA. In the period 1948-65, out of 172 officers there were only six resignations. Three of these were women dropping out due to pending marriages (which, as the reader will remember, disqualified them from continued service) and the remainder (less than two percent of the total IFS force at that time) resigned for reasons not given.[27] Even if these resignations occurred for policy reasons, dissent as expressed through this channel in 1948-65 was not strong. The journalistic leak, a common means of dissent in the West (as well as a tool for the manipulation of public opinion by elites), is not very frequently used inside MEA. Nayar relates that the entire text of the confidential Indo-Soviet talks of 1968 were leaked to the press, much to the Soviet diplomats' displeasure.[28] This seems to have been, for MEA, an isolated event.

The leak is a more common Ministry of Defence practice. According to one observer, defense officials have their "own little games" which they play with favored journalists.[29] Officials will approach carefully-selected journalists with a report or other

---

[26] See, for example, A.N. B'Crat (pseudonym), "the Uncivil Masters Who Rule India," *Perspective*, 1, September 1977, pp. 20-33; Badrud-din Tyabji, "Foreign Policy Set-Up: The Case for a Review Commission," *Statesman*, March 6, 1976; quoted in Tharoor, pp. 117, 172. See also the case of Nirmala Prasad, section 10.3.

[27] *Report of the Committee,* pp. 73, 81.

[28] Kuldip Nayar, *Between the Lines* (Bombay: Allied Publishers, 1969), pp. 99-100.

[29] Personal interview. Summer 1982.

information on a current topic, presenting the views of the officials as "concerned citizens," men afraid that certain defense decisions will damage Indian security. It is not known if these approaches to individual journalists are made with the approval of higher leadership. A couple of days, for example, after the announcement of the 1982 American decision to sell F-16 fighter aircraft to Pakistan a report was circulated to certain Indian journalists which set out the defense ministry's (unofficial) side in the matter. These forms of pseudo-dissent are practiced, but real bureaucratic disagreements are still not often openly expressed. Of course, India is not the only country in which pseudo-dissent is practiced; journalists can be in any society both a temptation and a threat to the bureaucracy's closure.

IV
The Procedural Hierarchy

As discussed previously, structure can have a variety of degrees of objectivity; lines of command, divisional structure, methods of administration, particularly when on paper, can be more paradigmatic constructs than precise delineations of behavior. What exists in a more objective analysis are lines of communication, which determine the flow of information within the total bureaucracy. The information and resources (manpower, budgetary) available to the subsets of the bureaucracy set in turn are essential to the determination of the outcome of plays of whatever bureau game we might study; subsets are defined as players. This chapter will demonstrate that a large proportion of bureau lines of communication can be generated by mapping a set defined as all members of a bureau onto a monotone transformation. That is, many of the relationships between bureaucrats can be characterized by what might be called a seniority operation, in which everyone is {superior, not-superior} to everyone else. In this chapter, we will be in essence establishing a strengthened monotone scale, in which equality of rank can be determined (through the institution of formal bureaucratic labels) and an identity exists (the seniormost official, who is never subordinate within the bureau). Any line-related group of individuals has game-assets strongly correlated with its seniority relation set.[1]

Administrative guidelines established during the British regime now form one generalized pattern for all the ministries. Just as diplomatic rank and title have changed little over the centuries, in fact since the Treaty of Westphalia in 1648, bureaucratic rank and title have changed very little. The changes to be chronicled in chapters 6-10 are those of the system of

---

[1] This information-theoretical analysis will be fully developed in the author's planned 1988 study.

ranks and procedures in the larger organization, in their arrangement and relationship, but not of the ranks and procedures internally, as members of the system. The ranks are the basic building blocks of the bureaucracy and perhaps are viewed as too much the bureaucracy's trivia to merit serious inquiry or alteration (by the central executive). Communist leadership in the USSR and PRC are exceptions; both experimented for a time with discarding rank and privilege in their armed forces, frequently a country's largest administrative hierarchy. In both countries, when state administration proved more complex than the predictions of Marxist-Leninist doctrine, the experiment was dropped (though the gradient of privilege-distribution between officers and enlisted men in the PRC's Red Army has been significantly reduced). In India, as noted, the British administrative system has been adopted virtually without change by the conservative (among post-colonial Third World states) Indian government. Both the system of formal ranks and their effect upon actual operations have been retained without significant intentional variation.

MEA's history is unique in both the frequency and purposiveness of change. Adaptations far greater in number than in any other ministry have had to be made in MEA, due to the special mission of this ministry, or the unusual character of the policy jurisdiction, and the close scrutiny which it has been under from the time of Nehru. Nevertheless, a general system of rank and command has come about which all the ministries, including MEA, share. The generalized system is desirable as it makes interministerial coordination easier and smooths the task of cabinet leadership. The particular adaptation of MEA to this general system is represented in Table 4.1. For most of the 1950s the administrative hierarchy was rather simpler than at present: (a) the secretary was the superior of the joint secretary; (b) the joint secretary was the superior of the deputy secretary; (c) the deputy secretary was the superior of the under-secretary, a simple quaternary chain of command. And instead of the present multiplicity of joint secretaries there were only three, who resembled more the additional secretaries of today's MEA than its joint secretary.[2] MEA has certainly become more complex in recent times, but mostly in response to external requirement stimuli rather than the internal momentum of the foreign policy bureaucracy. We can begin to understand the method behind administrative change by starting at the narrow top of

---

[2] See, for example, Ministry of External Affairs, *Annual Report 1951-52*, p. 1.

Table 4.1: MEA administrative hierarchy

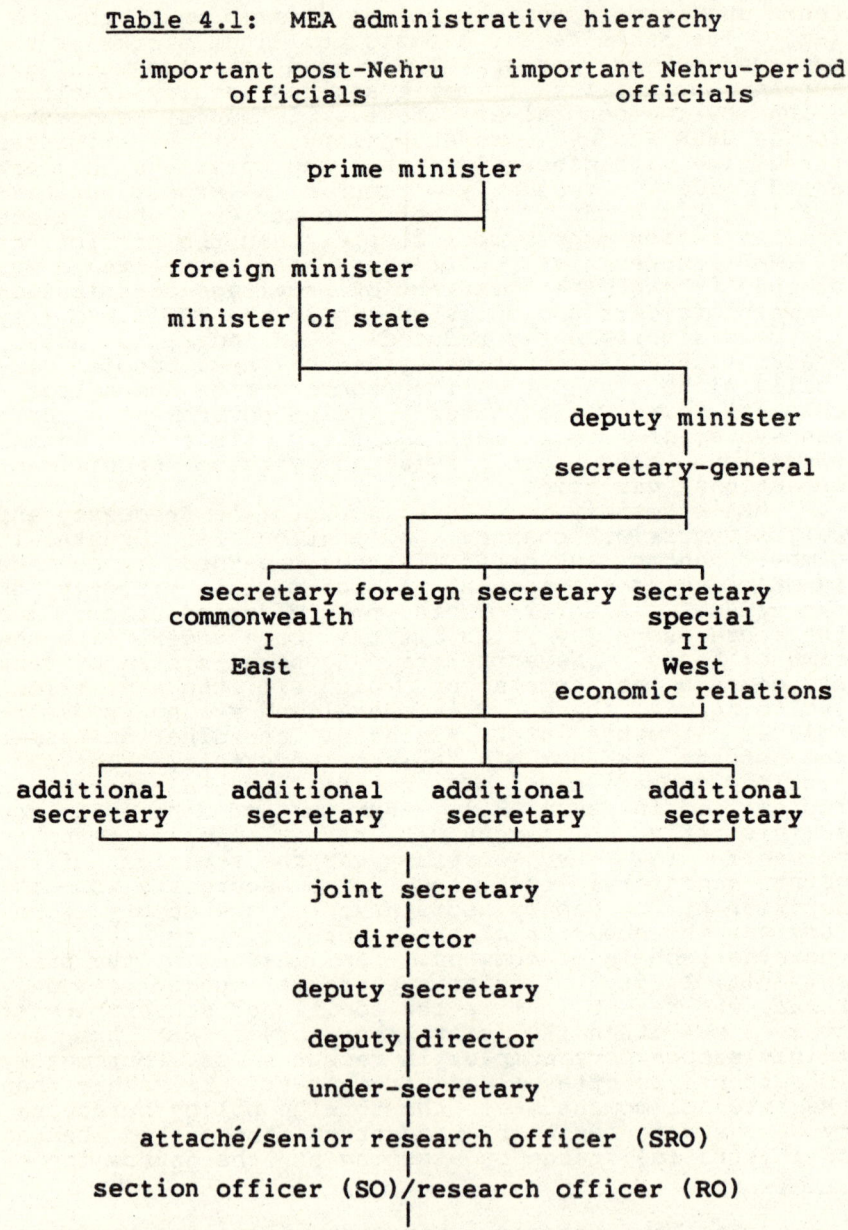

Procedural Hierarchy 65

Table 4.2: Hierarchy composition: 1952-55

1952-53
one secretary-general two secretaries four joint secretaries eight deputy secretaries twenty-four under/assistant secretaries

1953-54
one secretary-general two secretaries five joint secretaries nine deputy secretaries twenty-four undersecretaries

1954-55
one secretary-general two secretaries eight joint secretaries ten deputy secretaries twenty-four under-secretaries

source: *Reports, 1952-55.*

the pyramid, and working our way down into the administration.

4.1 QUASI-CENTRAL EXECUTIVE

At the very apex of Indian government is the council of ministers, the fraternity of cabinet officials and junior ministers responsible for carrying out the directives of the central executive. The hub of this organization is the prime minister and the central level-two group, the cabinet. The junior ministers who implement the orders of their cabinet superiors make up the remainder of the council. There is no qualitative difference in the responsibilities of junior and senior ministerial officials. The cabinet, which in the British system is a decision-making body, is used in India as a platform for the dissemination of policy decided by the prime minister and his or her inner circle of advisors. Therefore, when looking at the ministerial contribution to foreign policy below the prime minister, we are looking at the implementative and interpretative side of policy rather than the stage of its initial formulation. Despite its denial of the important formulative responsibilities given the ministers and cabinet officials in other governments, ministers and cabinet officials other than the prime minister have often gained distinction and sometimes power in their positions.

The MEA has not followed the standard mold in its relationship with the cabinet, and conversely neither have other council officials assigned to MEA followed a standard pattern of relations. During the Nehru period, there was for a time a minister without portfolio who worked very closely with MEA, and became probably the best-known (especially outside of India) cabinet official below the prime minister in Indian government. That was Krishna Menon, who held this unique position February 1956-May 1957.[3] Though not all as well-known as Krishna Menon, all senior and junior ministers have distinct and well-defended responsibilities as the political representatives to the bureaucracy.

4.1.1 The Prime Minister

The highest minister related to MEA is the prime minister, of whom in post-1947 India there have been five:

1. Jawaharlal Nehru (1947-64)

2. Lal Bahadur Shastri (1964-66)

---

[3] Other ministers without portfolio in Nehru's government were N. Gopalaswami Ayyangar (1948-49), C. Rajagopalachari (1948), and T.T. Krishnamachari (1963), the lattermost who was minister without portfolio several weeks before he was fully instated in a cabinet position. See N. Parameswaran Nair, *The Administration of Foreign Affairs in India with Comparative Reference to Britain* (New Delhi: School of International Studies, 1963), p. 215.

3.   Indira Gandhi (1966-77, 1979-)

4.   Morarji Desai (1977-79)

5.   Charan Singh (1979)

During the Nehru era, the foreign portfolio was held by Nehru, a practice followed in his first days as prime minister by Lal Bahadur Shastri and at times by successor Indira Gandhi. Two conditions were probably behind Nehru's decision to keep the foreign portfolio to himself. First, passively, it was unnecessary to have another man in that position. Nehru was quite able and willing to fullfill this role by himself and simply did not want a foreign minister. Second, actively, a separate foreign minister could very well have been an obstruction to Nehru's authority. While a minister would have been obliged to carry out Nehru's orders, he would have had, as a political appointee, much broader interpretative powers than a career bureaucrat. A foreign minister's resignation, had it occurred, would have been embarassing and might have jeopardized Nehru's supremacy in the sphere of foreign policy. Nehru did however tell Bajpai that he wanted a foreign minister but could not find anyone he considered satisfactory for the post. The person who most wanted that post, Vijaya Lakshmi Pandit, was rejected by Nehru on the grounds that ". . . he would be criticized if he appointed his sister." Other members of Nehru's family, though, were not stopped by this counterjustification from assuming many different foreign policy postings.[4] Probably a stronger motive for Nehru's denial to his sister of the foreign portfolio was that ". . . she would argue with him on foreign affairs."[5]

4.1.2   The Independent Foreign Minister

When Shastri took over, he found an administrative machinery best suited for a prime minister such as Nehru accustomed to monopolizing the foreign policy process. Shastri at first retained the foreign portfolio, as Nehru had, but soon relinquished it due to illness to Sardar Swaran Singh, who thus became the first independent Indian foreign minister. Since Shastri (and before 1984), the foreign portfolio has remained out of the prime minister's hands (except for a short gap

---

[4] See chapter 10.

[5] Escott Reid, *Envoy to Nehru* (New Delhi: Oxford, 1981), pp. 37-38, 194.

1967-69, though this occurred because Smt. Gandhi was not prepared to immediately replace Foreign Minister Chagla rather than because of her desire to take over foreign). After Nehru there were seven independent foreign ministers and eleven distinct ministerial periods, namely:

1.   Lal Bahadur Shastri (1964; less than 0.5 years)

2.   Sardar Swaran Singh (1964-66, June 1970-October 1974)

3.   M.C. Chagla (1966-September 1967)

4.   Indira Gandhi (September 1967-1969, 1.5 years; July 1984-)

5.   Dinesh Singh (1969-June 1970)

6.   Y.B. Chavan (October 1974-March 1977)

7.   A.B. Vajpayee (March 1977-1979)

8.   S.N. Mishra (1979)

9.   P.V. Narasimha Rao (1979-July 1984)[6]

The choice of who should be foreign minister in a time of transition has been determined largely but not only by politics. When Shastri made his first cabinet, Indira Gandhi (for whom the foreign portfolio would have been a stepping stone to political ascendency) was denied foreign because it might have made her ". . . too powerful." At the same time, the competent M.C. Chagla was denied the position on the policy-specific ground that he was considered too radically anti-Pakistani.[7] The first foreign minister, Sardar Swaran Singh, was given the portfolio when Shastri was stricken while in office by his first heart attack. Singh was the first of three choices for the foreign ministership, over M.C. Chagla and Indira Gandhi. Swaran Singh proved very much the Shastri man,

---

[6] The typical length of tenure for foreign ministers has thus been a little over two years. The ministerial (though junior) MEA official who lasted longest in that capacity was probably Surendra Pal Singh, who was a minister-ranked official from at latest June 1968 to October 1974, more than six years.

[7] Kuldip Nayar, *Between the Lines* (Bombay: Allied Publishers, 1969), p. 14.

". . . unflashy, but steady." His main influence over policy was in urging a softer line on Soviet arms shipments to Pakistan, on the invasion of Czechoslovakia by Soviet forces, and a softer line on the refugee influx from East Bengal, all during his second tenure under Smt. Gandhi. Swaran Singh did not have any great influence on policy outside of these issues and always was basically a spokesman for, rather than a maker of, policy. Perhaps that is why he served longer than any other independent Indian foreign minister.

M.C. Chagla, the second independent foreign minister, seems to have won the portfolio through the competence that he had shown in public life as a chief justice of the Bombay high court, though, as Tharoor suggests, there were political reasons as well for his appointment.[8] It is suggested that Chagla owed his place in the Shastri cabinet partially to his being the only Muslim in the cabinet, and that he gained foreign under Gandhi due to his lack of Syndicate ties (the Syndicate was the group of men under the Congress-notable Kamaraj, who took it upon themselves to find a successor in 1964 to Nehru). Tharoor believes that Chagla's training as a jurist prejudiced his work as a diplomat, by conditioning Chagla toward a paradigm of diplomacy as a judicial nexus, a set of "decisions," rather than as a flexible complex of communication. However, in view of Chagla's very successful service as ambassador in London and Washington before gaining the foreign ministership, that his experience in the Bombay high court impaired in any way his skill as a diplomat is doubtful. His knowledge of law, presumably extending into the international realm, could not but have helped him to understand many of the issues that he came to work with (the bar is as well a common background for statesmen). Chagla was probably the minister most aware of what was happening below him, and most conscious of the bureaucracy not as a machine but as a group of people with real needs and personal difficulties. In this concern for the affairs of the IFS, he might be called the career foreign minister, as opposed to Dinesh Singh. The latter was the consumate institutional foreign minister. When Foreign Secretary Azim Hussain was attacked by parliamentary opposition for supposedly harboring pro-Pakistani sentiments (a manifestation of apprehensions concerning Muslim officers noted in chapter 2), it was the anti-Pakistani Chagla who came to Hussain's rescue at considerable political risk to himself. Chagla also apparently remained open to meeting with subordinates of any rank,

---

[8] Shashi Tharoor, *Reasons of State* (New Delhi: Vikas, 1982), p. 156.

though other ministers have restricted contact to those of joint secretary rank and above. Of the ministers, Chagla was apparently the most accessible after office hours.[9]

Whatever else may be known, Chagla's antipathy toward Pakistan is certain. Chagla said in the heat of the 1971 Bangladesh intervention,

> I want to see the destruction of 'Pakistan' . . . the destruction of all those vicious principles that Pakistan has stood for[:] military dictatorship, military tyranny, hostility towards India, two-nation theory, destruction of democratic rights and [of] every principle which is enshrined in the United Nations Charter . . . Pakistan was conceived in sin and is dying in violence.[10]

Such a position taken in the United States about the Soviet Union would place an individual to the far right. During Chagla's foreign political ministership, immediately after the 1965 Rann of Kutch episode, this stance toward Pakistan might not have been too far from the official position, so that it is not clear that Chagla's strong feelings about Pakistan were a hindrance to Indian diplomacy. Tharoor's claim that Chagla's bias against Pakistan hindered his work in the MEA seems unfounded. It did not seem to affect the bureaucracy, but was manifest only over the negotiating tables to which Chagla was personally present. Despite his interest in the bureaucracy, his presence in MEA was too transitory for him to have built up any appreciable influence over the bureaucracy as a whole.

Chagla was followed by Dinesh Singh, not a strong foreign minister but perhaps a more colorful and stronger personality than Swaran Singh. Dinesh Singh started his career as private secretary to Nehru, and as deputy minister had a closeness to Nehru which probably no one else of like rank has had. At that time, of course, deputy ministers were only official spokespeople, answering questions in parliament. They had little say in policy other than as advisors. Dinesh Singh became identified during his term with the new radical policy currents initiated by a much stronger Indira Gandhi. Gandhi, after the 1969 contest, had

---

[9] Tharoor, p. 167.

[10] M.C. Chagla, *Roses in December* (Bombay: Bharatiya Vidya Bhawan, 1973), pp. 461-62.

emerged in strength and was able to put forward and carry into implementation the new policy ideational structure; they were emphatically Gandhi's ideas, not Dinesh Singh's. The events of the period which gave rise to this new radical image were the upgrading of relations with North Vietnam, the invitation sent to the North Vietnam's Nguyen-thai-Binh to visit India, and a closer identification with the socialist bloc.[11] Dinesh Singh in the end cut his career short by loudly broadcasting his assumed importance to Smt. Gandhi's foreign policy. It is believed that Smt. Gandhi fired Singh to demonstrate that she needed no one person to make her foreign policy work, least of all her flashy foreign minister.

Smt. Gandhi's last pre-Janata foreign minister was Y.B. Chavan. Chavan was the emergency (1975-77) foreign minister, and, typical of many emergency-period political personalities, colorless and impotent in the face of the powerful streams of political favor flowing before him. Before 1969 the ministers were generally independent of Smt. Gandhi, and the bureaucrats also enjoyed considerable freedom. According to Tharoor, after 1968 senior bureaucrats were given control of all civil service appointments, so that one very important way of checking the bureaucracy's power ceased to exist for the cabinet.[12] The Congress split (1969) hindered and the emergency crushed this way of bureaucratic life.

The Janata foreign minister A.B. Vajpayee was quite active in his office but somewhat distracted by Janata intrigues. He had a greater measure of control than his Gandhi predecessors, and was responsible for some of the important policy changes regarding the overseas communities. His Lok Dal successor, S.N. Mishra, was responsible for a number of diplomatic *faux pas*, and Mishra's lame duck foreign ministership was not one of the more memorable periods in Indian foreign policy annals. The most recent independent foreign minister, P.V. Narasimha Rao, seemed to be practicing an effective brand of quiet diplomacy of which the most visible success was shown in the progress made in Indo-Pakistan relations. Narasimha Rao seemed to be more sensitive to the need for tact and caution in his diplomacy than previous men in this position, and was apparently treated in policy as an equal partner to Gandhi. Narasimha Rao easily outlasted his predecessors, with his five-year tenure, though less is known about this foreign minister's policy contribution than

---

[11] Tharoor, p. 158.

[12] Tharoor, p. 116.

about that of many of his peers. Narasimha Rao lost his foreign ministership in July 1984, in a series of Cabinet reshuffles brought about by the Punjab crisis. Smt. Gandhi once again took over foreign, further demonstration of the principle of increased executive power over foreign policy in crisis periods. The Punjab crisis is partly an international one, with Indian fears of Pakistani intervention in the crisis exaggerated by the role of the Indian overseas communities in the agitation.

The foreign minister is in charge of the MEA and is responsible for the conduct of the total Indian foreign policy effort. This implies as a first cut the foreign minister's authority over MEA, but since the Indian foreign policy effort encompasses over a half-dozen ministries, certain cabinet committees and even some semi-public bodies, the foreign minister's authority is recognized not only at headquarters but in government offices kilometers from his South Block office. The foreign minister is the most visible member of the foreign policy community. The frequent newspaper photographs of visiting dignitaries usually show the foreign minister dealing out the first handshake; official documents are replete with mention of him, and the highest-level negotiations are led by this man. But he seems to be a man often associated with the broad generalities of Indian foreign policy rather than the specifics of the flow and administration of that policy. When dealing with the personalities of the bureaucracy, it is probably a mistake to dwell too long on the character and the stance of the foreign minister, as his is more the task of political representation than the work of the bureaucracy. His power (when in power) as representative of the prime minister is undisputed in the present Indian system, and in those diplomatic negotiations to which he is a party he plays a very important role in policy formulation and in high-level implementation. He is more than just a ceremonial leader or politician rewarded by the portfolio, but he is not the equivalent of an American secretary of state in his relationship to the activities of the foreign policy community.

The secretary of state, the executive head of the Department of State, on the other hand probably has a lesser role in ceremony. In the United States diplomatic ceremony is not exclusively State's function but is shared evenly between a great many of the members of the foreign policy community, with an important White House component. This latter executive departmental staff-component is missing in the Indian system, modeled as it is on the British pattern. The American secretary engages in ceremony, but has traditionally taken an interest more in State internal affairs and in the broad community rather than in the task of political representation for the president, for which the latter has a large pool of special envoys, ambassadors-at-large and others. Bureau leadership is generally thought to demand the very highest representation, with the negotiational and outside representative positions going to lower-echelon (though highly qualified) individuals. As a consequence the secretary of state is less visible but has a greater say in the particulars of foreign policy. The Indian foreign minister has contrarily been regarded frequently as more or less a rubber stamp for policy already decided by Gandhi and her innermost circle of advisors. As K. Subrahmanyam writes,

> [g]enerally, decisions in specific instances or even policies are initiated and brought up to the minister concerned to say 'yes' or 'no.' Very rarely a major policy is initiated by the Minister himself.[13]

M.C. Chagla and Dinesh Singh were the only foreign ministers to take serious interest in MEA itself, but their scrutiny apparently did not penetrate to any depth. Vajpayee might have played a greater part in the bureaucracy, but he was too occupied in party squabbles to do a great deal of internal work with the bureaucracy. Narasimha Rao is a very talented and intelligent diplomat, but it is too early to know whether he will be able to fashion a role for himself clearly distinct from prime minister Gandhi.

The characterization of the foreign minister as "rubber stamp" is probably extreme, but the occupants of this office have not done much to make their contribution known in the public realm. Even if the characterization is valid, the foreign minister in exercising his right to approve a document or otherwise to reject it is doing something quite important. "In the Indian conditions, policy is largely formulated by the senior civil servants and the political leadership functions as monitors of this policy formulation."[14] The foreign

---

[13] K. Subrahmanyam, "Foreign Policy Planning in India," *Foreign Affairs Reports,* January 1975, p. 3.

[14] Subrahmanyam, p. 3; see also N. Parameswaran Nair, *The Administration of Foreign Affairs in India with Comparative Reference to Britain* (New Delhi: School of International Studies, 1963), p. 248.

minister is a participant in a system of bureaucratic checks and balances, keeping the bureaucracy within the bounds of political reality. The foreign minister's primary contribution to policy lies in ensuring ". . . that political objectives take precedence over economic and military strategies and that the civil service plays no more than its legitimate role."[15] One thing which the foreign minister can do which no other South Block official can is determine the types of policies that will not meet with Smt. Gandhi's approval. He is not the cook, but he is the gourmet whom the cook strives to keep happy.

This is a strictly informal system, as is much of Indian governing practice, and is a product of Shrimati (Smt.) Gandhi's unique style of leadership, no more than that. It operates because a foreign minister or in fact any cabinet member will not approve ministerial policy output when the policy may lead to his political downfall. Through this the foreign minister fullfills at least the purely negative feedback function of keeping MEA in line with political currents. This same system of checks and balances governs the relationship between a secretary of state and the president (in the U.S. system).

4.1.3 The Minister of State

At the next administrative level is the minister of state, also a member of the council of ministers. The constitution gives the minister of state, known in 1952-57 as "Minister of Cabinet rank," considerable formal powers, including the ability to assume control of a ministry in lieu of the cabinet minister's control. The minister of state first came to MEA when Dr. Syed Mahmud was appointed to the office in 1954. He remained until 1957 (at which time the general elections were held). For five years no one occupied the post, which was viewed as inessential and a political reward (Dr. Mahmud was a friend of Nehru, and seemed to men like Mathai the very type of "old man" appointee who was supposed to have surrounded Nehru in these council positions). In 1962 the position was reactivated with Lakshmi N. Menon, then spokesperson for the Indian government on the China war.[16] Dr.

---

[15] K.P. Mishra, "Foreign Policy Planning: Some Suggestions," *International Studies*, Vol. 17, 1978, p. 829.

[16] Subimal Dutt, *With Nehru in the Foreign Office* (Calcutta: Minerva Publications, 1977), p. 31; Nair, p.

Mahmud had complained that he was often bypassed by Nehru in the MEA hierarchy, and that he did not seem to be able to make any important contribution to the real work of the organization. With Smt. Menon the minister of state became a much more influential office and after Nehru seems to have taken over many of the functions earlier handled by the secretary-general. Later, the Janata leadership seems to have vested much more confidence in their minister of state, Samarendra Kundu, than Congress leadership had previously vested in their own officers of that rank.[17] The minister of state fullfills only those responsibilities given him by the foreign secretary, so that his duties are not fixed or limited like those of most other MEA officials. He remains a "wild card," his duties conforming to whatever current needs may be.

4.1.4 The Deputy Minister

The lowest-ranking member of the council of ministers, the deputy minister, performs a function identical to that of the British minister of state. The post, created in 1952 to ". . . help the Prime Minister in his Parliamentary work . . ." is, like the minister of state, no more than an extension of the foreign minister's office.[18] The first deputy minister in MEA was B.V. Keskar, followed by three prominent Nehru-period deputy ministers, Anil K. Chanda, Lakshmi N. Menon and Dinesh Singh, all of whom used the post as a stepping stone to higher stations. During much of the Nehru period, or up to Smt. Menon's assumption of the minister of state posting in 1962, the deputy minister was the most important council member under Nehru in foreign policy. After Nehru the post seems to have declined in prominence, though in the period of Smt. Gandhi's assumption of the foreign ministership (1967-69) she was assisted liberally by deputy minister B.R. Bhagat, the most prominent deputy minister of the post-Nehru period. In constitutional terms, the deputy minister is never given independent charge of a ministry, but is attached to the foreign minister or the

---

213; Sudershan Chawla, *The Foreign Relations of India* (Encino, California: Dickenson Publishing, 1976), p. 66.

[17] J. Bandyopadhyaya, *The Making of India's Foreign Policy* (New Delhi: Allied Publishers, 1979), p. 194.

[18] Nair, p. 214; Dutt, p. 31.

minister of state and does what is demanded of him by these officers.

4.1.5 The Junior Minister

Another Nehru official very similar to the MEA junior ministers was the parliamentary secretary. The parliamentary secretary was a member of one of the *sabhaė* (houses) of the *sansad* (parliament), and functioned mainly as a spokesman for the ministry. Two parliamentary secretaries were necessary for the two *sabhaė*, but before 1957 there were three such secretaries assigned to do parliamentary work. In general, the junior ministers and parliamentary secretaries were utilized mostly by the Nehru regime. This was a much less common practice for Nehru's successors. These officials functioned as Nehru wanted them to function, as contacts with the *sansad* and as general policy spokesmen. However, this was not the general government practice, and other ministries usually had deputy ministers taking part less in representation than in the ministry's administration. Outside of the foreign minister, the junior ministers were regarded, like the career bureaucrats, as climbers, and it was expected that at least a few junior ministers would eventually become cabinet officials themselves. The frustration of these hopes in the MEA structure and the apparent disuse to which the hierarchy had fallen led certain critics to censure the ministerial arrangement.[19]

It is true that the junior minister in MEA held little in common with the officials of the other ministries. First, MEA officials in the Nehru period seldom stayed with MEA for a very long time. B.V. Keskar was appointed minister for information and broadcasting after his term with MEA. That is the right direction for a deputy minister to move in, but to the wrong ministry. It is widely observed that the movement of ministers in the promotion process should be vertical rather than lateral. Anil Chanda was also shipped off after a short experience with MEA to another ministry. S.N. Misra and Satish Chandra, both parliamentary secretaries (1951-52), both dropped out of MEA after their terms. The only junior minister who appears to have stayed on was Lakshmi N. Menon, who rose from parliamentary secretary to deputy minister and finally to minister of state. Besides the irregularities in promotion, the junior ministers' work was reported to be "vague" and "ambiguous." These MEA officials simply didn't have the clearcut responsibilities assigned to

---

[19] See, for example, Nair, pp. 217-26.

other junior ministers. In 1948 Gopalaswami Ayyangar in his *Report on the Machinery of the Government of India* suggested that junior ministers be given clearly defined administrative duties in their respective ministries. This advice was carried out in much of the Indian government, but not in MEA.

This critique of the junior ministers' part in the MEA hierarchy, while not undeserved, is probably irrelevant for the Nehru period. Nehru ran MEA the way he wanted, and seldom let standard operating procedures get in his way. The author believes that junior ministers did not rise in MEA because Nehru wanted a foreign minister made to his personal order, not to that of the system. The careerist secretary-general was given precedence over the political deputy minister because of the secretary-general's need for clear seniority over the Indian ambassador abroad, and because the MEA secretaries as a rule got their way in policy matters over the junior ministers. Nehru did, however, need junior ministers for parliamentary work, and thereby the MEA ministers remained tied to these duties.

4.2 OPERATIONAL BUREAUCRATIC LEADERSHIP

4.2.1 The Secretary

Below the "political" ministerial ranks are the secretary ranks. The secretary

> . . . is the administrative head of the Ministry, and he is the principal advisor of the Minister on all matters of policy and administration within the Ministry. The Secretary is not only responsible for the organization and efficiency of the Ministry, but also for the advice given to the Minister through the whole range of his duties.[20]

The secretary is the most important career official of the MEA, and at times, as in the case of Janata foreign secretary Jagat Subha Mehta, he has been in command of the entire grouping of foreign policy bureaux. The secretary has a continuity of power in the bureaucracy such as no other MEA official has, and becomes the

---

[20] *Organization of the Government of India* (1971), p. 45.

officer whom we most need to study to learn how leadership directs and channels foreign policy. As the wheel rotates, every point on the wheel but the hub moves. The secretary has maintained his power because of his pivotal position in the bureaucracy, arising from his specific, permanent responsibilities and jurisdiction within MEA. Knight and McDaniel establish as a central organizational characteristic the existence of a "locus of power," some group of interrelated bureaucrats who together control, say, over sixty percent of the information and resources of the bureau. The secretaries constitute that group within MEA (though perhaps not to that proportion of influence).[21] Either contributory to, or as a result of, this unique position, during the Nehru period no strong officers mediated between Nehru and the secretaries, making the secretaries the most important instruments of power during the formative years of Indian foreign policy. In 1947 the secretaries were three: (a) secretary-general; (b) foreign secretary; and (c) secretary(commonwealth). After Shastri took over as prime minister, the post of secretary-general was abolished with the retirement of the incumbent officer (that being R.K. Nehru, one of Pandit Nehru's cousins). This occurred at approximately the same time as the establishment of a separate foreign minister. Quite possibly many of the responsibilities formerly in the realm of the secretary-general were transferred at this time to the foreign minister.

The office of the secretary-general was opened to accomodate structural conditions within the early external affairs apparatus. For some years on both sides of 1947 the Ministry (pre-1950, the Department) of External Affairs was divided into a Department of External Affairs and a Department of Commonwealth Relations. As each of the departments was headed by a separate secretary, a new official was needed to supervise the work of the two secretaries and their disjoint departments. For this a super-secretary, the secretary-general, was created (suggestions had been afloat to name him the advisor but eventually the title of secretary-general was decided upon, to emphasize the fact of his executive control over the ministry). Besides his administrative burden, the secretary-generalship was also intended to relieve Nehru of the many routine meetings with members of the diplomatic corps which the prime minister had previously to attend.[22] The secretary-general was the cornerstone of

---

[21] Kenneth E. Knight, Reuben R. McDaniel, Jr., *Organizations: An Information Systems Perspective* (Belmont, Cal.: Wadsworth, 1979), p. 5.

Nehru-period policy implementation and lapsed with the end of the Nehru regime. By the time that Shastri had taken over, the two old departments within MEA no longer functioned as separate administrative units, and the need for a super-secretarial officer to supervise these units ended. The secretary-generalship lapsed temporarily May 1952-November 1952. Then in 1965 the post of secretary-general was eliminated permanently. At that time the foreign secretary, the senior-most of the three secretaries under the defunct secretary-general, headed the ministry. The commonwealth secretary and special secretary were presently renamed secretary(EA-I) and secretary (EA-II).[23] Although the Pillai report has advised the reestablishment of the secretary-general post, the post of secretary-general was set up against an administrative background which has since faded away and foreign policy professionals have seen no reason to cast a new super-secretarial post in that particular form (as it is now, a new super-secretary might be regarded as an excess layer which would only slow administration down, without improving overall coordination).

The present head of MEA, the foreign secretary, is best conceived of as the "jack of all trades" of foreign policy operations. He, the "career minister" or "political secretary," is most able to deal with the units of the community holistically rather than with just one level or particular grouping. His role in the foreign policy community is coordinative, controlling the flow of information both to and from the ministers, rather than formulative (the central and quasi-central executive) or implementative (the junior ranks). To the extent that such is required in order to maintain informational control, the foreign secretary dabbles in both formulation and implementation. His place in the policy process is distinct also from that of the joint secretaries who, while also control-coordinative, are in charge of only a division rather than, as is the secretary, of a group of divisions. The secretary is also able to talk to top political leadership, something that the joint secretary rarely does despite his capability. According to Nair, in the early sixties the seniormost of the three secretaries was even regarded as an "automatic choice" for cabinet member-

---

[22] M.O. Mathai, *Reminiscences of the Nehru Age* (New Delhi: Vikas, 1978), p. 195.

[23] *Report of the Committee on the Indian Foreign Service* (New Delhi: Government of India, 1966), pp. 1,2.

ship, though this was never formalized.[24]

The political relationship between the secretary and top leadership recently has acquired more importance with Smt. Gandhi's style of leadership. While Smt. Gandhi generally manages finished policies in cooperation with the foreign minister, the policies are initially devised hand-in-hand with the executive head of the ministry, the foreign secretary. While Smt. Gandhi's work is unchallenged in the foreign ministry, it is impossible for her to work out policies with very complex technical points completely alone. While it might have been possible for Nehru to have developed much of the substance of early Indian policy on his own and without much external assistance, both the sheer complexity of the task today and Smt. Gandhi's lessened interest in the subject make the foreign secretary a much more important person today than when Nehru and Shastri were prime ministers.

Though Gandhi has given a bigger share of early-stage policy formulation to the foreign secretary, this process is unlikely to go so far as to give the foreign secretary or foreign minister primary control over policy, with Smt. Gandhi only in a supervisory or advisory position. Smt. Gandhi cannot relinquish her proximity to foreign policy without giving up the power which foreign policy leadership emanates as a political symbol. Nevertheless, the secretary has earned an important role in policy formulation which he shares with the foreign minister. In more colorful terms, Smt. Gandhi lets the foreign secretary lead her by the hand through the jungle of policy formulation, but she then leans on the foreign minister on the long march through negotiations. During the 1971 Bangladesh conflict, Gandhi sent D.P. Dhar to Moscow, and "JP" Narayan and Sisir Gupta to a number of other countries to stir sympathy for the Indian role in the war, but the MEA secretaries, ordinarily the main participants in any such informational effort, stayed at home. Gandhi has generally tended to rely upon her political fellows and close confidants in outside negotiations, and upon the careerists for early formulations.

One reason for Gandhi's formulative reliance on the MEA secretaries is the ease with which they can be spoken to, which has made them attractive sources of assistance to other ministers in foreign policy matters. B.M. Kaul relates that when he was impeded by Krishna Menon in his pre-1962 quest for defense equipment, he immediately appealed to the foreign, finance and other secretaries for assistance.[25] The secretary,

---

[24] Nair, p. 206.

besides being accessible, generally controls resources comparable to those controlled by the ministerial rank officials of other governments. This makes them the essential allies of cabinet leadership as well as of anyone seeking to bypass cabinet leadership in hunting for resources.

The two junior secretaries have undergone a number of changes in title and powers. A secretary(special) was created in 1947 whose sole responsibility lay in the management of UN affairs. In late 1952, this secretary was abolished. For a time this left only two secretaries, the foreign secretary and secretary(commonwealth) (not including the secretary-general). The commonwealth secretary was the second-most senior secretary and ruled in the British period over the Department of Commonwealth Relations. When the secretary(special) was suspended, the foreign secretary took on most of the secretary(special)'s workload. Several years lapsed before it was decided that an extra secretary, even with a secretary-general, was needed. So in the late fifties the position of secretary(special) was reinstated. This time the secretary(special) was assigned only administrative duties, to which around 1963 was added the special supervision of the West Asia and North Africa Division.

As noted, in 1965 the secretary(commonwealth) and secretary(special) were redesignated secretary(EA-I) and secretary(EA-II), to eliminate the last vestiges of commonwealth-centric cognition in MEA's territorial issues management. Secretary(commonwealth) retained his seniority over secretary(special) even with this change of title. Eventually it was decided that the two junior secretaries would be regarded as equal members, and they were redesignated secretary(east) and secretary(west), respectively. These titles are used as secretarial designations today. J.S. Mehta, who previous to 1976 was additional secretary in charge of Administrative and Africa Divisions, took over as secretary(east) in early 1976, replacing the retiring V.C. Trivedi.[26]

The men who occupied the secretarial ranks had a particularly fertile opportunity to influence the formation of policy, particularly in the early years of India's nationhood. In the Nehru period the dominant secretarial position was the secretary-general post, then occupied by Girija Shankar Bajpai (not to be

---

[25] Tharoor, p. 168; B.M. Kaul, *Confrontation with Pakistan* (New Delhi: Vikas, 1971), pp. 287, 295.

[26] *Report 1951-52*, p. 1; Nair, p. 290; *Report 1975-76*, p. 128.

confused with U.S. Bajpai, presently with the India International Centre) who took the post of secretary-general in June 1947 and served in that capacity for five years (his son K.S. Bajpai entered the foreign service the year of G.S. Bajpai's retirement from MEA). Bajpai had served the British for a long time before this, his latest British executive position being that of the British Indian agent-general for the United States (1941-46; when he, as the British Indian propaganda officer for the U.S., cryptically called Nehru the "Hamlet of Indian politics"). Before that he had been secretary of the Department of Education, Health and Lands for over fifteen years. His dominant and expansive influence as a bureaucrat was well established under the British, when K.P.S. Menon said of Bajpai's Department, "I found the atmosphere there somewhat suffocating. One might say of Bajpai, as Dryden said of Shakespeare, that he laid waste his whole territory simply by occupying it so conclusively."[27] Bajpai had attained his position after joining the Department of Education, Health and Lands in 1919 as an under-secretary and a confirmed desk man, staying in Delhi rather than risking the perils of the NWFP or the easier lifestyle of the officer in the Indian states. As a desk officer he rose from under-secretary to deputy secretary, then to joint secretary and finally to secretary of the department. As secretary he shortly became a member of the viceroy's executive council. He gained all this by virtue of being "one of the most able men in the ICS" and carried this cachet with him into the modern period.

Bajpai's ICS background, however, did not endear him to some people who felt it opportunistic that a man could adapt to serving both the colonial and independent governments with equal ease.[28] He was redeemed in giving to MEA and the early foreign policy process an expertise in administration which was badly needed; as secretary-general Bajpai became Nehru's most valuable IFS officer, handling much of the cable traffic moving through South Block. Bajpai exerted his greatest influence on those policy decisions relating to Kashmir and India's stance toward the Cold War, areas in which Bajpai had a special interest. After leaving his mark on Indian policy through the office of the secretary-general, Bajpai left MEA in the summer of 1952 to take

---

[27] K.P.S. Menon, *Many Worlds: An Autobiography* (Bombay: Oxford University Press, 1965), pp. 134, 264.

[28] See, for example, M.O. Mathai, *My Days with Nehru* (New Delhi: Vikas, 1979), p. 119.

over the government of Bombay.[29] It is a tribute to Bajpai's standing in the opinion of Nehru that he should be given, immediately after Bajpai's work in MEA, perhaps the most important governorship in India. He is an example of continuity, not of policies, but of bureaucratic outlook and expertise between the British and modern periods, and shows the ease with which at least part of the old ICS staff adapted to the new political environment.

Bajpai's secretary-general successor was N.R. Pillai, also ICS, likewise coming from Department of Education, Health and Lands employment, and imbued like Bajpai with an ethics of equal and nondiscriminatory service to both the British and Indian governments. Pillai was quite a different secretary-general from Bajpai, in that he insisted on the close supervision of actual MEA operations rather than on the more aloof control of general policy. After Bajpai, in fact, no secretary-general would come to exercise predominant influence on the content of high-level policy. This was a weakness in the post-Bajpai secretary-general's internal power assets, compensated somewhat in 1956-58 when international tensions required stronger foreign policy leadership.[30] This two-year period saw the Suez and Hungary crises which shook Nehru's nonaligned foreign policy; the outbreak of violence, communal and otherwise, in the Punjab, Bombay, Orissa and Bengal areas; the death of one of Nehru's closest colleagues, Abul Kalam Azad, and the resignation of another, T.T. Krishnamachari. The strain that this period placed on Nehru was surpassed only by that of the 1962-64 period, six years later, when the secretaries were forced again to take on more policy responsibilities.

The last secretary-general was R.K. Nehru, cousin to Nehru (Nehru's other namesake cousin, B.K. Nehru, started in the finance ministry, rose to become the officer in charge of economic affairs in the Washington embassy, and was up to March 1984 the Jammu and Kashmir chief minister. He has since transferred to Bombay) and previous to the secretary-generalship the number-two man in Washington (with the rank of minister). R.K. Nehru was preceded by M.J. Desai as secretary-general; after them, Nehru's death brought the secretary-general tradition to a close.

---

[29] Dutt, pp. 5, 24, 87.

[30] Menon, p. 135 Michael Brecher, *Nehru: A Political Biography* (Boston: Beacon Press, 1961), p. 218.

There have been a number of exceptional foreign secretaries, beginning with foreign secretary Kumar Padmanabha Sivasankara Menon. K.P.S. Menon began his career as the only Indian member of the IPS in the position of under-secretary to the resident to Hyderabad state. In years of service to the British he saw both the world of the frontier officer and followed the urbane career of the British officer to the states. After a period of active field service K.P.S. Menon settled down as a desk officer in the Department of Education, Health and Lands, leaving a Foreign and Political Department where his chances for advancement as a field officer were practically nil. K.P.S. Menon was appointed deputy secretary in 1935, when in Education, Health and Lands N.R. Pillai was an under-secretary. These three men, crucial to the early Indian diplomatic effort, were in this way first brought together twelve years before independence. After one year in Bajpai's Department, Menon rejoined the Foreign and Political Department, though this time as a desk officer of deputy secretary rank. As a head of the Foreign and Political Department's X section Menon gained his first experience of dealing with the world outside of the British domain; that is outside of India, its neighbours and the Middle East. In 1943 K.P.S. Menon left his headquarters posting to become the agent-general for India in China, a position just vacated at that time by Zafrullah Khan. After independence, Menon served in the Indian delegation to the UN Korea commission, followed by an appointment as ambassador to China. By the time Menon became foreign secretary he was marked as one of the most experienced officers in the external affairs staff. He used the early secretaryship as an outlet for bureaucratic education, the inculcation of values, ideas and ethos. He saw himself as ". . . essentially a custodian of precedents . . ." and was very aware of the need to maintain some kinds of continuity within the government, despite the leadership's revolutionary global self-image.[31] He was involved heavily in protocol and was the architect of the fledgling IFS, in which connection he helped to reduce some of the very serious problems caused by an early shortage of trained manpower. K.P.S. Menon was one of the most popular officers in MEA at that time, and upon relinquishing the office in September 1952 he was given the Moscow ambassadorship, at that time one of the three most important Indian ambassadorships (the others being London and the United States). K.P.S. Menon finally retired in 1961.

---

[31] Mathai (1979), p. 118 Menon, pp. 140, 271.

His successor foreign secretary M.J. Desai took great interest in the implementation of the Forward Policy, which preceded the 1962 confrontation with China. He was, according to Maxwell, present in at least one top-level military policy meeting and was consulted on the siting of border posts and the direction of patrols.[32] We can assume, then, that Desai was fairly influential in late Nehru-era decision-making.

Since then, many have filled that post, but we would do best to comment only on three of the last six (up to 1984) foreign secretaries. According to one who has had contact with all three men, Jagat Subha Mehta was a "strong personality," who had to be strong to deal with a frequently intransigent MEA; his successor Ram D. Sathe was "very careful," but "not aggressive enough" and "too much a gentleman." It is felt that he often did not press hard enough on matters of importance. After him, foreign secretary Rasgotre (who had just previously headed the Paris mission), has not been at the ministry long enough to make a deep impression at the time of my interviews (only assuming the post in the summer of 1982), but he was thought of as "aristocratic" in bearing. Rasgotre was succeeded for a short posting by K.S. Bajpai, who left the China ambassadorship to take over the post (and of whom no attitudinal information is available). Of the three before Bajpai, Jagat S. Mehta will probably prove the most worthy of historical note, who during the turbulent Janata years came effectively to control the foreign ministry at a time when this was far from easy. The Janata leadership was unable to spend the time which the better organized Congress(I) had spent in the pursuit of foreign matters. Accordingly the bureaucracy gained unprecedented power over the policy process, but Mehta remained at the center. Foreign minister Vajpayee, while deeply involved in policy formulation, left Mehta in charge of most operations.

There were in 1982 four secretaries in supervision of MEA: the foreign secretary Rasgotre, who replaced Ram D. Sathe on May 1, 1982; secretary(ER) Romesh Bhandari, who is responsible for the Economic Division and all matters of relations with the Middle East ("West Asia"); secretary(West) Eric Gonsalves, who was previously posted in Brussels, and was for a time in 1982 conducting the talks held in that year with China; and lastly secretary Natwar Singh, who was previously ambassador to Pakistan and was in 1982 supervising PakIraf Division, along with his other responsibilities. Singh's position was created to administer the

---

[32] Neville Maxwell, *India's China War* (New York: Doubleday and Company, 1972), pp. 230, 242.

Table 4.3: Secretarial jurisdiction: September 1982

foreign secretary
coordination and supervision Northern Division Indo-U.S. relations Indo-U.S.S.R. relations coordination with regard to relations with Eastern, Western Europe

secretary(E)
East Asia Division Southern Division BSM Division External Publicity Division

secretary(ER)
Economic Division WANA Division

secretary(Chogm/PakIraf)
coordination of work arising from Commonwealth heads of government meeting 1983. PakIraf Division

source: courtesy of PPRD.

recent Commonwealth heads of mission conference, and probably lapsed at the end of 1983.

Table 4.4
Secretary jurisdiction: 1951-55

	1951-52	1952-53	1953-54	1954-55[a]
foreign secretary	continental Europe Americas Middle East Far East	continental Europe Americas Middle East Far East United Nations administration NEFA	continental Europe Americas Middle East Far East United Nations administration NEFA Nepal	American Division Western Division Eastern Division Southern Division[b] Administration "representation"[c]
Special[d] secretary	UN policy	---	---	---
secretary (Commonwealth Relations)	Commonwealth South East Asia, Africa	Commonwealth[e] South East Asia, Africa	Commonwealth[e] South East Asia, Africa	Commonwealth[e] Southern Division[f] Africa Division Pakistan Division

[a] division system reinstituted
[b] Middle East jurisdiction
[c] protocol-related work
[d] special secretary dropped 1952-55
[e] excluding Commonwealth
[f] South East Asia jurisdiction
sources: Annual Reports, 1951-55.

Table 4.5: Additional secretarial jurisdiction: September 1982

additional secretary UN and Conference
UN Division Africa Division America Division

additional secretary administrative
Administrative Wing Passport, Emigration and Consular Division Protocol Division

additional secretary policy planning
Europe Division-East Europe Division-West PPRD

additional secretary legal and treaties
Legal and Treaties Division

source: courtesy of PPRD.

Table 4.6: Joint secretarial jurisdiction: 1953-54[a]

joint secretary
Nepal, NEFA, Tibet, South-East Asia emigration-related topics

joint secretary
North, South America United Nations Africa foreign technical aid

chief of protocol[b]
Great Britain, Ceylon protocol work issue of passports

joint secretary
Europe

joint secretary
administration

[a] the beginning of the MEA's internal divisional organization.
[b] of joint secretary rank.
source: *Report 1953-54*, p. 26.

4.2.2 The Additional Secretary

The additional secretary has somewhat the same relationship to the secretary as the minister of state has to the foreign minister. The additional secretary, a senior joint secretary in charge of certain important MEA divisions, is a post not found in most Indian ministries. Three additional secretaries (designated I, II, III) were active in 1979 and during most of the recent past. In 1982, though, there were four additional secretaries, the chiefmost being Teja in charge of policy planning (and the Policy Planning and Review Division as the organizational reification) and S.K. Singh over PakIraf. The additional secretary posts were opened usually to give more emphasis to some topic or subpolicy of short-term high-priority. One example of this principle in action was the creation in 1974 of an additional secretary to supervise Indian relations with states in the Persian Gulf region. The additional secretaryship stressed the recent ascendency of the Persian Gulf in Indian reckoning, and was a child of both external situation and internal policy alterations. Another example illustrates a third force in the creation of positions within the bureaucracy, that of purely administrative expedience. In 1974-75 a secretary(economic relations) was created, at the same time that secretary(west) lapsed. The secretary(ER) post had long been desired by the ministry, but it had been difficult to implement with an existing officer fullfilling many of these functions. A change in bureaucratic circumstances, the retirement of secretary(west), made such an innovation possible.[33]

4.2.3 The Joint Secretary

Below the additional secretary, though in some cases directly in line with a secretary, is the joint secretary. Close to the joint secretary rank is that of the director, an officer of somewhat lower rank than the joint secretary (measured by a drop in salary), and created when in the fifties a number of officers of counselor rank were brought off the field to headquarters. The joint secretary, generally the control head of the division, had ambassadorial rank and was of limited number, but no other headquarters placement could have been given to the returned officers without such being considered a demotion. For this reason a new rank of director was created which by the mid-sixties headed most MEA divisions. This is no longer the case, with the director today in charge of the smaller divisions where the authority of the leading officer is not invoked so frequently in appeals to superiors. The joint secretaries share division leadership not only with directors but also, in some cases, with other joint secretaries. When a division has two or more units of substantial size, leadership is often shared

---

[33] *Report 1974-75*, p. 119.

between several officers. Examples would be the Pakistan Division of 1963, which was made up of Pakistan I, Pakistan II and Kashmir subsections, collectively headed by two deputy secretaries and an officer on special duty.[34] A more contemporary example is the Europe Division, which is separated into Europe Divisions East and West, each headed by a joint secretary. Despite these occasional separations of responsibility, the joint secretary is most frequently the sole head of the division. Usually his ranking superior officer is as well not the additional secretary but one of the three secretaries.

The secretary and joint secretary are both very important officers, who despite their proximity on the ladder are widely separated in the orientation of their tasks. The secretary is a supervisor and is able to view developments with a breadth denied the joint secretary. The joint secretaries, though, have in their own small areas something denied to the secretaries in large part: control over the flow of information. The world that the secretaries see is that shown to them by their joint secretaries. The difference between the secretary and joint secretary is in both the quantitative and qualitative breadth of their powers. The secretary has the power to interpret information flowing downward, but the joint secretary has the power to present alternative courses of action. The joint secretary is the widest link in the chain of command, the highest level to which a single integrated area of knowledge and decision corresponds.[35] Officers higher than the joint secretary are impeded in building solid expertise and cannot become, as the joint secretary can, a "specialized generalist" in some area. The joint secretary also has control, within the secretary's general mandates, over the precise course of action to be taken. Since the joint secretary can, among given alternatives, decide to delay acting upon orders, the relationship between the joint secretary and the secretary becomes an informal one based on the needs of the moment rather than on a formal, structured arrangement. Relations between the two depend largely on the personal rapport felt between the two. The corollary to this observation is that the way in which interpreters (the secretaries) and decision-makers (the joint secretaries) influence each other will be very fluid and unpredictable.

---

[34] *Report of the Committee,* p. 28; Nair, p. 272.

[35] Personal interview. August 31, 1982.

This informality is sustained by working relationships between the joint secretary and those below him. When subordinates need to communicate, they do so without the necessary involvement of the joint secretary; all communication on courses of action of facts and decisions are made with the joint secretary's knowledge only if subordinates upon their professional judgement so choose. Only when a communication goes outside MEA to another ministry or to parliament is the joint secretary's approval required. Other than for that decision, there is close symmetry between the decision-making process followed by the officers down to the under-secretary level. At each rank is a separate and semi-independent decision-making level; so that a great many papers never reach the joint secretary, having been dispatched by the junior officer at his own discretion. This is done nonarbitrarily, on the officer's own authority. Whenever a matter reaches an officer's desk where a decision would implicate subsections, sections, branches, divisions or ministries other than his own, then the paper is passed directly up to the officer having sufficient breadth of authority to make such a decision, without passing the paper through intermediary ranks. Knowing or determining sufficient authority is fairly routinized, so that junior officers, while not bound by any strict hierarchy, still do not have the personal control over the flow of information that the joint secretary does.

The counterpart to the joint secretary in the American system is the country director, the "action officer" of the Department of State. As a 1970 task force noted,

> His is the responsibility for initiating proposals, crystallizing issues, calling meetings, involving higher levels when necessary, and acting himself and taking the credit or blame later when circumstances do not permit full coordination or guidance.[36]

The chief difference between the country director and the territorial joint secretary is that the painstaking care taken for a single country in the country director programming system is missing in the MEA territorial division system, which administers regional rather than

---

[36] *Diplomacy for the '70's: A Program of Management Reform for the Department of State*, Department of State Publication 8551, Department and Foreign Service Series 143 (released December 1970), p. 347.

national diplomacy. This is not an omission but rather an admission of the lower stakes which India holds in the destiny of most nations. Venezuela, for example, means more as a vote in the UN than it does as a country which by itself could much affect the Indian welfare. Single-country divisions are probably advisable, though, for Pakistan, Sri Lanka, Bangladesh, Nepal and Bhutan. India should have a leading diplomatic presence in these countries, and they should not be treated as members of anonymous regional groupings. A final point to keep in mind is that the country director is expected to be an expert in matters that parallel his administrative jurisdiction. He must know something about that country above what he will pick up on the job. The Indian joint secretaryship demands no such special expertise.

4.2.4 Junior Officers

Under the joint secretary is the deputy secretary and deputy director (the latter slightly below the deputy secretary in rank). Under the two deputy officers are the under-secretaries, who with the deputies make up the most important and largest desk officer class in MEA, with most of the paper of the ministry passing under their gaze. Though one will find them everywhere in MEA today, the deputy secretaries of the 1950s were employed in only a few specialized tasks. In 1953-54, for example, there were two special deputy secretaries assigned, not to general duties, but rather to the administration of United Nations Division and to the External Publicity Division.[37] The lowest secretarial rank, that of the under-secretary, is in standard Indian government practice in charge of a branch, though in MEA this varies considerably. The under-secretary rank is the largest group of IFS postings in the MEA, and is the first headquarters posting for any neophyte IFS officer. Many of the under-secretary positions not held by first-year IFS are taken by IFS(B) inductees. The under-secretary is in rank equal to the first secretary in the mission abroad, while the under-secretary's direct subordinate, the attaché, generally also of IFS(B) cadre, is a senior section officer who has been put in charge of a branch. It is a peculiarity of the IFS that positions lower than the first secretary in the mission abroad are occupied by non-IFS personnel (a rule not followed in the smaller missions). Under the attaché in non-IFS posts are section

---

[37] *Report of the Committee*, p. 28; *Report 1953-54*, p. 26.

officers, research officers and low-level clerical staff.

4.3 PROCEDURAL "THEORY"

While the New Delhi foreign policy community is large, at no time does it resemble the profusion of bureaux, agencies and departments of the Washington D.C. foreign policy network. The Delhi bureaucracy is small enough so that it really is possible for the central executive or political leadership to manage the bureaucracy or to get a grip on what is happening in that community, something occasionally dreamt of in Washington but never realized. Responsiveness becomes a problem when, despite the good contact leadership may have with subordinates, subordinates do not understand the policy adequately or may have troubles keeping operations in line with policy. The problem lies not in the formulation of policy or in the communication of policy but rather in the implementation of operational policy. This is the result of the lack of specialists in MEA, inflexible and inadequate funding of projects, continuing shortfalls in meeting officer manpower requirements and a continuing Indian reliance on rhetoric to the exclusion of substantial projects and commitments. The overall gravity of the responsiveness problem is disputable, but the problem is indeed pivotal at the level of administrative leadership in foreign policy. The MEA officer is best thought of as a manager or political negotiator rather than as a departmental advocate or warrior.

The work patterns to develop in MEA are largely informal, though there are some formal guiding principles. The traditional unit groupings are the section and the branch, with the section the indivisible "atom" of the bureaucracy and the smallest MEA working group. The branch is built up of two or three sections of similar function, with the branch itself traditionally gathered into dyads and triads called, since the 1950s, the division. For several years after independence the basic administrative unit was the section, for which branches and divisions were conceptual but not working groups. The nearly sixty sections of MEA were in the early years shuffled between joint and deputy secretaries without much regard to their branch or divisional affiliations. This changed in 1954 when the division became a more or less fixed grouping for the formerly loose sectional structure. When this divisional practice was initiated there were sixty sections arranged into ten divisions.[38] Though MEA has changed considerably since then, the division is still the working unit of MEA operations.

In MEA today there are two hierarchies, the conventional or traditional hierarchy and the reorganized hierarchy. In the conventional set-up every section is run by a section officer, every branch by an under-secretary and above every under-secretary, in exactly this order, would be a deputy secretary, joint secretary, additional secretary and secretary. It is a simple hierarchical system adopted with few alterations from the British. Up to the late 1950s the entire ministry was governed according to this conventional arrangement, but it was decided about that time that business was being slowed too much by its inflexibility. In 1958 the territorial divisions (excepting UN Division and the Nepal unit of Eastern Division) were reorganized by abolishing the internal section/branch organization of these divisions, which considerably reduced excess layering and compartmentalization. Previously, individual sections, even when several made up one division, maintained separate files; after 1958 one section maintained the files of the entire division, while the other sections had no separate filing capacity at all. In the reorganized divisions the constant hierarchy was abolished, and different links in the chain of command began to be omitted over time. After 1958, then, MEA came under two separate designs of management, conventional and reorganized, in the non-territorial and territorial areas respectively, in which pattern it remains today.[39]

---

[38] Nair, p. 271.

[39] Nair, pp. 292-94.

V
Basic Administration

Thirty-seven years have passed since independence, but Indian foreign policy still means largely the work of the Ministry of External Affairs. MEA is the ministry which makes decisions on all questions of Indian conduct with the outside world. It decides, and implements a great many of its decisions, but leaves much of the implementation to other government bodies. MEA is given broad guidance by a central executive or political leadership, presently orchestrated by the prime minister Indira Gandhi. Gandhi has created mechanisms to bypass MEA in decision-making, but uses them for that purpose infrequently. MEA acts with the authority of the government of India, under the brief furnished it by the Indian government's *Rules of Business*. MEA's duties are kept distinct from those of other ministries by the *Rules of Business,* and its internal structure is devised with reference to this document. MEA is authorized to deal not just very generally with foreign policy, but has been given some very specific responsibilities. These rules may be understood as the specific adaptations to the Indian case of the three fundamental goals of every foreign policy bureaucracy, those being: (a) the management of diplomatic manpower; (b) the production of documents for elites; (c) the transnational distribution of governmental funds. The adaptations following from these are:

1. External affairs.

2. Relations with foreign states and the Commonwealth.

3. All matters affecting foreign diplomatic and consular officers, UN-assigned officers, and the specialized agencies of the UN in India.

4. Passports and visas, excluding the grant of visas or endorsements for entry into India, but including the grant of entry permits to South Africans of non-Indian origin under the Reciprocity Rules (South Africa) of 1944 and the grant of entry visas for Sri Lankan nationals except missionaries.

5. Extradition of criminals and accused persons from India to foreign and Commonwealth countries and visa versa, and general administration of the Indian Extradition Act (XV of 1903) and extraterritoriality.

6. Preventive detention in India for reasons of state connected with external and Commonwealth affairs.

7. Repatriation of the nationals of foreign and Commonwealth states.

8. All emigration under the Indian Emigration Act of 1922, from India to overseas countries and the return of emigrants; immigration to India from the Union of South Africa or any other country to which the Reciprocity Act may apply.

9. All consular functions.

10. Travel arrangements for traders, muleteers, porters and pilgrims from India to Tibet region of China and visa versa.

11. Liaison work connected with the Ministry of Education's cultural scholarship schemes and the nomination of private students of Indian origin domiciled abroad to receive seats in medical and engineering colleges in India.

12. Matters relating to the state of Nagaland.

13. Political pensions paid to foreign refugees and descendents of those who rendered service abroad.

14. Ceremonial matters relating to foreign and Commonwealth visitors, as well as diplomatic and consular representatives.

15. Matters in respect of Pondicherry, Goa, Daman and Diu, involving relations with France and Portugal (anachronistic).

16. Relations with states in special treaty relations with India (such as Bhutan).

17. Himalayan expeditions and permission to foreigners to travel beyond the northern "inner line."

18. Coordination and development measures in border areas.

19. United Nations, specialized agencies and other international conferences.

20. All matters concerning the IFS, A and B branches.

21. External publicity.

22. Political treaties, agreements and conventions with foreign and Commonwealth countries.

23. Both the:

    a. Pilgrimage to places outside India including the administration of the Port Haj Committee Act of 1932 and the rules made thereunder, the administration of the Indian Pilgrim Ships Rules of 1933, and pilgrim parties from India to shrines in Pakistan visa versa.

    b. Protection and preservation of non-Muslim shrines in Pakistan and Muslim shrines in India in terms of the Pant-Mirza agreement of 1955.

24. The recovery and restoration of abducted persons.

25. Evacuation of non-Muslims from Pakistan to India (when necessary).

26. Protection of the rights of the minority communities in India and Pakistan (excepting the rehabilitation of Muslim migrants who have returned from East Pakistan to West Bengal under the Nehru-Liaquat Pact [anachronistic], rehabilitation of Muslims internally displaced in West Bengal at the time of the communal disturbances during partition [anachronistic], and the restoration of mosques and other places of religious worship to Muslims in West Bengal).

27. Non-Muslim migration from Pakistan and Muslim migration from India.

Basic Administration   99

28. Recovery of advances granted to the evacuees from Burma, Malaya, etc. during the years 1942-47 and residual work relating to refugees given asylum in India during World War II (anachronistic).

29. Notification regarding commencement or cessation of a state of war.

30. Foreign jurisdiction.

31. Piracies and crimes committed on the high seas or in the air; offences against the law of nations committed on land, the high seas or in the air.

32. Inquiries and statistics for the purposes of any of the subjects alloted to this ministry.

33. Fees in respect of any of the subjects alloted to MEA.

34. The hospitality grant of the Indian government.

35. Demarcation of the land frontier of India.

36. Border raids and incidents on the land borders of India.

37. Diplomatic flight clearances for non-scheduled chartered flights of foreign civil and military aircraft transiting India.

38. Matters relating to the continental shelf, territorial waters or the contiguous zone, and the question of fishery rights in the high seas and other questions of international law.

39. Economic and technical assistance given by India to the government of Nepal under the Colombo Plan for cooperative economic development.[1]

We will be returning to these functional categories repeatedly in this study. Not each of these categories is performed by a separate section of MEA; some are carried out by one or two officers apart from the regular sectional structure, and other officers are secreted inside sections devoted externally to quite a

---

[1] The above is adapted from Indian Institute of Public Administration, *The Organization of the Government of India* (New Delhi: Somaiya Publications, 1971), pp. 49-50; also Ministry of External Affairs, *Report 1966-67*, pp. 123-24.

different purpose. Not only does the modern system have twice as many formal tasks as the British Indian bureaucracy had, but there is also little continuity between the type of the Indian and British responsibilities. Only categories 1-4 and 11 of the British list (see section 2.3), about one-third of its enumerated sixteen functions, are shared by the modern ministry, and these even in a very different context. Despite their sophistication and relatively greater command of resources, the British in their day had a much less extensive system than the Indians have today in the realm of foreign policy. While the quality of the work done today may be lower in some respects (mostly attributable to much reduced funding) the system today is more complex and sophisticated than that of the British, measured by the quantity of work accomplished and the much broader range of chores handled effectively by the organization. The Indian rulers do much more than the British ever did, and they do it with perhaps less personal incentive (for example, a leaner budget for salaries).

The early apparatus, despite similarities in the title of the office and the staffing personnel, was worlds away from the Department of External Affairs and Commonwealth Relations in structure and the extent of its responsibilities and resources. The pre-1947 foreign office had purely regional responsibilities, and the Indian foreign office's responsibilities were quite simiplified due to their colonial context. The Department had no missions abroad, and only a handful of agents-general in neighboring countries. The Department dealt with only a handful of sovereign nations, which were located on Indian borders. Even then, the small Department was called "most inadequate, unscientific and unsystematic" and may even at this early time have been experiencing organizational difficulties of some scale.[2] To transform such a body into the foreign office of a sovereign nation, to assume diplomatic responsibilities hitherto held by Whitehall, was undoubtedly a difficult task; Indian foreign experience was on a scale and of a quality totally unlike that of the British.

The foreign office had to develop aptitude in protocol (the end to which, as noted, the first foreign secretary K.P.S. Menon devoted most of his time).. Previously, protocol was the particular sphere of the London Foreign Office, and the Indian department had little of this kind of expertise. The skills of administering a large organization, different from

---

[2] Indra Datt, *Diplomatic Service in Free India* (Lahore: Indian Book Company, 1947), p. 84.

small bureau management, would also have to be learned. From dealing with less than a half-dozen nations before 1947, Indian representation abroad would develop into an organization of over ninety missions of various types, in every continent, only a decade after independence. To open in one decade such a diplomatic array from almost scratch is a feat of finance, negotiation and communication unmatched in diplomatic history (history in the long-term; in the short-term a number of nations such as Pakistan, Nigeria and Israel have had to make comparable efforts).

All of the nations emerging from colonial bondage had such problems, problems not shared by the Western or Eastern states. The West was able to develop its diplomatic facilities slowly, appropriate to its own needs. The emerging Third World had to force-fit diplomacy created to suit Western needs onto its own fragile body without the time or indigenous expertise to make a strong, unique initial national interpretation (Communist leadership such as that of Fidel Castro and charismatic leaders such as Nasser occasionally rebelled against diplomatic convention, but even they made few changes in embassy operation or the organization and responsibilities of their foreign offices. They ignored some elements of protocol, but did not succeed in creating a new protocol for all that). For the West diplomacy was tailor-made, but for India and much of the Third World it was factory-made, a standardized "one size of diplomacy for all." That India, through Nehru's leadership, aspired to a position not only of representation but also of global leadership makes what India did with its foreign apparatus all the more remarkable.

Within MEA throughout most of its history sixteen to twenty divisions have been responsible for the work of the Ministry. MEA also has certain subordinate offices, which ". . . function more or less as field establishments, responsible for the detailed execution of the decision of the Government."[3] Many ministries have attached offices, which are given by the ministry certain tasks and the funding to carry them out, but are not actually a part of the ministry. MEA has no attached offices, but the Indian missions abroad are very similar to attached offices in their relationship to MEA headquarters.

At present there are twenty divisions, or nineteen divisions and the Administrative Wing. As shown in Table 5.2, they are generally grouped as either administrative, functional or territorial in nature. Among the administrative divisions, Coordination (Coord) and

---

[3] *Organization* (1971), p. 43.

Finance (Fin) are recent creations, not in existence before 1970; among the functional divisions, Policy Planning (PP) and Economic (ED) were not known to Nehru; and among those territorial, only North (N), South (S), West Asia and North Africa (WANA) and America (Amer) divisions have continued through the years unchanged. Among notable divisions which no longer exist are Bangladesh (in existence for over seven years after the civil war), Historical and Kashmir Divisions, all assimilated into other divisions. Also, as late as 1971 there was a Naga Unit in charge of the NEFA security apparatus, no longer with MEA.

The number of divisions inside MEA has steadily increased. In 1977-78 MEA had twenty-one (of which twelve were territorial) divisions. The previous year MEA had nineteen divisions and in 1963 there were fourteen divisions. The reason that the division system was first implemented (as noted, originally there were no divisions, only sections) was to cut down the complexity of administering an organization of sixty sections (nineteen administrative, forty-one territorial and technical), each one following its own orbit, the entire mass pulling together only with the personal efforts of the three secretaries and their junior officers.[4] It was plain at that time that a formal system would have to be devised to supplement the secretaries' personal efforts; out of such the division system grew.

With four exceptions the divisions are housed in the southern complex of offices in the New Delhi Central Secretariat, known as South Block. South Block office space is also shared by the Home Ministry's internal intelligence organizations, who would not consent to freeing the space required by External Publicity and Policy Planning Divisions. External Publicity is presently accomodated in nearby Shastri Bhavan, and the Research Wing of Policy Planning with the MEA library are in Pathiala House (near India Gate), and the old army barracks next to the central secretariat are also used to house part of the Administrative Wing. MEA also has a subordinate office, the External Affairs Hostel, which furnishes temporary accomodations for returning diplomats (previously, they stayed in each other's homes upon returning from abroad). Finally, the missions abroad constitute MEA's most important extension outside of South Block.

---

[4] *Report 1975-76*, p. 129; N. Parameswaran Nair, *The Administration of Foreign Affairs in India with Comparative Reference to Britain* (New Delhi: School of International Studies, 1963), p. 271; *Report 1954-55*, p. 1.

Table 5.1: MEA divisions: 1955

	four directors[a] two directors[b]
American Division	North, South America
Western Division	UN, Europe[c]
Eastern Division	China, Japan, Korea
	Sikkim, Bhutan, NEFA
Southern Division	Middle East
	South-East Asia
African Division	Africa, Great Britain
	colonies
	emigration topics
Pakistan Division	Pakistan

	joint secretary
protocol division	protocol and consular work
	passports and visas
	abducted persons

	director[a]
Administrative Division	administration

	deputy secretary
External Publicity Division	external publicity

	director[d]
Historical Division	historical research

[a] of joint secretary rank
[b] of deputy secretary rank
[c] excluding Great Britain
[d] specialist officer
source: *Report 1954-55*, p. 1.

Table 5.2: MEA divisions: 1970

territorial	non-territorial
	administrative
America Division	Protocol Division
Europe Division	UN and Conference Division
West Asia and North Africa Division	Passport, Emigration and Consular Division
Africa Division	Legal and Treaties Division
Pakistan Division	External Publicity Division
Northern Division	Historical Division
East Division	Economic Division
South Asia Division	Policy Planning and Review Division
	administrative
	Personnel, Security, Communications and Civil Defense
	Administrative Division

source: K.P. Misra, *Foreign Policy and its Planning*, p. 59.

In 1981-82 headquarters had a staffing of 506 officers. The total staffing of IFS and IFS(B) cadres at headquarters and abroad was 3,684, 1,226 of which were officers. Three years previously the total staffing of headquarters in 1978-79 was 542 officers and 2,010 clerical ("non-gazetted" in King's English) staff.[5] In 1970-71 the manpower strength was at 3,409. From 1970-71 to 1976-77 there was a 7.6 percent rise in the diplomatic staffing of missions abroad. Tables 5.4 and 5.5 show well the sharp increases in staffing during the post-independence period. It is worth noting that the original IFS had only 130-odd officers, with a clerical staff not much larger than that. MEA's budget has also rapidly increased.

In the ten-year period 1966-67 to 1976-77 total MEA expenditures more than tripled, from Rs. 305 million to Rs. 1.08 billion; total missions' cost rose

---

[5] *Report 1978-79*, p. 67; *Report 1981-82*, p. 59.

Table 5.3
MEA divisions: 1982

Name	Abbreviation	Bureau goal
Administrative		
Administrative Wing	AD	Administration, security
Coordination Division	C	Coordination with other ministries
Finance Division	F	Budgeting
Passport, Emigration and Consular Division	PV	Consular services *Functional*
Policy Planning and Review Division	PP, PP&R	Policy planning theoretically, actual work research; bureau-elite staff role; MEA's "wild card"
Economic Division	ED	International economic policy, ITEC
External Publicity Division	XP	External publicity, monitoring world press, communications, relations with international press
UN & Conference Division	UN	United Nations policy, international conferences, disarmament
Legal and Treaties Division	L&T	Legal topics
Protocol Division	P	reception of foreign VIPs, hospitality
Territorial		monitoring missions in:
Pakistan, Iran & Afghanistan Division	PakIraf	Pakistan, Iran and Afghanistan
Bangladesh, Sri Lanka and Maldives Division	BSM	Bangladesh, Sri Lanka, Maldives
Northern Division	N	Nepal and Bhutan
Southern Division	S	South East Asia
East Asia Division	EA	China, Korea, Japan
West Asia and North Africa Division	WANA	Middle East, North Africa
Africa Division	Africa	sub-Saharan Africa
Europe Division West	EW	Western Europe
Europe Division East	EE	Soviet Union, Soviet-bloc Europe
America Division	AMS	Western hemisphere

Table 5.4:   Expansion in headquarters staffing: 1948-66

	1948-49	1956-57	1965-66
officers[a]	86	152	376
staff	828	1,329	1,705

[a]section officers, research officers included.
source: *Report of the Committee*, p. 6.

Table 5.5: Total staff strength: 1957, 1969

	1957	1969
headquarters	1,462	1,289
subordinate officers	4,413	415
missions abroad	990	1,274
miscellaneous	98	-----
total	6,963	2,978

The drop in strength is due mostly to the removal of the Inspectorate-General, Assam Rifles from MEA jurisdiction.
Source: IIPA, *Organization of the Government of India*, 1958, 1971 editions, pp. 44, 60 respectively.

from Rs. 90 million to Rs. 223 million, and the headquarters budget doubled, from Rs. 26 million to Rs. 52 million (most of the increase in this period was taken up by MEA revenue expenditures other than headquarters and missions abroad).[6] MEA revenue expenditures in 1981-82 are Rs. 1.54 billion (broken down into

---

[6] Figures adapted from Jayantanuja Bandyopadhyaya, *The Making of India's Foreign Policy* (New Delhi: Allied Publishers, 1979), p. 197; 1971 edition of the same book, p. 60. Bandyopadhyaya's "Table 10" is, incidentally, not of the individual staff strengths of "India's Resident Missions Abroad," as he writes, but of total staff strength, headquarters and subordinate offices included.

Table 5.6: MEA revenue expenditures: 1981-82

headquarters	70.216[a]
missions/posts abroad	459.648
supply wing, London and Washington	25.708

other items

contribution to UN, Commonwealth secretariat, other international organizations	35.746
Central Passport and Emigration Organization	31.503
other miscellaneous items	313.482

aid

to Bhutan	386.388
to Nepal	157.500
to other developing nations in Asia and Africa under ITEC	46.874
to Bangladesh	12.749
personnel payments under social security, welfare	4.411

[a] in millions of rupees
source: adapted from *Report 1981-82*, p. 84.

---

component expenses in Table 5.6), a forty-three percent rise over a five-year period, seven to eight percent annually. The expenditures of missions abroad have gone up as rapidly as in past years, a 106 percent increase in five years, 15.6 percent annually. Despite the speed with which the MEA budget has been growing, the entire Indian diplomatic apparatus is still run off of a paltry sum of US$ 172 million.

> The External Affairs Ministry's budget is a mere 156.54 crore, or around 0.72 per cent of the Central budget. It is less than what Japan spends in a year just on External publicity! The Indian Embassy in Washington D.C. must do with less money than the Indian Tea Board branch in Frankfurt. 'No country in the world operates on that kind of shoestring budget and still expects so much from its foreign policy and diplomacy', said

an official ruefully, 'One result is that when the foreign minister goes abroad, his visit cannot even be properly publicized'. India maintains 132 diplomatic missions abroad, staffed by 689 diplomatic personnel. Around 200 of them man the missions in Washington, Moscow, London and Kathmandu, leaving an average of about three diplomats per mission--an absurd state of affairs.[7]

5.1 ADMINISTRATIVE METHOD

Before talking further about administration, we must make a distinction between administration and leadership. Leadership concerns itself with policy, the grand issues around which the organization revolves. The organization serves leadership by responding to its directives. Administration, on the other hand, serves the organization by responding to needs of the organization which develop in the implementation of policy commands. Administration is not concerned with the esoteric issues of policy but with the exoteric problems of employee welfare, building maintenance, clerical chores, communication, etc. Perhaps it might seem that administration would not interest the international relations specialist, concerned as he is with more lofty and essential subjects, but a little thought will reveal that administration, even as a topic of study, is important. Unless the administration of the Ministry of External Affairs is efficient and unencumbered, the Ministry will not concentrate on matters of policy with the single-mindedness that is required. An organization in which bureaucrats could not obtain the proper materials for their work, one in which there are grave dissatisfactions with pay and perks, or one in which infrastructure is neglected, is bound to have morale and bottleneck problems which will sooner or later embarrass the implementation of policy.

This is an acute problem for the Third World bureaucracy plagued by economy drives and reduced funding for infrastructure. The developing nations suffer also from shortages in skilled administrators, and from insufficient exposure to modern managerial techniques. Modern management training is not a high-powered frill indulged in by only some rich and advanced nations, but rather a response to problems of social organization with a range encompassing every modern nation.

---

[7] Bhabani Sen Gupta, Dilip Bobb, "In Danger of Isolation," *India Today*, December 16-30, p. 57.

Shortcomings in just this one area, adaptation to modern management techniques, can impede India's attainment of foreign policy goals. This will happen, for example, when other nations find that Indian bureaucrats, even in branches of the government other than the MEA, cannot carry out their assistance programs (this lately occurred with the U.S. AID-financed Madhya Pradesh Social Forestry Project).

In 1963 the Administrative Division was the largest in the MEA, having within it thirty-five of the seventy-seven sections into which MEA was divided. The joint secretary who headed the division had a close working relationship with secretary(special) similar to that which director(Economic Division) had with the secretary-general. Joint secretary (Admin) had six deputy secretaries, sixteen under-secretaries and an ancillary staff under him. These men were organized into five wings, namely:

1. Personnel wing.

2. General administration wing.

3. Supplies and services wing.

4. Communications wing.

5. Security.[8]

The Administrative Wing of the present-day is similar to this, especially in its independence and size. The tasks of administration can be divided into two categories, labeled here housekeeping and efficiency management. Housekeeping is the fairly urbane labor of maintaining the organizational status quo, keeping institutions running in the present as they have in the past. Efficiency management is the obverse function, consisting of the alteration of the status quo when it has become disruptive to the smooth operation of the total organization and the fullfillment of its assigned mission. Often, sections become obsolete due to a changing environment, or because routine procedure becomes outdated. The removal or revision of such when it occurs is a normal part of administration, or of the efficiency managerial portion of administration.

The *toshakkhana* (Persian for "storeroom") is an exemplary housekeeping function, a storeroom for gifts given to Indian diplomatic personnel. Since gifts cannot be retained by officials, they are kept in the *toshakkhana* until sold off at an annual public auction.

---

[8] Nair, p. 290.

Another part of housekeeping is the Recording and Indexing (R and I) Unit, which cuts down on the inevitable growth of files by weeding and indexing them, reducing a giant hoard of papers to human proportions (R and I in 1968-69 alone eliminated or recorded over 90,000 files). Also in housekeeping is the Welfare Unit, which looks ". . . after the general welfare of all the officials serving at Headquarters and Missions abroad including admission of their children in Educational Institutions including Medical and Engineering Colleges . . ."[9] Welfare, like the External Affairs Hostel (which might also be included, were it not a subordinate office, in administration), serves the human interests of the employees of MEA. If we were to draw a diagram of "policy relevance" as a circle whose center was designated "high foreign policy relevance" and whose circumference signified "low foreign policy relevance," we might find such bodies as the Ministry of Education near the circumference but indeed inside the circle. The Hostel and the Welfare Unit would not even find a place within the circle, despite their great physical and superficial policy proximity to those divisions and their connection with individuals involved regularly in foreign policy. We might regard these housekeeping bodies as trivial in the study of foreign policy, but the inability of these bodies to do their jobs well could adversely affect other more political divisions and eventually final policy products.

One somewhat more interesting housekeeping section is the Central Cypher Bureau (CCB), also in the Administrative Wing. The CCB is entrusted with encoding outgoing messages and decoding those coming in from missions abroad. The CCB was created in 1903 with view to improving Indian security in the face of what appeared to be an awakening spirit of new European adventurism. At that time, as of now, the CCB dealt only with telegraphic communications. With the rapid expansion of its work the CCB achieved branch status in 1910. The CCB's task in the early Nehru years must have been very difficult, when missions communicated with headquarters by means of commercial telegraph rather than direct lines, and at a time when they probably lacked sophisticated cryptanalytic machinery. India even today is probably hampered in this field by the cost of electronic equipment. The CCB at present has 195 employees of Grade II Cypher Sub Cadre status, as well as a few IFS(A) officers-in-charge and some

---

[9] M.O. Mathai, *My Days with Nehru* (New Delhi: Vikas, 1979), p. 180; *Report 1968-69*, p. 79; *Report 1977-78*, p. 55.

IFS(B) employees not directly involved with the cryptographical work.[10]

There are other housekeeping bodies, but our purpose here is not to enumerate but to illustrate. There is not such a proliferation of efficiency management bodies, so it will be possible to treat them more comprehensively. The Organization and Method (O and M) Section, Reorganization Unit and Vigilance Unit are three of the bodies within Administrative Wing which function to keep MEA in line. O and M is an operations research body, which examines work methods and how work is organized and tries to find more efficient means of management. It was set up in November 1954 and is now under Administration, but keeps in close touch with the O and M Division in the cabinet secretariat. In May 1973 "routine work measurement studies" of Africa, America and Southern Divisions were carried out, typical of the work O and M and related units do.[11] O and M is also known as the Work Study or Internal Work Study Unit.

The officer in charge of O and M in 1963 was also the vigilance officer in charge of the Vigilance Unit for MEA. Vigilance, an institution in Indian government and business, is deployed against bribery and other corruption in desk-level business, and works closely with the Administrative Vigilance Division of the Home Ministry. There are also a number of ongoing reorganization projects concerned with the divisions and their larger groupings. The Reorganization Unit, also under the Vigilance Officer's charge, is concerned with preventing bureaucratic inertia from bringing these improvements in ministry organization to a halt. The efficiency management process also sometimes brings other ministries into the act. In 1973 the Staff Inspection Unit of the Ministry of Finance began to assess the manpower requirements of various divisions in the MEA, finishing the review in late 1976. At the same time, certain of the suggestions of the Department of Personnel and Administrative Reforms were taken up.[12]

The Foreign Service Inspectorate (FSI), set up in 1954, is also an efficiency management body, but its operations are directed to the missions abroad rather than to headquarters. Its purpose is to suggest improvements of efficiency and economy in missions abroad. When originally set up it consisted of an

---

[10] Nair, p. 61; *Report 1981-82*, p. 82.

[11] *Report 1973-74*, p. 124.

[12] *Report 1975-76*, pp. 132-33.

inspector with joint secretary rank, one financial advisor of joint secretary rank (from the Ministry of Finance), one accountant and a personal assistant (stenographer) for both the inspector and advisor. The FSI is under Administration and originally reported to secretary(special). Every year the FSI carries out a large number of on-the-spot inspections in missions abroad. In 1977-78, the FSI held inspections in the missions of Kathmandu, Rangoon, Cairo, Rabat, Rome, Madrid, Tunis, Lisbon, Algiers, Belgrade and Teheran.[13]

5.2 THE PILLAI COMMITTEE

Besides the standard MEA review mechanism, special measures have been taken in the past. An important administrative achievement of the Shastri period, to be ranked with the establishment of the Prime Minister's Secretariat (later Office of the Prime Minister), was the establishment of the Committee on the Indian Foreign Service. This was a timely act of organizational introspection, following the year of administrative mourning of the end of the Nehru period. It was time to see what had been accomplished, and what might further be done. The first meeting of the committee was on July 9, 1965, with seventy-seven meetings in all. The chairman of the group was N.R. Pillai, and under him was the member-secretary N. Krishnan. Basically what the committee set out to do was to find if the administrative machinery which had been appropriate during the Nehru period was still germaine. The recommendations focussed on manpower requirements, but considered a great many other topics as well. The conditions that gave birth to the Pillai Committee were present as early as 1952, when the *Annual Report* of MEA commented that "[h]aving regard to the increasing range of the Ministry's work and responsibilities, the present strength is quite inadequate. Proposals for the reorganization of the Ministry are under consideration."[14]

This type of Indian government review is infrequent, and in thirty-seven years of service there has been only one such committee established in MEA to help sort out organization difficulties. Even so, many of the recommendations of the Pillai report were not acted upon, such as its recommendation to re-establish the secretary-general's office. But the Pillai report was

---

[13] Nair, p. 295 *Report 1977-78*, p. 55.

[14] *Report 1952-53*, p. 1.

read and exegesis performed by bureaucrats and academics, and was not passed by by the central executive. Smt. Gandhi wrote in 1967 to foreign minister M.C. Chagla that the report reflected ". . . her desire for bold and radical changes in the administration of the Ministry and a more frequent discussion of foreign policy issues at the highest level."[15] However, the committee suffered in having only five members and a secretary, who all in turn had little access to materials and investigative funding. Besides the committee, itself an ad hoc creation, there is an ongoing process of cadre review known as the Board. The Board looks into payscales, perks and other aspects of employee welfare, but does not deal with more serious organizational questions. The Administrative Wing serves as secretariat for these Boards.[16]

Table 5.7: Indian foreign policy community

Ministry of Finance, Department of Economic Affairs
Ministry of Commerce
Ministry of Petroleum and Chemicals
Ministry of Education, Department of Culture
Ministry of Defence
Ministry of Information and Broadcasting
Ministry of Tourism and Civil Aviation

Department of Space
Department of Atomic Energy
Department of Cabinet Affairs
Planning Commission
Cabinet Secretariat
Office of the Prime Minister

cabinet and parliament
Indian Council for Cultural Relations
state governments

---

[15] A.G. Noorani, *Aspects of India's Foreign Policy* (Bombay: Jaico Publishing House, 1970), p. 48.

[16] Due to their uninvolvement in policy formulation, the Boards are ignored by this study. Nair, p. 291; the Boards are dealt with in Nair's work in depth (albeit dated).

5.3 COMMUNITY COORDINATION

Foreign policy is a group effort, of several ministries and non-ministerial bodies, and not just of MEA; it is the task of the Administrative Wing to coordinate the efforts of all these bodies. Communication falls within the sphere of administration, and coordination in India seems more the problem of communication than the complex political one of negotiation (though the political element exists as well). The Indian foreign policy community has seventeen main members, not including MEA (listed in Table 5.7). At every level inside MEA the three processes of data collection, policy formulation (or decision) and implementation are carried out without predominance of one of the three functions at a level. Within the foreign policy community, however, there is a polarization in which MEA has a stronger formulative role and the other ministries have a more salient implementative role. This distinction is only relative, though. When we compare MEA and the Office of the Prime Minister, MEA appears more implementative and the Office more formulative.

The extent to which these bodies become involved in the foreign policy process will only gradually become clear, though certain basic relationships can be grasped immediately. In the bureaucratic vehicle of diplomacy, the mission abroad, several ministries are represented and participate in representation, negotiation and reporting. Until a few years ago the Ministry of Information and Broadcasting furnished the external publicity manpower for the missions, and most of the large embassies today have defense, labor and even education attachés. The ministries are severally represented in many important tours of representation, as, for example, when in the 1975-76 emergency period the minister of state for tourism and civil aviation toured a large part of South-East Asia.[17] The joint commissions which India holds with several nations are composed of members from the economic and domestic ministries, as well as of diplomats. For MEA's economic assistance programs, dependence on other ministries for technical staffing is total, and in arms purchases and sales the Ministry of Defence plays a far larger role than the diplomats.

The international organizations, such as the International Labor Organization (ILO) and the UN, deal more with the Indian domestic ministries than with MEA itself. To differ with Tharoor, there is really no great problem with breaking up responsibilities for

---

[17] *Report 1975-76*, pp. 1-28.

foreign affairs among several separate ministries.[18] Due to the very specialized nature of the international organizations concerned (UNIDO, WHO), very little that a ministry initiates with such is likely to become a bone of serious policy contention. But even if this weren't true, there would be little that leadership could do about the division of labor. MEA does not have the resources or (being staffed by a generalist IFS) the expertise to manage all these functions. Even the Economic Division within MEA has had frequently to ask other ministries for aid in its own labors. There is just no way that all this can be brought under one roof. In contending that all foreign policy functions should ideally be managed by one ministry Tharoor contradicts one of the foundation premises of his book, that the degeneration of pluralism in Indian domestic politics has led to a degeneration in foreign policies. Pluralism in the policy-process may lead to better policy, at least according to some actors' interests, than a centrally restrictive machine.

Indian work in high technology presents a very interesting aspect of extra-MEA foreign relations. Work in these areas has high policy relevance in that it gives India the potential to develop nuclear weaponry, and in that there is strong outside involvement by nations assisting India in the development of these technologies. The Department of Space becomes involved with foreign policy on issues of joint space ventures, of which India has had several (generally with the Soviet Union). The United Nations Outer Space Treaty comes under the attention of the Department of Space. The other high technology government body, the Department of Atomic Energy, is concerned with the implementation of treaties regarding the supply of nuclear fuel or equipment for nuclear reactors from foreign countries. Its only responsibility is to look after India's nuclear reactors and the treaty relationships which concern their operation. If India ever comes under International Atomic Energy Commission (IAEC) guidelines, the Department of Atomic Energy is likely to be the body to carry on liaison with the IAEC.

The state governments also come into the implementation process when UN and other aid projects are discussed which will eventually be carried out within a certain state. Involvement of this sort, though, usually only grants the state some control over the technical aspects of the project, as the general project outline has already been set forth by New Delhi.

---

[18] Shashi Tharoor, *Reasons of State* (New Delhi: Vikas, 1982), p. 166.

The Indian foreign policy community must be bound together to facilitate communication and prevent drifting, as a raft of logs on turbulent policy currents. Counter to Bandyopadhyaya, it is not possible for the foreign minister or foreign secretary by themselves to coordinate the community, despite the status of coordination as the formal function of these officers.[19] MEA bureaucrats insist that the informal coordination which exists presently between divisions and with other ministries is sufficient for general community needs, but the Pillai report (a product of the bureaucracy) contrarily advised that "organization mechanisms" be set up for coordination with the Ministries of Defence, I and B, Civil Aviation and Atomic Energy.[20]

We label separately community coordination and interministerial coordination, both because of the cabinet committees and because of formally autonomous bodies such as the Indian Council for Cultural Relations. In the American foreign policy community staffs have developed, a staff being a group of men and women outside of the organization empowered by the secretary or another high-ranking official to act in their name. The staffer has a relationship to the secretary similar to that which an Indian private assistant (P.A.) has to a secretary. The difference is that staffs are usually regarded as unified groups, whereas a P.A.'s value lies in the personal individual assistance that he gives the officer whom he serves. In India, a coordination body similar to and yet quite different from a staff has developed. The Coordination and Information Division was set up in 1964 for community coordination, a responsibility which before lay with the secretary-general. This division was first headed by I.J. Bahadur Singh, who was at that time also the official government spokesman, a responsibility which now rests with the External Publicity Division's head. IFS officers Teja (now secretary[PP]) and Hiremath (now retired from service) were connected with the early Coordination and Information Division. Possibly the need for a coordination staff existed before 1964, but because of Nehru's monopoly over policy functions, no move to create such a body was made. The Coordination Division was similar to a staff in terms of both purpose and internal composition, having a relatively large, well-trained staff devoted to tying the foreign relations efforts of many otherwise unrelated bodies to one central policy movement. It was quite unlike a staff

---

[19] Bandyopadhyaya (1979), p. 276.

[20] *Report of the Committee on the Indian Foreign Service* (New Delhi: Government of India, 1966), p. 22.

effort in that it was in the charge of a director (of roughly joint secretary rank) and did not have the kind of special relationship to a very high-ranking officer that the Planning and Coordination Staff (S/PC) in the Department of State enjoys. It is probably this lack of a high-level relationship that has most greatly impaired Coordination Division's operation.

To argue that such a special relationship with a secretary or higher-ranked officer is unnecessary, is to put too much faith in the power of formal procedures. The Coordination Division, which handles not just interministerial but also interdivisional intra-MEA coordination, would have to be in the business of giving orders. But how can a joint secretary-ranked officer give this kind of leadership at a divisional or, with even more difficulty, at a ministerial level? Only an organization headed by a cabinet-level official could deign to steer the courses of the mighty ships of state, the ministries, even if only on such a specialized topic as foreign policy. Such a body would operate outside of the confines of any of the ministries or policy bodies under the coordinative body's jurisdiction. A coordination staff, serving the foreign secretary or the foreign minister, not within the MEA but whose members are empowered to act in the secretary's or minister's name, could operate well without endangering pluralism.

The Coordination Division's Parliament Section of the present-day is quite active during parliamentary sessions, as in addition to its more serious duties it acts as an information outlet for the *sansad*. The Coordination Division also organizes regular intraministerial meetings where briefs on current topics, prepared by concerned territorial divisions, are discussed. Such discussions allow a larger community involvement by the concerned territorial divisions.[21] At present the Coordination Division consists of one under-secretary, one director and a joint secretary. The joint secretary (in 1982, U.C. Soni) is also in charge of the Policy Planning and Review Division (PPRD). Coordination presently functions much like the switchboard of the ministry, connecting individuals and issues outside MEA with the appropriate division inside the ministry. If a cabinet official is going abroad he will, rather than contact all the divisions concerned with the countries involved, give his itinerary to Coordination. It will then bring all the concerned divisions together to work out their part of the tour abroad. If an external agency contacts MEA on a topic likely to concern more than one division, it is

---

[21] PPRD letter to author. September 1982.

referred to Coordination. Coordination factors the problem into separate policy-tasks that can then be acted upon by individual divisions without their joint coordination. Inside MEA, if a division needs to contact, say, ten other divisions on a single topic, the contact will be handled through Coordination rather than division by division.

Another method by which members of the community are coordinated is through the interdepartmental group (IG). The IG is a common Indian practice, though rarely formed on anything but an ad hoc basis. As an example, for the first Indian expedition to Antarctica, a project with important political and international implications, a committee was set up consisting of the cabinet secretary, the finance secretary, the foreign secretary and the chief of naval staff. Upon the successful conclusion of Operation Gangotri, as the secret project was called, the committee was disbanded. Another example: for the recent Cancun, Mexico North-South summit, a committee was formed consisting of the head of the Office of the Prime Minister G. Parthasarathi, one of the joint secretaries in charge of the Economic Division, K.K. Bhargawa, the foreign secretary R.D. Sathe, and the secretaries of the Ministries of Commerce and Finance, to name the principal members. After Cancun, this group was disbanded.[22]

An important permanent coordinating body exists in the committee of secretaries, under the cabinet secretariat. Levi claims that the proposal to form the committee was never followed through, but Tharoor notes in fact that the committee, devised by then cabinet secretary S.S. Khera in 1962-63, still exists and was used by Smt. Gandhi in her pre-emergency rise to power.[23] Little is known other than its main foreign policy priority and that it exercises a substantial policy input into the macroprocess, unlike the cabinet. As for coordination between divisions, foreign minister Dinesh Singh organized weekly meetings with senior officials and monthly meetings with all staff (meetings of an hour to an hour-and-a-half in length) at which policy was discussed.

---

[22] Dilip Bobb, "Operation Gangotri," *India Today*, March 31, 1982, p. 91; confidential interview, July 30, 1982.

[23] Werner Levi, "Foreign Policy: The Shastri Era," in K.P. Misra, ed., *Studies in Indian Foreign Policy* (New Delhi: Vikas, 1969), p. 194; Tharoor, pp. 143, 167.

Other more subtle techniques are used to build awareness of what the total foreign affairs effort looks like. The secondment (deputation, in Indian terms) of IFS officers to other ministries is common. In 1975-76, for example, twenty-seven IFS officers were under deputation to other bodies; one to the Ministry of Finance, four in the Ministry of Commerce, one to the Ministry of Petroleum and Chemicals, one in the Ministry of Education, two in the cabinet secretariat, one in the Department of Space, one in the Department of Atomic Energy, two in the National Defence College, one in the ICCR, one in the Trade Development Authority, and the remaining officers on deputation to areas not directly concerned with foreign policy.[24] The officers deputed will return to MEA probably better educated about the role of peripheral organizations in the formulation of policy, and more able to keep the MEA aware of work being done elsewhere. At least deputation is justified that way. The IFS officer generally asks to be deputed to another ministry not due to their desire to gain a more holistic understanding of the foreign policy process, but because for noncareer reasons (an impending marriage, perhaps) they wish to prolong their stay in India before being sent to a mission abroad (as most new IFS officers are during the training period).[25]

---

[24] *Report 1975-76*, p. 128.

[25] Personal interview. Summer 1982.

VI
Research, Intelligence and the Foreign Policy Bureaucracy

We have so far dealt with only the Administrative Wing and Coordination Division in MEA. Outside of these service bodies, divisions are categorized as functional and territorial. The territorial divisions are easily defined as those divisions which are assigned the task of maintaining contact with the overseas missions in a particular section of the globe. The functional divisions cannot be grouped in this way, and are a potpourri of different and unrelated groups providing a variety of services. The first topic covered in our treatment of the functional divisions will be that of research and planning, how the analytic requirements of the MEA are met. We will then cover a related topic, how MEA stands in relation to the intelligence apparatus.

While Nehru did not himself use formal research bodies to supplement his foreign policy judgements, such facilities did exist in various forms throughout the Nehru period. These bodies, with one exception, were of a temporary, ad hoc nature. Three of the temporary bodies were the Kashmir Unit, the Disarmament Cell, and the Goa Research Unit (attached to the now-defunct Western Division), all set up to investigate particular issues as they arose. These single-issue research bodies could not help but be provisional, highly specialized and for this reason unable to participate in a permanent research and analysis grouping. Such a niche was instead reserved exclusively for the first Indian foreign policy research body, the Historical Division (HD).

There were small research staffs attached to the Economic Division, some territorial divisions, and the UN mission in New York, but the HD was the only division in MEA totally devoted to research (a Historical Division of similar function can also be found in the Canadian Department of External Affairs). HD was not

Table 6.1: Functional divisions: 1963

Protocol and Consular Division
Passport and Emigration Division
External Publicity Division
Historical and Research Division
Legal and Treaties Division
Economic and Coordination Division
UN and Conference Division

Of these, only three existed when the divisional system was instituted (1953). These were:
Protocol and Consular Division
External Publicity Division
Historical Division

source: Nair, p. 277.

---

oriented toward the future and the analysis of trends, but rather toward the past and preparation of deep historical briefs on topics of current relevance. In this role the HD bears the amateur historian Nehru's imprint, though it was set up by the first foreign secretary, who personally selected its first director, Dr. Zachariah.[1] The HD was naturally weak on a contemporary outlook and was not generally consulted for advice.

Historical data was valuable, but HD's research had not the urgency of current affairs research. The HD, to the degree in which it specialized in deep historical briefs, was unable to make a great contribution to the formulation of foreign policy. It aided policy-makers in their deliberation upon matters of substance, much as an encyclopedia might, but did not have anything to say directly about the current policy. However, when the HD through its work built up legalistic arguments to support international claims, its work became of immense value to policy-makers, though still it did not have any great effect on policy. It was an obedient servant of policy, but not a trusted advisor. In this connection its prize work was a voluminous study of the Sino-Indian border dispute drawn up to serve Indian negotiators in the 1958-62 talks with China. The HD study turned out to be perhaps the most

---

[1] K.P.S. Menon, *Many Worlds: An Autobiography* (Bombay: Oxford University Press, 1965), p. 271.

powerful weapon, albeit propaganda weapon, in the Indian arsenal.[2]

The HD was headed by a director, and on July 1, 1961 consisted of six research officers and seven assistant research officers, of which three were assigned to the Goa Research Unit. The first director was not IFS but research cadre, and was chosen for his expertise as a historian rather than diplomat. The HD's functions around this time also included:

1. ". . . the printing of selected old records for official use . . ."

2. Preparation and issue of monthly summaries of the activities of the Indian government for the information of Indian diplomatic missions.

3. The assistance of scholars working on official research projects, as well as the limited assistance of private scholars.[3]

During the Nehru period, the HD had also been doing surveys of public opinion so that Nehru might know how the public felt about Indian foreign policy. However, this liberal policy task was not favored by the radical Smt. Gandhi, and the function no longer exists. The background studies which the HD did were done at the request of other MEA divisions, and completed work was forwarded to the relevant territorial division.

The HD's resources consisted of a trained research staff, the MEA library, and the MEA's Intelligence Unit. The library was quite large, having in 1968-69 67,000 volumes and in 1975-76 a staff of seventeen non-IFS cadre officers. The Research and Intelligence Section (also: Research and Intelligence Branch, Research and Reference), a very old part of the HD's work, no longer, unlike the library, exists. Research and Intelligence Section's work was very limited, consisting only of the preparation of monthly intelligence summaries. The information contained in the summaries was drawn from reports of heads of mission and from the library's resources. Preparing these reports demanded

---

[2] K.P. Misra, "Foreign Policy Planning Efforts in India," *Institute for Defence Studies and Analyses Journal,* April 1970, p. 384.

[3] N. Parameswaran Nair, *The Administration of Foreign Affairs in India with Comparative Reference to Britain* (New Delhi: School of International Studies, 1963), p. 280; Ministry of External Affairs, *Report 1968-69,* p. 83.

some skill, and the HD was staffed by highly professional personnel, non-IFS regional specialists with high linguistic competence.[4]

The HD's dominance over the research process ended with the disastrous conclusion of the 1962 border conflict with China. Though the 1962 war had its most profound effects on the defense machinery, it also set into effect a chain of administrative events within the MEA with important contemporary consequences. The 1962 war was important organizationally, and only Nehru's death two years later has resulted in greater changes in MEA's structure and outlook. The 1962 war resulted in the creation of the Foreign Affairs Committee of the cabinet, the Emergency Committee of the cabinet, and, within the MEA, the East Asia Research and Coordination Division. The Division originally had a small staff of a joint secretary, deputy secretary and four research officers.[5] It was established in 1963, initially a group of Indian China watchers with a "distinguished" (according to one source) China specialist heading it.

Outside of the MEA, the cabinet was also engaged in planning efforts. The Defence Committee of the cabinet was served in this respect by the Joint Planning Committee, created after the 1962 conflict. It was recognized that planning for Defence had an even greater urgency than its counterpart in foreign policy.[6]

A major responsibility of the MEA and of its diplomatic missions was in reporting and in the evaluation of those reports. The final analyses of the MEA are ideally, formally, sent to the prime minister and his immediate subordinates to aid them in making policy and deciding specific action based on that policy. But what happens when the prime minister does not want analysis of information, when he does not make decisions based on the weighing and integration of all available facts but rather on entirely different criteria? It was well known among his associates that Nehru relied heavily on his intuition in making foreign affairs decisions, bringing into play what Arthur Lall calls the "intuitive factor" in Nehru-period foreign policy. K.P.S. Menon comments,

---

[4] *Report 1968-69*, p. 83; *Report 1975-76*, p. 129; *Report 1951-52*, p. 2.

[5] K.P. Misra, *Foreign Policy and its Planning* (New Delhi: Asia Publishing, 1970), p. 22.

[6] P.V.R. Rao, "Government Machinery for the Evolution of National Defence Policy and the Higher Direction of War," *IDSA Journal,* July 1968, p. 1.

> Our foreign policy . . . necessarily rested on the intuition of one man, who was Foreign Minister as well as Prime Minister, Jawaharlal Nehru . . . his intuition was based on knowledge--knowledge which he had gained by a close study of international problems and meditation thereon during long years of enforced inactivity in jail.[7]

Judging from his close emulation of Mahatma Gandhi, his style of speech-making, his spontaneity in public and quick temper in private, it becomes apparent that Nehru valued intuition very highly. It seems that intuition played a role in deciding the outcome of issues in the MEA as well, and in fact this conclusion must be drawn to explain the arrest of bureau research facilities' growth.[8]

6.1 RESEARCH AFTER NEHRU

After Nehru a policy planning organization was established, but it was regarded by many policy-makers and academics alike as little better than what had existed before: nothing. According to a senior government official, the policy planning apparatus faces serious

---

[7] Arthur Lall, "Change and Continuity in India's Foreign Policy," *Orbis*, Vol. 10, 1966-67, pp. 91-105; Menon, p. 271.

[8] A very important part of the MEA's responsibilities lie in analysis, and this function has been carried out by various research bodies inside the MEA. However, during the Nehru period, the only research body inside the MEA was the HD, the only responsibility of which was the preparation of briefs on deep rather than recent history, without the capability of making policy recommendations on current problems. If Nehru had been an inductive logician, his policy would have required more extensive research facilities than in fact existed. The structure of the HD suggests that Nehru was looking for fundamental historical patterns and was therefore in policy-making a predominately deductive reasoner. General research on current topics was not accomodated until after Nehru's death; in 1965, a Current Research Division was set up in the building that housed the HD, Pathiala House, enabling, *a priori*, a rough processing of reports.

problems even today.[9] It fits very awkwardly into the general processes of the MEA, being regarded more or less as the "fifth wheel in the coach," and is tolerated but not encouraged by leadership. During most of 1976, for example, its staff was practically without work to do. It was employed that year finally in a make-work briefing for a heads of mission conference.

The only reason that the Policy Planning and Review Division (PPRD) is tolerated is that it does serve as a useful resource body for whoever might on occasion need it. There is nothing to keep it employed full-time. The PPRD is also apparently very weak in creative and innovative work. This is less its own fault than that of the people who utilize it, as the PPRD is told to just look up the facts, but no brilliant analysis please. The PPRD is generally directed by bureau leadership to compile the available facts on some topic, after which the report is turned over to the soliciting division for comments, elucidation and courses of action. The research officer is regarded as a fact-finding drudge and a servitor to the IFS officer. Naturally, creative and innovative work would be stifled by such an atmosphere. PPRD officers are not oblivious to what is happening, and are, as sources relate, "frustrated" and "insecure" in their work, but have little idea of how to reverse the situation.

Also, the (now-defunct) overseeing committee (the PPRC) was twice headed by people who were not, being too involved in other matters, able to conduct policy planning. One committee chairman, D.P. Dhar, was too deeply committed to the management of the Bangladesh crisis, and Parthasarathi retained his committee position because of this value as confidant to Smt. Gandhi, not because of his competence as PPRC chair. At other times, the foreign secretary (who normally heads the committee) had not been strong. The committee has at present been disbanded which, in the opinion of one senior official, has harmed the policy planning process considerably. In fact, the process has been so deficient in resources and challenges that Bandyopadhyaya writes that ". . . the major function of the PPRD over the years has been the writing of speeches for the Foreign Minister and the Prime Minister."[10] To understand what is happening in policy planning today, and to prove or disprove the legitimacy of the complaints that surround it, we should examine its early post-Nehru

---

[9] Personal interview. August 6, 1982.

[10] Personal interview. September 29, 1982. Jayantanuja Bandyopadhyaya, *The Making of India's Foreign Policy* (New Delhi: Allied Publishers, 1979), p. 260.

history and subsequent developments. There are problems within the policy planning process, but are probably intrinsic to the nature of overall foreign policy formulation and implementation. It is not a local weakness or specifically-rectifiable fault.

After Nehru's death a prime minister came along who preferred a more pluralistic decision-making machinery. After the committee of secretaries, the most important intrabureau move made by Shastri was to continue the operations of the East Asia Research and Coordination Division well after the cessation of the immediate China threat.[11] He did this by changing the name of the division to Current Research Division, in which form it remained for slightly over a year, until Indira Gandhi assumed power after Shastri's second heart attack and death. The transient Current Research Division was headed by a joint secretary, who had under him a deputy secretary and four research officers. It was dependent on the HD for resources, and was located with the HD in Pathiala House. The most pressing administrative problem for the Current Research Division lay in the determination of jurisdiction. The Current Research Division (clearly named such in contrast to the HD) failed, according to the Pillai report, because there ". . . was no clear procedural arrangement laid down for the discussion of papers produced by the Division." In other words, the Division fitted into the administrative structure but not into the policy formulative process. It was unclear where research responsibilities should be drawn between the HD, Current Research Division and the territorial divisions.[12] Though this was not the central cause of the Current Research Division's termination, it was probably a contributing factor (it was terminated centrally due to leadership rather than intrabureaucratic dynamics; the Current Research Division did not suit Gandhi's early policy goals).

After Shastri passed away the Current Research Division became the PPRD. With the name change came changes in internal structure, the number of research officers was increased somewhat, two under-secretaries added to supervise them with one more deputy secretary. The entire division was now headed by a director (of

---

[11] The committee of secretaries will be discussed further in chapter 10.

[12] Misra, *IDSA Journal,* p. 386; *Report of the Committee on the Indian Foreign Service* (New Delhi: Government of India, 1966), p. 25; Bandyopadhya (1979), p. 255.

slightly lower rank than the previous joint secretary).[13] Jagat Subha Mehta was the first PPRD head in its fledgling years 1966-68. There was talk in 1969 of upgrading the rank of PPRD head above that of joint secretary, but this was not done until 1971. With the growth of its assigned personnel strength, the PPRD became a better research division, but with the change in name the PPRD was not changed into a planning body, as much as leadership might have wanted such a body.

Table 6.2: PPRC membership

```
  chairman: foreign secretary, MEA
 secretary: joint secretary, PPRD, MEA
   members: two remaining secretaries, MEA
    member: chairman, Joint Intelligence Committee[a]
   members: two secretaries, cabinet secretariat
    member: secretary, Ministry of Commerce[b]
    member: secretary, Ministry of Defence[b]
```

[a]with rank of additional secretary, MEA
[b]late addition to PPRC
source: Misra, *IDSA Journal*, p. 390; Bandyopadhyaya (1979), p. 255.

To supervise the PPRD, later in 1966 the Policy Planning and Review Committee (PPRC) was formed, a body which Misra called ". . . a new version of the Committee of Secretaries" and which apparently came about in an attempt by the new Gandhi leadership to do what the new Shastri leadership had attempted, but had failed to do; to open a secondary policy pathway of direct contact with the secretaries, supplementing the primary policy path running through the foreign minister.[14] Why were two such attempts to create a secondary policy informational pathway made in such rapid succession after the end of the Nehru era? The creation of a foreign ministership separate from the prime minister's person after Nehru's death might have been the

---

[13] Misra, *IDSA Journal*, p. 391; *Foreign Policy and its Planning*, p. 27.

[14] Misra, *IDSA Journal*, p. 390.

stimulus, as Nehru had always had direct access to his secretaries, and this contact was eliminated with a separate foreign minister. With Shastri and Gandhi a separate foreign minister existed (with short lapses during Gandhi's regime) to coordinate between the prime minister and the secretaries. Both the committee of secretaries and the PPRC can be seen as attempts to restore the direct contact with the secretaries so typical of the Nehru bureaucracy, apparently very desirable even to later leadership. Table 6.2 reveals an interesting PPRC structure. Outside of MEA on the committee were representatives of the Ministries of Commerce and Defence and the Joint Intelligence Committee. There is also a high proportion of secretary-ranked officers, as was true of Shastri's committee of secretaries. Additionally, P.N. Haksar apparently sat in on the meetings when he was deputy chairman of the Planning Commission. As Misra notes, the PPRC-PPRD paired mechanism was similar to the Planning Group/Community and Policy Planning Council (later the S/PC) in the American Department of State apparatus, though the American grouping has had more success than the Indian one.[15] The American staff was directly responsive to the secretary of state. I hypothesize that the PPRC, not part of any line organization, must have been held directly responsible to the prime minister Indira Gandhi. It does not seem credible that such a high-powered group would be concerned only with the fate of the PPRD. Only when the PPRC knew that its primary customer would be the prime minister could it be expected to do effective and meaningful work in the face of disintegrative influences from high-level MEA political appointees and the coordination problem posed by having four radically different government bodies (MEA, JIC, Ministry of Commerce, and the cabinet secretariat) represented on the same committee. This committee would have the support of the prime minister, and in return would, in theory, give the prime minister a useful contact with his secretaries.

The influence of the PPRC was further broadened by the simultaneous transformation of the Current Research Division into the PPRD. Though the PPRC was created after the PPRD, it came to control the PPRD immediately, eventually transforming the PPRD into its resource body. PPRD studies could be initiated at three levels, the ministerial, secretarial and joint secretarial (at the initiative of other divisions or of the joint secretary in charge of the PPRD himself). With the

---

[15] Misra, *Foreign Policy and its Planning*, p. 27; Shashi Tharoor, *Reasons of State* (New Delhi: Vikas, 1982), p. 176.

elimination of the word "research" and replacement with "planning" this division underwent a conceptual role shift. No longer was it the passive, receptive background producer, but now became a prescriptive policy input itself, defining values, priorities and alternate courses of problem resolution for the other divisions to follow. In addition to the above-mentioned 1966 improvement in this division's staffing (by 1970 the PPRD had somewhat less than sixteen officers), the powers of the PPRD relative to the other MEA divisions were broadened.

When the PPRD was first instituted, it was known also as the Policy Planning and Communications Division, and was apparently in charge of overseas missions communications. The PPRD through this was given immediate access to all important communications from the diplomatic missions, making it independent of the policy output of the other divisions. The PPRD also could initiate any policy studies which it found important on its own behest, and did not have to wait, as the HD had generally to do, for requests from the other divisions (it is not clear that the PPRD at that early stage availed itself of these opportunities). However, the policy studies for which the PPRD was responsible assumed the nature more of research than planning. As real long-term planning would have required a much larger staff than the PPRD commanded, the PPRD degenerated rapidly into ". . . a flexible facility available to the Foreign Minister and Secretary for collection of data, background material, reports at short notice etc." Such complaints about the ineffectiveness of the PPRC/PPRD process in policy planning do not take into account that these bodies were never primarily policy planning bodies, but rather short-term background research staffs with a Planning title.[16] This is not necessarily a failure on the part of the PPRC, as bureaucratic bodies often perform tasks quite unrelated to their titles.

So it was that the research process was made administratively contingent on the planning process, making the flow of policy information to the prime minister predominately that of processed summaries of policy alternatives and less that of raw data. This preference for processed policy summaries is an important difference between Nehru's and Smt. Gandhi's styles of leadership. It both signals a greater trust in the

---

[16] *Report of the Committee,* p. 2; Dilip Mukkerjee, "Decision Making for Defense," *IDSA Journal,* January 1969, p. 107; K. Subrahmanyam, "Foreign Policy Planning in India," *Foreign Affairs Reports,* January 1975, pp. 1-12; see also Bandyopadhyaya (1971 edition), p. 207.

skill and integrity of MEA professionals and an end to the Nehru-period policy monopoly. The result of dependence on processed policy summaries is that less time had to be spent by the prime minister on foreign policy, in return for which the MEA professionals gained a greater degree of freedom in manipulating the flow and nature of policy information inside the bureaucracy.

The senior research division, the HD, maintained until recently, throughout all MEA structural variation, its separation from the PPRD. The separation of functions between HD and the PPRD was a cause for dissatisfaction within both divisions, and suggestions for the merger of the two divisions began to emerge in the sixties. Other recommendations toward the improvement of research included the upgrading of the PPRD's head to that of a secretary (putting it on a level with Economic Division), increasing the staff, giving the PPRD access to foreign intelligence reports as well as the standard missions' reports which it (in theory) automatically received, getting first-hand information for the PPRD by stationing its officers abroad, and commissioning the PPRD to do a series of policy papers, rather similar to the Nixon administration's National Security Study Memoranda (NSSM).[17] By April 1970 the PPRD was headed by a joint secretary with one deputy secretary and two research officers. Because MEA leadership had sanctioned three deputy secretaries and several more research officers, it is clear that improvements could have been made in staffing. The total MEA research staffing, including PPRD, Economic Division and research staffs attached to the territorial divisions (c. 1970) consisted of one joint secretary/director, six deputy secretaries/deputy directors, sixteen senior research officers and five research officers.

6.2 RESEARCH AFTER 1971

The PPRD reached its peak in animation in the period between the Bangladesh insurgency and the declaration of the emergency. Before the Bangladesh war and soon after the emergency, those two great and catalytic events in modern Indian history, the PPRD's performance was mediocre. This happened not because of the type of men making up the PPRD but because of the powers assigned to PPRD leadership by Gandhi. The policy planning apparatus was in part a tool created and

---

[17] K.P. Misra, "Foreign Policy Planning: Some Suggestions," *International Studies* 17, 1978, p. 830.

utilized in a larger extrabureaucratic political struggle. The Congress split occurred in 1969, and Smt. Gandhi gained full control over the Congress political machine by breaking the Kamaraj syndicate's power over the executive office. From 1969 to 1975 Gandhi was flexing her political muscles, learning to take on steadily larger tasks which culminated in the emergency. The emergency was the act of a woman confident but not yet skilled in the use of power. She gained this confidence partially through the handling of the Bangladesh adventure and through the events which followed the civil war, particularly the signing of the Indo-Soviet Treaty of Friendship. Our concern will be how the PPRD has fullfilled political needs extending far beyond the realm of foreign policy.[18]

The PPRD met with a strange fate when in 1971 it was used by D.P. Dhar[19] to direct a large part of the Indian Bangladesh operations. In this role he was functioning as the chairman of the PPRC. Dhar's appointment was an important variation on PPRC routine since the foreign secretary was the *ex officio* chair of the committee. Dhar owed his new position to the close working relationship which he had with Gandhi, and not to any institutional provisions. As PPRC chairman Dhar's main task was to convince the world of Indian rectitude in intervening in the civil war, in which capacity he travelled extensively. D.P. Dhar and the PPRD were not only in charge of the Bangladesh political (not military) operations, but were also in control of the Research and Analysis Wing's (RAW) work in this area (immediately previous to the large-scale intervention the Bangladesh military operations were the reserve of the RAW).[20] In 1971 the PPRD was more than active, it was also very powerful. After the war the PPRD would slow down somewhat, but its days of glory were not yet over.

---

[18] For a more complete treatment of Smt. Gandhi's slow rise to power, see Tharoor, pp. 50-153. The reader is warned that Chawla's treatment of the 1971-76 period (Sudershan Chawla, *The Foreign Relations of India* [Encino, California: Dickenson Publishing, 1976], pp. 69-70) is not organizationally accurate.

[19] Former chief minister of Jammu and Kashmir and ambassador to the Soviet Union.

[20] Bandyopadhyaya (1979), pp. 257-58 Chand Joshi, "Out in the RAW," *India Today,* April 1-15, 1977, pp. 29-30.

In June 1972 D.P. Dhar was appointed head of the Indian delegation to the Simla talks being held at this time between India and Pakistan, simultaneous with his PPRD chairmanship. This was an indication of the high esteem with which D.P. Dhar was held by prime minister Gandhi, and correlatively the high value which she must have placed in the operation of the PPRC (the PPRD joint secretary position has at times also been a valued post in MEA, serving as a stepping stone to other plum jobs. The first head, of course, became the foreign secretary in 1976, and the second joint secretary became in the same year ambassador to China). Several months later in August 1972 Dhar entered the cabinet as planning minister (a post that had not existed before he assumed it), still the head of the PPRD.[21] Thus for the first time the PPRD had a cabinet-ranked official in political charge. The foreign secretary regained his status as head of the PPRC at this time.

A couple of years later, in early 1975, G. Parthasarathi gained the chair of the PPRC and became the political head of the PPRD with the rank of minister of state, replacing Dhar as head of the PPRC-PPRD process.[22] Parthasarathi was (and still is) a close confidant of Indira Gandhi and had retired just previous to his PPRD appointment from the vice-chancellorship of Jawaharlal Nehru University. While minister of state, Parthasarathi apparently met foreign minister Y.B. Chavan privately twice weekly. At the same time, D.P. Dhar was additional secretary (Admin) in MEA. Besides his PPRD appointment, Parthasarathi has figured very prominently in the Office of the Prime Minister. Until Parthasarathi found himself out of a job under Janata in 1977, the PPRD continued to function with the same even, high performance. Indeed, the 1971-77 period was a plateau in the PPRD's performance, a performance not repeated since.

In the eighties, the PPRD seems to have given up the great ideal of policy planning and has instead become an earnest research body. Several post-1977 conditions support this transformation. With the

---

[21] Bandyopadhyaya (1979), pp. 257-58.

[22] Tharoor's account, p. 176, has, for its strengths, a few errors. The PPRD was created in 1966, not 1965; the PPRD was not put in the charge of an additional secretary until May 1980, not 1974 (this from PPRD sources); and Parthasarathi was given his minister of state position in early 1975, not 1974. See also Bandyopadhyaya (1979), pp. 257-58; K. Subrahmanyam, "Foreign Policy Planning in India," *Foreign Affairs Reports*, January 1975, p. 1.

Janata victory Parthasarathi lost the chair of the PPRC, which again reverted to the foreign secretary. Very soon afterward the PPRC stopped meeting altogether, and has not, though not formally disbanded, met up to the present day. The PPRC-PPRD process was seen by Janata leadership as an instrument of Gandhi's authoritarian rule, and suffered accordingly.

With the Janata victory a new perspective also was gained on the Indian overseas communities; whereas before they were ignored, they became suddenly important to Indian foreign policy. Indians were now exhorted to remember and retain their cultural identity despite their emigration abroad, and were assured that they were not forgotten by their motherland. Besides the permanent and second- or third-generation Indian communities, there was a transient Middle East labor community to look after. To take care of all this was virtually no organization, the overseas communities having been eclipsed by thirty years of a head-in-the-sand policy. Before 1947 there had been a Department of Commonwealth Relations whose raison d'etre had been to look after the overseas Indians, but upon its early assimilation into the MEA that function ceased.

To assist in the development of a government policy for the overseas communities, in late 1977 an Overseas Indians Cell was created, within the PPRD, which still exists. It is not a detailed implementative body, but rather is looking into the long-term prospects of the communities' role in the Indian national interest and is investigating means of the assistance, influence and utilization of the communities abroad.[23] For more mundane issues, a variety of bodies are presently consulted. For Indians on labor contracts to other countries (largely the Middle East) the ministering body is the Ministry of Labor. Consular aspects are the charge of the Passport, Emigration and Consular (PVC) Division. While no large organization has been established to put aspects of the overseas Indian philosophy into action, the Cell seems to indicate that policy-makers are of serious intent in their change of heart, one of the few lasting contributions to foreign policy which the short-lived Janata government made.

After Janata only two important changes have been made in the PPRD's operation. In May 1980 Dr. J.S. Teja was made head of the PPRD with the rank of additional secretary (a position which he held up to gaining the foreign secretaryship in 1982). The PPRD could have had no better qualified leadership than in Dr. Teja, a very experienced academic who has had none of the usual difficulties in adapting his skills to

---

[23] To be discussed further in chapter 10.

diplomatic service. When Dr. Teja (of IFS cadre) was ambassador to Afghanistan in the months immediately after the invasion, the Indian embassy was spoken of as the best-informed in Kabul.[24] The additional secretary (PP) is generally regarded as a permanent position, which will be handed on to someone else rather than be disbanded when an incumbent steps down. Despite Dr. Teja's skills, he was not, lacking cabinet rank and the special relationship with Gandhi that Parthasarathi and Dhar had earlier enjoyed, able to duplicate the successes of the 1971-77 period. This will probably have to wait until another crisis comes along and the unique services of the PPRD are again demanded.

The second important change was in the merger in December 1980 of the HD and the PPRD, resulting in a much larger PPRD with an organizationally intact HD (now known as Research Wing) inside it and under its control. As the Division itself points out, there was no special reason for the merger. "There was no specific recommendation from source to this effect. The whole thing was a part of the regular on-going review of the Ministry's working."[25] It was part of an organizational modernization process, and its main effect has been to give the PPRD a much larger research component. The merger, besides resulting in a new PPRD self-image as a research body, has also created frustrations. The new Research Wing is located in Pathiala House, as HD was, but the rest of the PPRD staff is in South Block, several kilometers distant. This has resulted in a significant communications difficulty within the PPRD, and conferences or the transfer of materials between Pathiala House and South Block result in big time delays. A division in many ways already enfeebled is thus weakened further.

6.3   RESEARCH: 1982

In mid-1982 there was created within the cabinet secretariat a Policy Assessment and Review Staff, of three or four men who, according to a senior government official, "spend all of their time reading."[26] Little is known about the Staff other than this, but it seems to be an attempt, as the PPRD was, to bring some thinking

---

[24] *India Today,* April 16-30, p. 53.

[25] PPRD letter to author. September 1982.

[26] *Report 1981-82,* p. 47; personal interview, August 6, 1982.

and critical assessment into the policy process. It may be an imitation of the Canadian Central Policy Review Staff, a very successful planning body. Besides the Staff, the Indian cabinet secretariat has no research and planning organ. However, the Staff may be germinal to an extensive future extra-MEA planning network, so great changes in that system may be forthcoming.

Table 6.3: PPRD structure: 1982

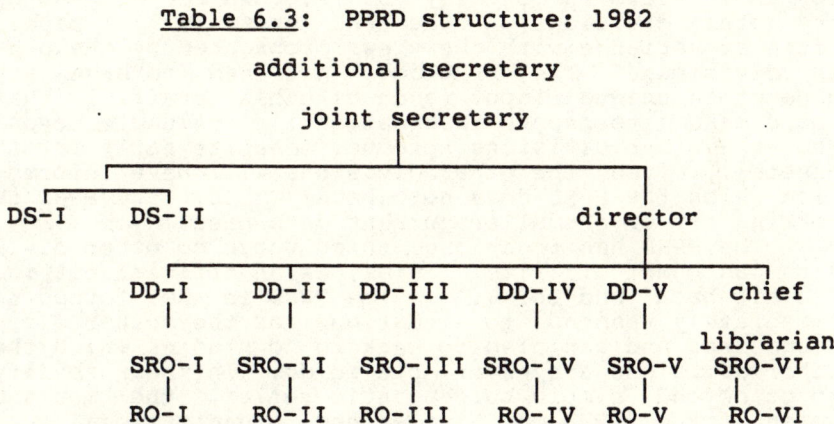

DS deputy secretary
DD deputy director
RO research officer
SRO senior research officer

source: courtesy of PPRD.

Today the PPRD (as shown in Table 6.3) is one of the larger divisions and functions under the general supervision of the foreign secretary. It is curious that a division of such unremarkable talents and uncertain future, as some would have it, should still exist today. It does, however, play a certain role in the policy process which has saved it from total abandonment. To understand this we will have to look at how the PPRD participates in policy, the paper-writing process. When an important issue comes up before the ministry, the PPRD automatically writes a paper, as well as whichever other territorial or functional divisions involved are consulted for their views. The ideas which the PPRD discusses with other divisions are often "half-baked," as one official put it, but are still brought into the picture. Discussion with the other divisions can bring an element of realism into the paper which PPRD officers lacking current value data may have difficulty in engendering. The PPRD, as the division involved with the broad aspects of policy, considers it necessary to take the broad organizational perspective as well. After consulting other divisions for their views (a courtesy not returned to the PPRD by the other divisions), the PPRD presents its paper, often at variance with the views propagated by the other divisions. The PPRD does not seem to have any dependable unique input (such as cable traffic) that would make its papers informationally valuable beyond what the other divisions produce (despite early formal assets). Often, the other divisions will have information which the PPRD does not have; thus, the PPRD is working off of a smaller current data base.

The PPRD has today one thing which no other division can boast of: time. Time, as an official put it, "to sit back and think."[27] The PPRD is not forced to immediately respond to situations as the other divisions are, and can also do background studies which the other divisions are never able to do. In their ability to go beyond simple bureaucratic reflex, the men and women of the PPRD may have earned organizational survival. An analytic perspective is needed badly in a bureaucracy where thought takes a back seat to action (a description not only of the Indian but of most national foreign policy bureaucracies, relative to most domestic bureaucracies, in the author's opinion). The PPRD may not always supply this analytic perspective very well, but at least some iota of that product is provided.

Besides participation in policy discussions, one of the PPRD's tasks is non-policy-related research. If the mission in Sweden wanted a chronology of nonalignment for their publicity efforts, or if a Swedish group expressed the desire for such information, then the PPRD would be employed in the research. The PPRD would also do topical backgrounds on request from Indian governmental agencies or officials. The PPRD, because of its academic orientation, also handles scholarships.

A possible future role for a policy planning division lies in a coordinative role similar to that undertaken by Coordination Division. Coordination Division

---

[27] Personal interview. September 29, 1982.

allocates tasks and information at the request of the division, and thus does not coordinate broad policy. But if a policy is composed of several only partially intersecting sub-policies, affects values of high national priority and draws upon informational, budgetary and manpower resources which involve most of the ministry, it is possible that, without coordination, a long interval may pass between the emergence of the need to decide and the complete (or optimal) formulation and implementâtion of the policy. This occurs because, without coordination, divisions rely upon their own independent informational networks in order to become activated toward the policy. The ensuing interval imposes costs upon the national society, which the bureaucracy serves. Put another way, the Indian central executive may allow an American multinational to set up a smelting plant in Kerala. It is possible that the Ministry of Commerce and Industry is better equipped (has a closer to optimal mix of bureau resources) to do effective liaison with the multinational than any other government bureau. But possibly the Economic Division has been better informed of the outcome of the political leadership's talks in past months with the multinational, and is in a position to win the liaison role through, say, an implicit threat of the joint secretary in charge to resign. Thus, through the happenstance structure of information, costs are imposed on the national society which could be avoided through the use of coordination (an informational override). The planning-programming-budgeting system movement in the Department of State is one way to implement such a policy-generated coordination (as opposed to coordination to serve the interests of the bureaucracy or the needs of political leadership). This, whose principal vehicle is the Program Analysis and Resource Allocation (PARA) system, utilizes manpower and procedures most similar to those available to the PPRD to determine optimal bureau-policy area mixes. PARA thus suggests a direction in which the PPRD may facilitate a move from the current bureau-generated coordination (of the Coordination Division).[28]

---

[28] Michael K. O'Leary, William D. Coplin, *Quantitative Techniques in Foreign Policy Analysis and Forecasting* (New York: Praeger, 1975), pp. 145-46.

6.4 CADRE AND ACADEMIA

The men who do the PPRD's research and analysis work belong to the non-IFS Combined Research Cadre. The cadre was instituted in 1973 and by 1975-76 comprised forty-eight officers. In 1981-82 it had only forty-five officers, entailing either a research personnel shrinkage or cadre redesignation. Cadre personnel have specialized training in some area, and have as a rule much stronger academic credentials than IFS officers. Perhaps because of the feeling that only generalists can lead, research cadre employees are generally of low, sub-deputy director rank. This rule has though been broken from time to time. K.P. Jain, 1982 director in charge of the Disarmament Unit, is, as an example, research cadre. Combined Research Cadre officers are scattered throughout MEA, and there are also a large number under deputation to other ministries. Discussions have been underway for some time on whether the research cadre should be assimilated into the IFS or allowed to remain separate. No decision has yet been reached but the problem at least is being considered.[29]

Foreign policy planning has stimulated a debate (which has, however, died off since the mid-seventies) among Indian thinkers such as no other topic in foreign policy organization. The leading example of this line of thought is K.P. Misra's *Foreign Policy and its Planning*. The debate itself has, perhaps surprisingly, not been among academics, as that community seems unanimously in favor of policy planning. The debate is rather between academics who want a greater say in foreign policy formulation, and bureaucrats who wish to limit non-cadre involvement in the policy process. This cooperation between bureaucrats and academics would depend a great deal on the degree of attunement of the universities to the needs of Indian foreign policy. The only Indian universities having international relations programs of any sophistication are Jawaharlal Nehru University (JNU) in New Delhi with its School of International Studies and Jadavpur University near Calcutta, with its Department of International Relations. The only Indian university with a staff devoted to the study of one country rather than a regional grouping is Benares Hindu University, Varanasi, with its Centre for the Study of Nepal. To supplement this there are a number of study institutions or "think tanks," such as the Institute for Defence Studies and Analyses or the

---

[29] *Report 1975-76*, p. 129; *Report 1981-82*, p. 82; interviews, Dr. Satish Kumar, May 25, 1982, and confidential, September 29, 1982.

Centre for Policy Research (both in New Delhi) both which sometimes sponsor foreign policy research or study, or have a handful of academics on their staff in this connection. Another government-affiliated study institution, one that no longer exists, was the School of International Studies. Once located on Ferozshah Road, it was established by Jawaharlal Nehru in 1956. It did training and research in diplomacy and international relations, and was eventually absorbed in 1971 virtually intact into the newly established JNU diplomatic programs. The last director of the School was Dr. M.S. Rajan, and during its existence received "generous grants-in-aid" from the government.[30]

The extent of government-academic cooperation is shown in a couple of cases. The Centre for Policy Research, in Spring 1982, began a review of Indian foreign policy which involved a number of semi-independent task forces. The Centre was in constant communication with the MEA through the PPRD. Questions were submitted to the PPRD in writing, and answers were given, but no access to files or ministry documents allowed (there being no counterpart in India to the unusual American Freedom of Information Act, nor provision for special security clearances). Even though the thirty-year rule says that files up to 1954 may now be opened, very few of these papers have been released (due to the lack of processing personnel). A second avenue for academic-government coordination is the India International Centre's Foreign Affairs Group, which holds one or two private seminars annually. Attendance at the seminars is by invitation only, and consists of government officials and selected academics. This does not constitute an official endorsement of such cooperation, though, as one year an official invitation was extended to MEA and was turned down. Since then bureaucratic participation has been strong but strictly off the record.[31] These ad hoc or periodic groups do exist, but none of the social science institutes have permanent foreign policy staffs or sponsor regular work in foreign policy. The number of places in which an international relations specialist might seek employment in his field is very low, and one of the tools which might bring up the number of foreign policy specialists in India, the social science study institution, has been scarcely utilized.

---

[30] *Report of the Committee*, p. 94; personal interview, S.D. Muni, JNU, May 26, 1982.

[31] Personal interview, Bhabani Sen Gupta. August 3, 1982.

In MEA, the involvement of academics in the direct process of policy formation is very low. Besides Dr. Teja there were in 1982 two scholars in the PPRD with PhD. qualifications, both senior research officers. In 1981-82 the Combined Research Cadre made up only forty-five of 506 officers in headquarters alone, giving a non-IFS academic representation of much less than nine percent.[32] And by predominately staffing only the PPRD and Legal and Treaties Division with Combined Research Cadre personnel, their contact with the total policy process is further restricted. Territorial divisions are entirely staffed, in the MEA set-up, by IFS generalists. Within MEA, and particularly within the IFS, there is a strong feeling that MEA is "for" the IFS, that no one else has the "right" to give MEA postings to too many non-IFS personnel (this is apparently an attitude shared toward the Department of State by the United States foreign service). Connected with that is the strong rivalry between IFS(A) ("true" IFS) and IFS(B) personnel, and the recommendations of the Committee on the Indian Foreign Service, whose manpower guidelines have been consistently unattainable because they do not seriously explore the possibility of staffing important MEA posts with non-IFS personnel. We may think in terms of a complex within the IFS cognitive structure which gravitates against the attempts of specialists to attain important, policy-significant positions within MEA.

Appointment of academics to high-powered positions in foreign policy circles has also not been seriously utilized. Eighty percent of all ambassadorships (sixty to eighty percent of ambassadorships for the U.S. foreign service) are as a rule closed to any but IFS, and academics do not make up an appreciable part of the remainder. In talks with various men in the past several months, the author could find no more than one example other than Dr. Teja of an academic being appointed to an ambassadorship, that man being JNU's Sisir Gupta, around 1982 appointed ambassador to Vietnam. Syed Mahmud, minister of state for external affairs under Nehru, was an academic, but because of his advanced age, among other things, Dr. Mahmud exerted no influence on policy. At present, the powerful men under Gandhi owe their positions not chiefly to Gandhi's respect for their intellectual abilities and achievements, but rather to Gandhi's trust in them as faithful deputies. That is how the position for the academic now stands, one of hopelessness for those interested in giving their expertise to the direct

---

[32] *Report 1981-82,* pp. 59, 82; personal interview, September 29, 1982.

administration of foreign affairs. That is not to say that the official MEA is unaware of the importance of academic participation in foreign policy. The 1968-69 *Annual Report* says in commendation of the PPRD's work that it ". . . has enabled the Ministry to increase its contacts with academic institutions whose work relates to foreign affairs."[33] But the cooperation has not been on a sufficiently large scale.

6.5 INTELLIGENCE AND INDIAN FOREIGN POLICY

The following section deviates from the central discussion of the MEA, though remaining close to the topic of research and analysis, and takes a community perspective on the problem of foreign policy organization. The many bodies in India concerned with foreign policy are not disjoint mechanisms grinding out policy without central purpose. They rather, together, compose a system. In a formal sense the foreign policy bodies are provided relational *gestalten* by service to the cabinet and prime minister, as well as common service to Indian national interests. Informally, there is an exchange of personnel and records, living and recorded experience. In missions abroad representatives of the various foreign policy bodies must learn to subordinate their own departmental interests in presenting a united front to the world. But the bodies nonetheless compete internally a great deal, and because civil war or schism in the governmental entity (unlike in other political organizations) is never possible, always a compromise must be reached between differing viewpoints. At the present time a conflictual relationship exists between the MEA and the Indian intelligence community, similar to that which exists in the United States at times between the Department of State and Central Intelligence Agency. Because the Indian intelligence and diplomatic communities examine many of the same kinds of questions, the prime minister must often choose between two perhaps widely diverging analyses to arrive at an agreed policy. Intelligence is an important policy input, and any discussion of how organization affects policy cannot, despite the shadowy policy contributions made by such bodies, neglect intelligence.[34]

---

[33] M.O. Mathai, *My Days with Nehru* (New Delhi: Vikas, 1979), p. 118; *Report 1968-69*, p. 83.

[34] The following chronology draws upon Bandyopadhyaya(1979), pp. 243-48 Asoka Raina, *Inside RAW* (New

The Nehru period gives us a few examples of an intelligence effort of policy relevance. At that time the only effective intelligence organizations were the Intelligence Bureau (IB, under the Home Ministry) and the branches of the three military services. Up until 1949 only one desk in the IB was devoted to foreign intelligence. In early 1949 the first IB director, Sanjivi Pillai, decided to post intelligence officers in Pakistan, Germany and France. In 1950, a misunderstanding between Pillai and Home secretary R.N. Bannerji led to Pillai being replaced by B.N. Malik, who in the period 1950-65 greatly expanded the IB's foreign intelligence network. Further work was done in this direction in 1965-68 by directors S.P. Verma and M.M.L. Hoja.

Delhi: Vikas, 1981); Kuldip Nayar, *Between the Lines* (Bombay: Allied Publishers, 1969), p. 178.

Table 6.4 The Indian intelligence community

```
cabinet ─── prime minister
secretariat   cabinet
              CCPA
              Steering Committee, JIC·
              Joint Intelligence Committee
                                                                              home minister
                                          chiefs of staff                     Ministry of Home Affairs
    director                                                                         │
    Research &                                                                Intelligence
    Analysis                                                                  Bureau (IB)
    Wing
                  Directorate    Directorate    Directorate
                  Military       Naval          Air
                  Intelligence   Intelligence   Intelligence
                  (DMI)          (DNI)          (DAI)

Directorate-General  Additional
Security (DG/S)      Director
        │
  Aviation   Special      Office of
  Research   Services     Special
  Centre     Bureau       Operations
  (ARC)      (SSB)        (OSO)

  joint        joint        joint        joint         joint
  secretary    secretary    secretary    secretary     secretary
  area I       area II      area III     area IV       Electronic,
  Pakistan     China and    Middle East  other         Technical
  Desk         South East   and Africa   countries     Sections
               Asia

                                         Administration   Internal
                                                          Security
```

sources: Raina, p. x; Bandyopadhyaya(1979), p. 248.

Table 6.5: JIC, JIC Steering Committee membership

JIC

chairman	additional secretary cabinet secretariat
representative, MEA	joint secretary[a]
representative, Defence Ministry	joint secretary
representative, Home Ministry	joint secretary
IB representative	joint secretary
RAW representative	joint director[b]
military intelligence representative	director(DMI)
naval intelligence representative	director(DNI)
air intelligence representative	director(DAI)
member-secretary	air commodore, Defence Ministry

JIC Steering Committee

chairman	cabinet secretary
members	foreign secretary
	defence secretary
	home secretary
	director, RAW
	chairman, chiefs of staff
member-secretary	chairman, JIC

[a] in 1977 the then incumbent IFS officer in this ministerial role was promoted to the rank of additional secretary, and continued as a JIC member at that rank.
[b] post-1971 addition to the JIC.

6.5.1 Military Intelligence

For the first four years after independence the IB shared responsibilities with the military intelligence groups. In 1951 the Himmatsinghji Committee found the foreign intelligence work of the Defence bodies inadequate in keeping an eye on neighboring countries, so all such responsibilities were given over at that time to the IB. Conflict between the IB and Defence erupted again during the 1962 war, with each side blaming the other for their separate intelligence failings. The

Ministry of Defence attempted to bring foreign intelligence back under its control, but this was stymied by the IB and the Home Ministry. There was also an attempt in 1962 to set up a Military Intelligence Organization under the guidance of an American advisor, an attempt which for political reasons also failed.[35]

Military intelligence was a somewhat disjoint composite of the intelligence branches of the three military services, the Directorate of Military Intelligence (DMI), the Directorate of Naval Intelligence (DNI) and the Directorate of Air Intelligence (DAI). These were quite similar in purpose and organization to the military intelligence bodies of the British raj. In 1948, the Joint Intelligence Committee (JIC) came into effect as an attempt to coordinate the military and and civilian intelligence bodies which existed at that time. Up until 1965 the JIC had virtually no impact on policy, but, as a result of the 1962 war, in 1965 a revamping of the organization was initiated. Failure of intelligence, among other things, was blamed for the unfortunate outcome of the war, and the JIC as the chief intelligence coordinative body felt the greatest impact. The JIC, whose chairman was originally a joint secretary in MEA, in 1965 was given an additional secretary of the cabinet secretariat as its permanent chairman, and a Steering Committee was set up to oversee and evaluate the JIC's work.

---

[35] In order to counter the growing Tamil Tiger movement, Sri Lanka's leadership, headed by Mr. Jayewardene, has decided to

> . . . hire former members of the elite British commando organization, the Special Air Service, and active members of the Israeli intelligence organization, Mossad, to set up a Sri Lankan intelligence organization and train a paramilitary force . . . The Israelis have now set up a 'special interests section' in Sri Lanka under the auspices of the US embassy. It is the first time the Americans have acted in such a capacity for the Israelis anywhere in the world.

The establishment or revision of intelligence organization under foreign auspices does not, therefore, seem a rare crisis reaction. *Christian Science Monitor,* July 11, 1984, p. 9.

The Steering Committee presently reports to the Cabinet Committee on Political Affairs, and the chairman is in close touch with the prime minister. Senior MEA officers in charge of territorial divisions are sometimes invited to meetings of the Steering Committee, and MEA participation in this body is greater than in any other intelligence IG. The JIC's membership composition has changed somewhat, with the most important alteration being that the JIC became no longer subordinate to the Chiefs of Staff Committee in the Ministry of Defence. It was instead now under the supervision of the cabinet secretariat and was responsible only to that body. We see here an attempt not only to upgrade the JIC and to increase its policy impact but also to reduce the Defence monopoly over Indian intelligence. This move seems to have been ineffective, as the JIC (like the PPRD) has not been given a large enough staff and sufficiently broad support from the top to do its job.

The JIC in 1975 had a secretariat of only four or five service and civilian officers, it lacked any significant research staff, and the chairman's time was taken up by many chores unrelated to his JIC duties. The other members of the JIC were as well occupied with their own organizations, having little time on balance to spare on the JIC (the JIC continued to meet three times a week in 1979, one session devoted to the preparation of a weekly military, political and economic intelligence report, and the other two meetings devoted to the preparation of papers on specific topics, all forwarded of course to the prime minister).[36] The JIC and the PPRD have suffered similar fates, having started with broad designs and having failed to achieve the missions expected of them due to inadequate infrastructure and weak top-level support. If the JIC were a more powerful body, the Steering Committee with its broad interministerial secretary composition and MEA participation would be quite effective intelligence management.

Another Defence body came into being in 1956, the Joint Intelligence Organization, whose purpose was to compile published papers for the Ministry of Defence. This body does not seem to exist now, and seems to have had little effect on the collection and analysis of intelligence. Defence seems by now to have lost permanent control over broad foreign intelligence, but the three service intelligence bodies remain, and they have to their record some sporadic successes. In 1971, for example, the chief of army staff set up an assessment

---

[36] K. Subrahmanyam, "Foreign Policy Planning in India," *Foreign Affairs Reports,* January 1975.

group for intelligence in East Pakistan under the vice-chief of army staff, which was useful in the conduct of the Indian operations during the Bangladesh intervention.

6.5.2 The Cabinet Bodies

The cabinet-sponsored intelligence bodies, in contrast with those of Defence, have been very successful. Besides the transfer of the JIC and related bodies to cabinet supervision in 1965, a new cabinet intelligence body was conceived with Gandhi's assumption of the prime ministership in 1966. The External Intelligence Organization was set up in 1967 under the cabinet secretariat with the task of military intelligence collection from neighboring countries. In September 1968 this body was superceded by the Research and Analysis Wing (RAW) of the cabinet secretariat. The RAW was first headed by Ram Nath Kao, a Kashmiri Brahman distantly related to Nehru, and was organized on the lines of "Force 136" of British intelligence. Force 136 operated during World War II and had at the time many Indian participants.[37] The RAW came about through cabinet efforts, but was originally not subordinate to the cabinet secretariat. The body was originally to have been under the Ministry of Defence (according to the suggestion of Brigadier M.N. Batra in a pre-1968 government paper on the topic) but apparently the Home Ministry wanted it under its supervision. Home would have been well-equipped for such a takeover, as it already had a large domestic intelligence apparatus easily adaptable to the task of external intelligence. It was decided eventually by Gandhi and her principal private secretary P.N. Haksar that the RAW should be brought under the cabinet secretariat so as to be directly responsive to the prime minister, and so that it would not suffer from a parochial ministerial outlook. Smt. Gandhi also undoubtedly realized the need for a personally responsive intelligence organization in her climb to power. Despite bringing the RAW under her supervision in 1968, the RAW did not come into full secretariat control until 1969, about the time of the Congress split (at the same time, Revenue Intelligence was moved from the Finance Ministry to the Ministry of Home Affairs, and the Central Bureau of Investigations in the Home Ministry was put under its Department of Personnel). According to Tharoor, the RAW reported to the JIC, but it is likely that the most important

---

[37] Dharmendra Gaur, "Rs. 22 to Write a Letter," *Sunday*, October 2, 1977.

intelligence found its way to Gandhi before it went to any institution such as the JIC.[38]

The RAW, a large organization with a budget of over Rs. ten crores (over Rs. 100 million, or US$ 11 million), is headed by a director with secretary rank. In effect, the director (in times when the RAW is in favor) enjoys more power than the ministerial secretary due to his direct and unparalleled contact with the prime minister, unbroken by the need to report to any intermediary officials. The work of the RAW expanded after its successful involvement in the 1971 civil war, and Gandhi seems now to have given at least equal time to RAW reports and analyses as to MEA studies. This policy equilibrium was maintained through the emergency and up until the Janata coalition took over in 1977, when the RAW was cut apart by Janata in a general purge of Congress(I) emergency instruments. Upon the Janata victory, R.N. Kao was relieved of his directorship and K. Sankaran Nair, who had been before that joint director, became the director. This meant little happiness for Sankaran Nair, as cabinet secretary N.K. Mukerjee suggested that the RAW head's rank should be cut from secretary to additional secretary equivalency, as it was inappropriate that a secretary-ranked officer should be in a line to the cabinet secretary. This suggestion was put into effect, and the head of RAW no longer reported directly to the prime minister, but rather only to the cabinet secretary. Prime minister Desai met with Sankaran Nair only three times, the first time less than ten minutes long. MEA was also told by Janata leadership to take over all responsibilities for foreign intelligence (which meant depriving RAW of most of its responsibilities).

RAW was cut in rank, responsibilities and strength during Janata obstensibly because of Gandhi's misuse of RAW personnel and resources during the emergency period. It was alleged that far from being exclusively a foreign intelligence organization, it was being used against the opposition inside India, carrying out the "dirty work" of Congress(I). Whatever evidence for these charges may exist, it seems that the pruning of RAW may not have proceeded for purely domestic political reasons (as we shall come to shortly). When Janata took over, the MEA probably was a major antagonist in the decision to cut down on RAW resources, and so this move may have been one of both bureaucratic and political expedience.[39]

---

[38] Tharoor, p. 148.

[39] The charges brought against the Congress(I) by Janata in reference to the misuse of RAW are very simi-

6.5.3 Community Fission

Since Janata, the intelligence apparatus has more than recovered. Ram Nath Kao now holds for the purpose of coordination and control the position of advisor-in-charge of the RAW, IB and CBI. The RAW, still headed by Sankaran Nair, had in the late seventies perhaps over forty stations, both inside India and abroad. No great changes have occurred, though there was talk in 1980 of establishing a "watchdog committee" to oversee intelligence activities. It is unclear whether anything ever came of this talk and whether the committee would coexist with or replace the JIC. At present foreign intelligence is the reserve of both the IB and RAW, the IB collecting most of its information on the neighboring countries or on foreign "influences" (the official term for international-national penetration) within the country. The RAW is generally concerned with foreign intelligence but has Special Bureaux in most of the larger Indian cities and state capitols.[40] While the IB collects foreign-related intelligence, only the RAW has employees stationed in missions abroad as diplomats, and it is with the RAW that foreign policy is most closely concerned.

The entire intelligence set-up, despite initial recover, is threatened with fracture. Inside the IB is an ongoing battle between deputationists, officers who got into the IB through deputation from the other law enforcement agencies, and direct recruits who were brought into the IB after the first communist electoral victory in Kerala (when the IB was expanded greatly to keep the communist movement under surveillance). The RAW's work is interrupted by continuous strikes, usually called by the lower-grade employees. The Aviation Research Centre (ARC), established in 1963 under the directorate-general of security (DG[S]), is torn by

---

lar to those brought in 1969 against the CPI-M government in Kerala, that the CPI-M had attempted to subvert and gain control over that state's police administration. The connection between the two cases lies in the attempt of a monolithic party structure to gain control of police powers, and the fall of the party from power partly for this reason. Interestingly, at least the failures of monolithic parties, whether Congress or Communist, seem to occur in similar ways and for similar reasons.

[40] Tharoor, p. 148 Asoka Raina, "Touching a RAW Nerve," *India Today*, June 16-30, 1980, p. 29; K.C. Khanna, "Bugs that Bedevil the IB and RAW," *Illustrated Weekly of India*, May 23-29, 1982, p. 26.

accusations of improper promotion practices, the abuse of deputation, and the like. Internal dissension also threatens the Special Frontier Force and the Special Services Bureau (third wing of DG[S]).[41] Besides these internal intrigues, the intelligence set-up has had clashes with non-intelligence sectors of the government, particularly MEA.

Intelligence, mainly the RAW, has been involved in the foreign policy process in a number of ways, to the consternation of Indian diplomats. While it is not known at present exactly what contribution RAW makes to the formulation of policy, we can discern the reaction of MEA diplomats to this invasion of their realm. There is absolutely no coordination between the MEA and RAW organizations. There may be some communication between the RAW director and the foreign secretary (Asoka Raina writes that foreign secretary T.N. Kaul and RAW chief R.N. Kao worked well together[42]), but when it happens it is a capstone without a base to support it. MEA officials as a group are not only uncooperative but, for several reasons, actually obstructive of RAW's activities. First, MEA officials understand that RAW often prepares reports on the same topics that the diplomats do, and that Gandhi and key advisors such as Parthasarathi may ignore MEA papers in preference for RAW reports. MEA officials have no idea how often this happens, or what the best way to counter this may be. They are thus frustrated, aware that many of their efforts may be to no avail. This is a result of RAW's bargaining advantage of secrecy, which a MEA within government circles does not possess.

There is also, in the author's opinion, a resentment within missions abroad and at the MEA secretary level that they, the foreign policy professionals, should be kept in the dark about RAW operations abroad. Officials must ask, why should a group of junior police officials with no understanding of the international arena be given a license to conduct operations perhaps with a profound influence on Indian international relations? MEA officials consider themselves the ministers of Indian foreign policy, and the secretaries would like to be kept informed about what the RAW is doing, and even to have some say over how things are done. Diplomacy may be, as U.S. president Johnson believed, a

---

[41] Rajat Sharma, "Civil War in Intelligence Bureau," *Onlooker*, June 30, 1982, pp. 8-13; "Crying or Spying," *India Today*, August 16-30, 1980, p. 39; Dilip Bobb, "School for Scandal," *India Today*, May 15, 1982, p. 101; also, *India Today*, September 16-30, 1980, p. 7.

[42] Raina, *Inside RAW*, p. 93.

"black art," but MEA officials consider themselves the magicians and the intelligence people the raw apprentices.[43] So long as no Indian equivalent of the American Forty Committee (which supervised intelligence operations during the Nixon era) exists to which the foreign secretary at least in principle is privy, we can expect Indian diplomats to harbor much professional resentment against RAW operatives who use "their" missions abroad for intelligence escapades. Exceptions to this general tension do exist. Apparently Apa B. Pant, G. Parthasarathi and D.P. Dhar were as ambassadors all very friendly to the RAW staff.[44]

Related to this is the very human concern for the promotion process. In several of the more important missions abroad the RAW man occupies the number-two position, creating difficulties.[45] If an IFS officer knows that his promotion is being delayed because the post which he would ordinarily be advanced to is being occupied by an Indian Police Service (from which most high-ranking RAW employees are drawn, and a less prestigious service than the IFS) officer several years his junior, there will naturally be resentment. This is a more personalized grievance than the others already mentioned, and probably more potent. This complaint will be made by the more senior officials, who will also be disturbed by the other above-mentioned factors more than the average junior officer. Finally, one point of difference between MEA and RAW will affect all IFS officers stationed abroad. That is the difference in background and outlook held by IFS and RAW officers. The RAW officer is generally from a lower social background and most of his previous experience would have been of the dull routine of police work in the cities and countryside of India. Because of his awkwardness in diplomatic high society, he is easily spotted and ridiculed by the more sophisticated IFS officer. IFS officers sometimes point out the RAW officer to the diplomats of other countries at social receptions, thinking that it must be obvious anyway who the RAW man is.[46] All of these factors have acted to close off

---

[43] I.M. Destler, *Presidents, Bureaucrats and Foreign Policy* (Princeton: Princeton University Press, 1974), p. 105.

[44] Raina, *Inside RAW,* p. 93. The latter two will figure prominently in our study of the Office of the Prime Minister, chapter 10.

[45] Personal interview, Dr. Bhabani Sen Gupta. August 3, 1982.

contact between the intelligence and diplomatic communities, erecting a wall between these two vital sources of policy.

---

⁴⁶ Raina, *Inside RAW*, pp. 91-94.

VII
Economic and Political-Military Policies

International economic relations is a responsibility of MEA, and within MEA is handled in its policy formulative phase by the Economic Division. We have seen already how the PPRD has survived and become a a permanent institution in Indian foreign policy formulation, but only after a prolonged (for many years) debate. The Economic Division was also the result of a debate, but one which was resolved so long ago as to have been forgotten by most. An Economic Affairs Division was set up in 1947, but was closed from lack of funds in 1950. Throughout the entire 1950-59 period there was no body inside MEA to handle economic relations and international economic policy, though the territorial divisions dealt with what work came up in their areas. The lack of an economic body in MEA was regarded by many ". . . as an unfortunate weakness in the structure of the Ministry responsible for handling international relations in the conditions of the modern world . . .," but attempts to correct the situation had no effect.[1] At that time, international economic functions were dominated by the Ministries of Finance and of Commerce and Industry, who had been handling this international relations issue area successfully for some time. They had their own sources of overseas data; Commerce and Industry had commercial sections in overseas embassies and Finance had commissioners-general in London and New York. Because of this it was very difficult for MEA to control Indian external economic policies, possibly resulting in disparities between basic foreign and international economic policies. Throughout the 1950s, though, no move was made to center responsibilities in

---

[1] H. Dayal, "The Organization of Diplomatic and Consular Services, with Special Reference to India," *India Quarterly*, XII, 3, July-September 1956, pp. 275-76.

MEA.

The situation was changed partly by the report of the 1960-61 Estimates Committee, which stated that

> [t]he Committee consider that the time for a full-fledged Economic Division in the External Affairs Ministry to replace the functions presently performed by the Commerce and Finance Ministries may not have risen immediately, but even so it would be desirable to take a decision on the pattern to be evolved ultimately in consultation with the Ministries concerned so that the necessary organization may be gradually worked out towards that end.

Armed with this conclusion, MEA was able to set up an Economic and Coordination Division in 1961. The Division was originally quite small, headed by a director who had three research cadre subordinates (from the Planning Commission) and an auxiliary staff.[2] Like his successors, the director had a special relationship with a secretary of the MEA, at that time the secretary-general, to whom he reported exclusively. The title was shortened in 1964 to Economic Division, and over the years since 1961 the Economic Division has risen steadily in intraministerial influence. From one joint secretary in 1961, by 1969-70 two joint secretaries were in charge of the division. At that time, Economic Division was thought of as two separate divisions, Economic Division I and Economic Division II (the designation is no longer followed but an internal dichotomous structure still exists). The first major expansion of ED's responsibilities was in the early 1970s, when the first joint commissions were set up at the initiative of the Soviet bloc nations. This marked the ED's first experience with bilateral economic relations.[3] A new UN and Third World emphasis toward North-South relations was prefaced by the Paris Conference of 1976, for which a special unit was established inside ED to help prepare India for this crucial North-South meeting. In August 1978 major changes in ED's

---

[2] *Estimates Committee 1960-61, Hundred and Thirty-Eighth Report*, no. 49, p. 12, para. 31; N. Parameswaran Nair, *The Administration of Foreign Affairs in India with Comparative Reference to Britain* (New Delhi: School of International Studies, 1963), p. 289.

[3] Personal interview, July 30, 1982.

responsibilities occurred, mainly a *geographisation*, the shift of bilateral economic issues back to the territorial divisions.[4] At the same time ED was made the center for both North-South and South-South policies. In 1981, much of the regional South Asian economic work was given to ED, and in the future South-South and regional matters will continue to incrase in importance. Even today, ED's greatest expertise is probably in South-South affairs.

By 1977-78 the ED was headed by a secretary(economic relations) with a staff of nineteen officers, making it not only the largest but also the most powerful MEA division. Secretary(economic relations), who gave ED its priority in the MEA, was previously secretary(ED), a post which came about when Avtar Singh, the last secretary(West), retired. When this occurred in 1974 B.K. Sanyal, who was at that time additional secretary(ED), was promoted into a new secretary(ED) post, replacing the obsolete secretary(West) position. The division which secretary(economic relations) supervises was created with three goals in mind, namely:

1. promotion of close Indian external economic and cultural relations, bilateral agreements, coordination of the implementation of Indian international economic policy and in particular the coordination of policy generated by the intergovernmental joint commissions;

2. administration of the Indian Technical and Economic Cooperation (ITEC) program;

3. support for generally stronger economic cooperation at the regional and international level, even when not directly involving Indian interests.

The ITEC program, initiated in September 1964, is the largest part of the ED's responsibilities, and itself has five objectives, namely:

1. provision of training facilities in India for other Third World countries;

2. long and short-term secondment (deputation) of technical specialists abroad;

---

[4] Personal interview, Summer, 1982.

3. gifts to other Third World nations of equipment, drugs, medical supplies, etc.;

4. financial assistance for the conduct of feasibility studies and technical-economic surveys;

5. cooperation with other nations in third-party economic development projects.[5]

When the ED was first set in permanent or continuous operation it was only to administer the ITEC program, and had not the broad purpose that it has today. Even today, though, over half of ED's regular staff is working with ITEC, and it is still the main Indian assistance program. The financing of the ITEC program has expanded to over two hundred times what it was in 1964. At present, it has jurisdiction over aid to any developing nation except Nepal, Bhutan and Bangladesh. The particulars of how ITEC assistance is to be conveyed are worked out in the joint commissions which India has with most developing nations. In 1975-76, the nations which benefited most from the ITEC's trainee program were Maldives and Sri Lanka, both of which had twelve participants.[6]

The ITEC program is impressive as a piece of creative governmental thinking, and is to the credit of the Indian bureaucracy. As impressive is the diversity of the ED's tasks. In 1978-79 alone, ED was handling talks on establishing joint economic commissions with Mauritius and Nigeria; an agreement to give tariff preferences to Sri Lanka; Indian participation in the Canton fair; gifts of medicine and rice to Laos; the dispatch of an eight-member medical team to South Yemen under ITEC, and a feasibility study for production cooperation for growing cashew nuts in Tanzania.[7] In 1976-77 the officers of ED were responsible for maintaining contact with ninety-five economic and commercial posts in fifty-two countries (it is obviously due to the size of this task that bilateral economic policy and relations were finally returned to the territorial divisions).

ED was in 1982 supervised by secretary(economic relations) Romesh Bhandari, and was the charge of two joint secretaries. One joint secretary, in 1982 K.K.

---

[5] Ministry of External Affairs, *Annual Report 1974-75*, pp. 88, 118; *Report 1966-67*, pp. 68, 94.

[6] Personal interview, July 30, 1982; *Report 1975-76*, p. 203.

[7] *Report 1978-79*, pp. 48-50.

Bhargawa, was in charge of multilateral and South-South economic policy, while the other joint secretary handles ITEC. Under the joint secretaries are two directors, two deputy secretaries and four or five undersecretaries. It, with the PPRD and XP Division, is one of the three largest divisions in MEA. Despite its size, contact between ED and top leadership is at present not great, and Gandhi met with secretary Bhandari only once a month.[8] The most important contact between Gandhi and the ED is in economic briefing. For example, before her August 1982 trip to the United States Smt. Gandhi was given an exhaustive background on the discussions that she would hold, a briefing conducted by ED officers. Other than on these occasions, Gandhi does not take an active interest in Indian economic programs. Her early decision to devalue the rupee is an example of a decision taken by the bureaucracy to which Gandhi capitulated, due to lack of active involvement in program supervision. She is unlikely to want to let such a major decision go by her again, but still takes no regular interest in the work of ED and associated economic relations bodies.

ED's reception of information from missions abroad is continuous and substantial. Those missions send cables to ED whenever multilateral, South-South or ITEC policies are involved, as well as another copy to the territorial division. ED, both within MEA and in the government community, carries a strong mandate (unlike the PPRD in its own area) to plan for broad external economic policy. The staff carrying out this mandate is overwhelmingly IFS generalist, with (at present) only two specialist officers, both economists. The lack of specialists inside ED is not a serious problem, as it is able within *Rules of Business* guidelines to draw heavily upon the staff of other ministries. This gives it a degree of flexibility which it would not have if it had a permanent specialized staff. Even for ITEC, ED's "own" program, there is great dependence upon other ministries for manpower and support. This, due to a harmony of interests in the area of economic policy, has been a satisfactory resource system. Besides ED, economic relations is in the jurisdiction of the:

- Ministry of Finance, Department of Economic Affairs, which deals with foreign aid policy and the Colombo Plan;

---

[8] Personal interview, July 30, 1982.

- Ministry of Commerce, Department of Commerce, which manages all foreign trade issues. The sixth conference of UNCTAD is a good example of its area of specialization. It also has several trade missions abroad under its own jurisdiction.

- UN Division, of MEA, which handles some multilateral work arising in conjunction with the UN, and coordinates contributions to UN programs.

- Legal and Treaties Division, of MEA, which is in charge of Law of the Sea work. These all constitute ED's resource bodies, for which it is the coordinative and formulative source of policy.

7.1 POLITICAL-MILITARY POLICY

Since 1945 the foreign policy endeavors of the Western nations have seen increasing cooperation between diplomatic and military specialists. This cooperation is seen particularly in the American conduct of the war in Vietnam, where diplomatic negotiations with the North Vietnamese were conducted by men well-trained in military science, and bombing halts were engineered to further the success of negotiations. Organizationally, political-military policy in the United States is processed by the Bureau of International Security Affairs of the Department of Defense, and within the Department of State by the Bureau of Politico-Military Affairs (PM). However, that it the United States, and we only cite these agencies as contrasts with the Indian conception of political-military coordination. Though the Cabinet Committee on Political Affairs (CCPA) provides at the ministerial level for defense planning and coordination, and the National Defence College organizes courses for senior IFS officers, the political-military organizational lacunae are almost complete. The National Defence College's training is devoted only to battlefield tactics in force-arrays of greater than battalion strength, and does not deal with sophisticated ideas such as strategic planning or political-military policy or coordination. IFS officers ask to be seconded to the College only because they do not wish to be posted overseas immediately (as noted in chapter 4), and they are not given significant military training.

The PPRD additionally has no officer with military specialization, and until 1969 the defence secretary was not even a member of the PPRC (he eventually gained membership through his own efforts). While there were representatives of both MEA and Defence in the JIC, the

CCPA and the PPRC, this did not lead necessarily to their collaboration. These groups were created with purposes other than political-military coordination in mind, and the representatives were too occupied with other business to be concerned with political-military coordination.

IFS probationers receive no training in military science, and there are no divisions or sections within either MEA or the Ministry of Defence responsible for political-military policy. The military attachés accredited to several Indian missions report to the Directorate of Military Intelligence (DMI), separating them from the mainstream of foreign policy formulation. They consider themselves to be diplomats accredited by their service branch to the armed forces of the other country, and their reports go directly back to the DMI, for purely military consumption, and do not contribute to the lofty aims of political-military policy formulation. Attachés have no special training before being posted, and postings are regarded as rewards for good work rather than as serious postings with importance for Indian foreign policy.

We deduce that, due to the lack of a political-military policy organization, Indian foreign policy lacks a substantial political-military element. The author believes that, due to the lack of a political-military policy or cognitive system on the part of policy-makers, unnecessary costs are imposed upon Indian defense policy. Political-military coordination has been, during modern Indian history, least apparent before the Sino-Indian border conflict, with a peak in 1958-64, a higher (but shorter-lived) peak in 1971 with the Bangladesh intervention, but with hardly greater prominence for political-military coordination in 1964-71 or 1971-84 than in 1947-58. In the 1962 conflict, MEA served as the station for American, British and other foreign advisors with their respective nations' aid efforts. Biju Patnaik's guerilla resistance project was under MEA (though it never quite got off the ground). And naturally the success which India had in obtaining military aid was partially dependent upon the persuasive skill of Indian diplomats. It was their mission to "sell" the Indian case for intervention in Bangladesh. Despite these areas in which political-military coordination clearly existed, the diplomats and soldiers continuously worked at cross purposes.

The cause of the 1962 conflict lay in the arguments of Indian negotiators for a position in the Aksai Chin and NEFA which military realities did not support. The political contribution to 1962 military planning was largely that of the central executive, and did not include the operational bureaucracy or experienced, IFS cadre diplomats. Of the central executive, it was Krishna Menon who controlled political policy contributions during the conflict, with foreign secretary M.J. Desai representing MEA (Defence was represented in these talks by the minister of defence rather than the secretary of defence). B.M. Kaul suggests that the political-military coordination as it existed was more deleterious than helpful, perhaps due to the lack of a responsible support body. Kaul further quotes Desai as having ". . . told the Army at official meetings that time [sic] had come to give a crack to the Chinese at least in one place to show that we meant business." Desai also said ". . . that an effective method of stemming the Chinese advance in Ladakh would be to give them an occasional knock during our encounters with them in our territory and to engage them in a short offensive action aimed at inflicting casualties and for taking prisoners." This gives us a good idea of the quality of "political" commentary during the 1962 war.[9] In the author's opinion, had a political-military body existed before 1962, the conduct of the war would have been much improved, though the lack of such a bureau was not the only or most important factor in the conflict's outcome.

Existence of a political-military bureau would have forced at least some components of military leadership to consider the political roots of the policy, if the political-military bureau enjoyed the proper informational assets. If they had done so, they probably would have been less prone to simply "follow orders." They could still, as General Kaul was, have been in favor of the Forward Policy and carried it through, but under the influence of a political-military body they might have thought more about the actual military needs of such posts if they were to come under Chinese attack. Such a body might also have forced the political experts to reduce some of their singular dependence upon international legalisms and to examine with a critical eye India's actual (rather than supposed) ability to obtain what it felt it was entitled to. One can examine at great length the Aksai Chin question in terms of treaty legalities and come to no clear conclusions. One can also look at the 1962 debacle in terms of purely military capabilities, and

---

[9] Personal interview with Dr. K. Subrahmanyam, Institute for Defence Studies and Analyses, July 29, 1982; Kuldip Nayar, *Between the Lines* (Bombay: Allied Publishers, 1969), pp. 174, 178; B.M. Kaul, *Confrontation with Pakistan* (New Delhi: Vikas, 1971), pp. 287, 292.

some will argue, like Kaul, that such a course of action was militarily sound, and for this reason should have been carried through. Real answers, something apart from rhetoric, can only be found when the political and military experts are brought together, preferably through the agencies of a permanently established, not ad hoc, political-military group.

Indian foreign policy has sometimes been accused of being more talk than substance. In India, there will probably always be a lower proportion of substance to rhetoric due to the difficulty of funding projects in scale with her international aspirations. This is natural. But India, by separating the military and foreign policy establishments and ideals has reduced her ability to make substantive policy. Consider how successfully all the great powers have learned to use their militaries in support of foreign policy objectives. What aspect of American or Soviet foreign policies (or, in the past, French, British or German) can be considered in total ignorance of military capabilities and objectives? This does not mean that India should emulate the great powers of past and present, but rather begin to acknowledge the role which the military plays in a successful foreign policy. India's military must be designed at least in harmony with her foreign policy, but before this can occur a political-military bridge must be built between MEA and Defence, as well as between all their satellite organizations.

That the political-military idea did not exist in India up to 1962 is not surprising. The political-military conception is contrary to Nehru's general conception of nonalignment, and Indian experts probably did not think that an idea so closely following the European experience applied to the Indian case. Dr. K. Subrahmanyam of the Institute for Defence Studies and Analyses has suggested that political-military bodies don't exist because policy-makers simply haven't learned to think of using the military in the projection of national interests, despite it being used so (and by no means always aggressively or offensively) in numerous examples throughout history. Dr. Subrahmanyam writes,

> ... an elite which is not used to using power as an instrument of policy and has been used to a static power structure has been reluctant to admit the legitimacy of power either in internal politics or in the international arena. Consequently a schizophrenic attitude has developed among the Indian elite towards power. They want to hold the power

they already have, want to acquire more but are reluctant to fight for it. Having been used to power being conferred by hierarchical social system [sic] they have similar expectations in internal and international political arenas.[10]

These basic inhibitions are probably what has kept the political-military approach from being implemented in India even after the 1962 war. There has been one important exception in the 1971 war, where through the involvement of the PPRD and RAW, under D.P. Dhar's supervision, political efforts gained credence as a tool in securing victory.

Within the Defence set-up there are committees that could serve as political-military forums, but they are not designed to do so. Before the 1962 war there existed a Defence Committee of the cabinet, which consisted of Nehru, the Defence Minister, the Finance Minister and other cabinet members. The cabinet committee had a strong informational input, being served by the Defence Minister's Committee, the Chiefs of Staff Committee, the JIC, and the Joint Planning Committee. This system was old, created by Lord Ismay, principal advisor to Lord Mountbatten, to serve the needs of defense coordination. It might, though, have easily been made a forum for modern political-military issues by the active inclusion of the MEA secretaries in the work of the Joint Planning Committee. As it was, the only MEA officers were the foreign minister, in the person of prime minister Nehru, and a joint secretary of MEA, not a very powerful officer, to head the JIC. Within the Ministry of Defence there are purely military planning bodies. In 1978 for the first time there was created a permanent defense planning body, the cabinet Committee on Defence, which reviews the military five-year plans. Before that, in 1973 under D.P. Dhar and in 1975 under P.N. Haksar were instituted the Apex groups, ad hoc bodies concerned with planning. The Defence Committee's title was changed after 1962 to the Emergency Committee of the Cabinet. The Joint Planning Committee was at the same time reorganized, but phased out after two years. Under Gandhi the Emergency Committee became the Political Affairs Committee, and finally the CCPA, in which form it is presently frozen.

---

[10] K. Subrahmanyam, "Security and Elite Attitudes," *Niti*, October-December 1970, pp. 9-12.

VIII
Participation in International Organizations

India became part of her first international conference with the Paris peace conference. Throughout the modern period India's heavy involvement in international organizations has been managed through the United Nations and Conference (UN) Division. The UN Division was created only in 1959, previously existing only as a section in the Indian UN diplomatic mission in New York, the various UN agencies, and multilateral conferences. The UN Division also acts in matters affecting them as a coordinative agency between ministries and other bodies in UN operations. While it is now headed only by a joint secretary, before 1953 UN affairs were considered so important that one of the secretaries, secretary(special), had that as his only responsibility.[1]

The UN relational apparatus in MEA has at its base the UN mission in New York. When one reads of events in the UN, one most frequently encounters the deliberations of the General Assembly, or decisions made by the Security Council. But most UN activity takes place within the seven main committees, those of disarmament (located, though, in Geneva), economic matters, human and social issues, decolonization, budgeting and administration, legal issues, and finally the Special Political Committee. The Indian UN mission has one member accredited to each of these committees. Heading the mission is a permanent representative (PR) who represents India in the General Assembly, and under him a

---

[1] N. Parameswaran Nair, *The Administration of Foreign Affairs in India with Comparative Reference to Britain* (New Delhi: School of International Studies, 1963), pp. 278-79; Ministry of External Affairs, *Report 1951-52*, p. 1; in late 1952 secretary(special) was abolished, a third secretary not emerging for several years.

- 163 -

deputy permanent representative (DPR), who coordinates representation on the seven committees, and replaces the PR in the General Assembly when he is indisposed. The member on disarmament in Geneva and the New York mission are treated administratively as one mission, but the Geneva representative reports directly to headquarters rather than in coordination with New York (at times, UN Division has been titled UN, Conference and Disarmament Division, to stress the importance of disarmament as a separate topic). The mission staffing is not only small but skeletal, and requests were made in 1982 by UN Division to increase the UN mission strength by three officers.[2]

The successful UN diplomat, according to the Indian conception, is a lobbyist and a deliberator. In a country mission, lobbying is frequently difficult for the understaffed Indian embassy or consulate. Even for the large Washington embassy, effective lobbying on Capitol Hill is a feat beyond the mission's capability, a quandary very frustrating for Indians stationed there. Lobbying in the UN is quite the opposite, consisting as the UN does of well-defined and bounded groups, who make decisions based on well-ordered voting procedures. Lobbying here becomes for the Indians manageable and a realistic means toward diplomatic success. Skill at deliberations is not frequently found helpful in many world capitols where India is represented, as the atmosphere in these capitols is competitive, not "pushing things through" but rather getting one's point of view represented irrespective of differences with other representatives, and having that point of view believed. In the UN, and especially in the Economic and Social and Human Committees, the skills of slow, plodding deliberation, the skills of the bureaucrat, are favored. In the General Assembly, as opposed to the committees, straight, undiluted representation is still in demand.

As would be expected, the UN mission attracts more senior than junior diplomats, and as a rule no one is given the United Nations as his first posting abroad (the first posting is chosen generally for the development of language skills). The UN is considered by Indian diplomats to be a much more high-powered posting than by American or perhaps other diplomats, due to the proportionately higher gains which the Indian government can expect from UN involvement in terms of resources and national prestige. It is also felt, in accord with the globalist international paradigm, that the UN could function as a credible international government (if the developed nations only gave it a

---

[2] Personal interview, September 14, 1982.

chance). Thus, serious Indian investments of time and effort are put into achieving this goal. The present-day Gandhi regime does not seek the personal involvement in the UN which Nehru did. Nehru was either involved in person or through a strong deputy such as Vijayalakshmi Pandit or Krishna Menon, but Gandhi has never considered this close, constant, personal inclusion in UN activities necessary, relying entirely on her usual UN diplomatic staff for adequate Indian representation. The UN has not become less important for India, but the way in which its relations are managed has shifted, in cybernetic terms, from "manual" to "remote control." The consequence of this is that India's visibility in the UN has lessened, an effect exaggerated by the growth of the UN from the chummy little club of Nehru's time into a large, almost impersonal legislation of over 150 nations.

At home, the UN Division is as small as the New York mission, with only a joint secretary, under him a director, and finally three deputy secretaries managing the seven UN committees. Coordination between the joint secretary and secretary(East) (who is now supervising the division), though informal, is very close. Leadership is apparently as interested in UN Division's work separately as in most of the other divisions collectively, thereby making the joint secretary of UN Division one of the more prestigious headquarters posting. UN Division has an important task in the coordination of other ministries' involvement in UN policy and in the host of other international organizations. UNIDO maintains liaison with the Ministry of Works and Housing, UNESCO with the Ministry of Education, UNCTAD with Commerce. The International Atomic Energy Authority (IAEA) is in closest touch with the Department of Atomic Energy, WHO with Health and Family Planning, and the Ministry of Food and Agriculture is in charge of work with the FAO. The Ministry of Labor handles India's old relationship with the International Labor Organization (ILO). The UN Division decides on the broad policies to be followed toward these organizations, but then passes the matter on to the other ministries for detailed implementation. The most important area in the determination of broad goals is the settling of contribution figures for the UN and non-UN international programs. Though the initial budgetary assessment is carried out by the UN Division in MEA, the actual monies are paid to the organization by the relevant ministry. Expenditure on the United Nations and other international organizations comes to only about five percent of the MEA's 1978-79 expenses, so that the UN definitely does not weigh heavily on the

MEA's pocketbook.³ It is clear, though, that India's trade relations with other nations do not determine her political relations. In the same way, her economic commitment to the UN is not strongly correlated with her political commitment.

8.1 INTERNATIONAL LAW

A number of experts are employed by the MEA to help unravel the subtleties of international law. They are organized into the Legal and Treaties (L and T) Division, and have as their duties:

1. inspection of treaties and agreements to which India is a party prior to notification;

2. investigation of topics brought up by the International Court of Justice.

3. investigation of bilateral and multilateral legal issues.

The L and T Division, run by a legal advisor with joint secretary rank, was established in 1957. Previous to that MEA relied upon honorary advisors and the Ministry of Law, although a Legal Affairs Department had been planned in 1948 and a legal advisor appointed who held office for a short while. In 1963 the L and T Division was headed by a deputy secretary and advised by an honorary legal advisor. These were assisted by three legal officers. None of the officers are IFS cadre, belonging instead to the Combined Research Cadre as do research officers elsewhere in the MEA. In 1975-76, L and T Division had a staff of twenty-three officers not considered to be regular IFS cadre.⁴

---

[3] *Report 1978-79*, p. 68.

[4] *Report of the Committee on the Indian Foreign Service* (New Delhi: Government of India, 1966), p. 3; Nair, pp. 281-82; *Report 1975-76*, p. 129.

IX
International and Domestic Services

9.1 INFORMATIONAL SERVICES

An important part of the projection of national power and the protection of national interests is effective international image-building. In wartime this is known as propaganda. While in peacetime it is as important and of a similar nature, it is then, in tribute to its less spurious character, designated as information. Information, as dealt with in this chapter, refers not to direct diplomatic communications between governmental elites but rather top-down appeals to other less powerful but potentially, in the long run, more important groups in other national societies. A nation's informational services use the international media to project a suitable image of its national society. This is done in the recognition that lobbies can wield influence over other nations' elites, and also in the knowledge that having a favorable international public opinion can be desirable in itself. Such is likely, for example, to lead to increased tourism. Information, besides using media as a tool, can regard it as an object. The Western media can be a powerful ally, as Jack Anderson has shown in his publication of the National Security Council proceedings on the US involvement in the Pakistani civil war. It is, though, generally regarded as a foe by Indian policy-makers, who chafe at what they feel is an exaggerated portrayal of Indian national weaknesses and disaster, while at the same time frequently ignoring Indian achievements. Indian informational work is known as external publicity, and with cultural relations shares the task of building an advantageous Indian national image.

The MEA did not gain control of the external press services until some time after independence. Before 1947 the Department of External Affairs handled the international press through its External Publicity Organization (EPO), a public relations wing of the British Indian government. In 1943 the EPO was taken over by the Department of Information and Broadcasting, and remained in the Department's hands until March 1948, when it was brought into External Affairs. However, after 1947 the organization that in fact handled all external publicity in New Delhi was the Press Information Bureau of the Ministry of Information and Broadcasting. The Press Information Bureau's activities were curtailed in 1958, when these responsibilities were taken up in earnest by the MEA and the External Publicity (XP) Division. The XP Division is at present headed by a joint secretary, who presides over an organization which was in 1963 divided into seven sections, namely:

1. External Publicity(Press Relations), created July 1958;

2. "   "   (Material)

3. "   "   (Administration)

4. "   "   (Policy)

5. "   "   (Reference)

6. "   "   (Services)

7. "   "   (Issue)

In 1963, the organization was headed by a director, assisted by the director and deputy director of the Information Service of India (ISI); also by a director(press relations) and a number of information officers and assistant information officers. Of the above, perhaps the most important XP section was Press Relations, which was something of a hospitality unit for visiting journalists, providing, as well as background, the "proper" facilities for them to pursue their investigations. The section strived to use its gentle influence to gain favorable press coverage, and its work was central to XP's operation. In addition to its headquarters set-up, there were fifty information units in missions abroad in 1961-62 serving as XP's overseas representatives (five years later, for over 100 missions and posts, there were only forty-nine publicity units).[1]

XP was in its early years much smaller than today. In 1953-54, the deputy secretary in charge of XP was assisted in its work by only one director and four information officers. In 1966-67 the XP Division employed in all 566 personnel, consisting of one deputy director, eleven public relations officers, thirty-eight information officers, thirty-nine assistant information officers/attaches/registrars/research officers/editors, 145 other India-based personnel and 322 locally-recruited persons. In 1956-57 XP Division had a headquarters budget of Rs. 2.10 million, and a missions budget of Rs. 6.29 million, for a combined budget of Rs. 8.39 million. Later, in 1964-65 the headquarters budget was placed at Rs. 5.23 million, and diplomatic overseas budget at Rs. 13.41 million. The XP Division's budget at that time, then, was expanding at an annual rate of 10.5 percent.[2]

Several problems can be identified of which XP Division seems to be aware. There is a lack of sufficient resources, an effective training program, and a specialized staff. Finally, XP headquarters does not enjoy efficient communication with missions abroad. The first two problems are shared with the other divisions and are endemic to the organization as a whole. The third difficulty has been partially dealt with by the establishment of specialized training programs (particulars are not available). The fourth is chiefly technical, depending on the modernization of equipment, and for this XP is likely to have to wait in its ministerial budget queue. The fourth problem will be solved only by a shift in the MEA's divisional preference ordering. Another problem is that of interdivisional conflict within the bureaucracy. Some of the greatest rivalries in the Indian foreign policy community have been those between the MEA's XP Division and the Ministry of Information and Broadcasting. Resolution of these jurisdictional difficulties are in the eighties a somewhat high priority. The foreign and I and B ministers held "periodic meetings" in the 1981-82 period. At a lower level they formed from the MEA and I and B, as well as from All-India Radio and Doodarshan (the

---

[1] N. Parameswaran Nair, *The Administration of Foreign Affairs in India with Comparative Reference to Britain* (New Delhi: School of Internation Studies, 1963), pp. 283-84; *Report of the Committee on the Indian Foreign Service* (New Delhi: Government of India, 1966), p. 58.

[2] Ministry of External Affairs, *Report 1953-54*, p. 26; *Report of the Committee*, p. 58.

Indian government-controlled television network), the committee which implements those joint ministerial-level external publicity decisions and helps All-India Radio to develop its programming. The effectiveness of these measures remains to be seen. In order to reduce some interservice tensions, in 1975-76 forty-four ISI officers were newly considered part of MEA's regular workforce.[3] Before, they had been regarded almost as outsiders. Recruitment of ISI officers into MEA slots ended in 1959, but the merger of ISI into IFS cadre did not begin until 1969. In 1982 only eight ISI officers remained in MEA.

Establishing good relations with other ministries is especially important, as the XP Division works more closely with branches of the other ministries than it does with most divisions within MEA. For example, XP's relations with the Commercial Publicity Wing of the Ministry of Commerce or with the Department of Culture in the Ministry of Education are very close, much more so than XP's relations with the UN Division, or with WANA.[4] It is here that nineteenth century British Indian administrative precedent is little evidenced. The bureaucracy of that area, small and high in task-redundancy, could be easily divided into boxes or distinct departments with largely internalized communications, corresponding in a certain way to the mechanistic mode of cognition and perception prevalent in the nineteenth century. Today, however, quantum field theories shape our perception of the cosmos, and perhaps correspondingly we see organizations best as fields with extensive overlap and cross-connections with other organizations. XP Division is not so much a subset of MEA as it is a part of the association of bodies that make up external publicity, a line operation with a strong staff element.

There have been some interesting recent developments inside XP Division. In 1977, under the well-known journalist Chanchal Sarkar a committe was set up "to review the External Publicity set-up of the Ministry with a view to making it more effective." This study was completed the following year with apparently good results, and was one of the small but important organizational reforms undertaken by the Janata regime. Another important development has been the shift in the Indian external publicity philosophy, from "image-building" to "the "projection of national interests." This shift, engineered by Janata and largely

---

[3] *Report 1975-76*, p. 129; *Report 1981-82*, pp. 48-49.

[4] *Report 1973-74*, p. 110.

implemented by the 1982 head of the XP Division, Mani Shankar Aiyar, means a more aggressive publicity effort, less the passive defensive steps taken in past years. In the Nehru period, as Aiyar said in an interview with the author, XP Division focussed on "information generation," on keeping interest in India alive and also on providing the world with a source of information about India other than Rudyard Kipling.[5] At that time the concern was not that the international public would take too much interest in India but rather that India might fade from global consciousness with the retreat of the British. In the 1960s this fear proved groundless, as an explosion of interest in Indian culture occurred. The Beatles, the Hippie movement, Transcendental Meditation and Krishna Consciousness created a permanent interest in India and things Indian, but also projected an image of India which many for good reason found misleading.

Nothing, though, had been done until toward the end of the Janata period to reflect the new global interest in India. The problem, it is now reasoned, is not information generation but information orientation, directing public enthusiasm over India into channels advantageous to India. The new approach is also one of disseminating "appropriate" information, information which not only depicts India accurately but which is biased toward Indian interests. An example is in order. The older Nehru-period efforts distributed just about the same material to every nation, only doing, where necessary, direct translation. Today a more sophisticated approach, sensitive to deeper differences in national conditions, has been adopted. The new material is custom designed, a good example being XP Division's wide-circulation booklet, "India--A Democracy on the Move." This is thought to be the best piece of work turned out yet by the XP Division, though it was originally designed by the Washington embassy. A version for Middle Eastern consumption was assembled, but the title of the Arabic version is "India--A Nation on the Move," changed to suit Islamic ademocratic sensibilities. There are corresponding alterations in the text. The third version produced in Russian for Soviet consumption is simply "India on the Move."

XP Division is organized very simply for these new responsibilities. The secretary in supervision of the Division in 1982 was secretary(East) Vajpayee, and the joint secretary in charge was Mani Shankar Aiyar. The joint secretary exercises a freedom from ministerial conventions which is unusual, probably partly resulting

---

[5] Personal interviews, September 7-8, 1982; *Report 1977-78*, p. 43.

from the XP Division's physical separation from South Block in Shastri Bhavan. The joint secretary runs a headquarters apparatus with a staff of 115, probably the largest headquarters arrangement. The Division is divided into three sections: XP Materials (XPM), XP Spokesmen (XPS) and XP Administration (XPA). Each is the charge of a deputy secretary.

XPM is divided into two sub-sections, Printed Materials and the Audio-Visual Directorate, both headed by under-secretaries. Responsibility for producing printed matter does not rest wholly with headquarters, as much of the material is produced by the overseas missions, and only cleared with headquarters before distribution. Printed materials have increasingly taken on a glossy look, and the texts have been more carefully chosen than in the past, but beyond this the work of Printed Materials has changed little. Audio-visual in its work depends heavily on the Films Division of the I and B Ministry, and like Printed Materials is especially active on the occasion of state visits. It is responsible not only for preparing Indian and foreign audiences through film presentations for these visits, but also for recording these visits when they occur. XPM has been the most handicapped of the three branches, as it is unable to keep up with expensive new information technologies. Video-cassette recorders, word processors, data retrieval systems and the new film-making techniques all cost money. Unless XP can remain state-of-the-art, they are going to have a much more difficult time holding a sophisticated international audience captive. Another potential problem for XPM is the role of the specialist in work which often demands special knowledge. Might not ad men or PR professionals be included with benefit in XP's work? Aiyar answered this question in the negative, countering that external publicity is considered just an extension of diplomacy, and thus could be satisfactorily handled by IFS generalists. He qualified this in adding that for some more difficult or technical problems consultants were hired on a temporary basis by the XP Division. The author believes that here, again, IFS generalist resources may not be most effective and that non-cadre positions should be opened within XP and maintained as a percentage of XP middle-grade posts.

The second branch, XPS, is probably more important from the policy formulative perspective. The joint secretary as the government spokesman, in which connection he holds a daily meeting with the Indian and foreign press, has a special interest in this branch. Below him the XPS employees produce a number of "special supplements" for inclusion in foreign newspapers, and do guided research, so that queries from the press may be answered in a policy-effective fashion. XPS works closely with the Consultative Committees in the *sansad,* thereby serving an informational role in the legislature. XPS is additionally given the responsibility of lending support and direction to foreign journalists inside India. Determining how best to help foreign journalists do their job and at the same time to keep their production as favorable to India as possible is an interesting problem, which is XPS's to solve. Not all of XPS's work is concerned with output. Through production of the *World Press Review,* XPS keeps track of what newspapers in different parts of the world are writing about India, on topics of interest to policy-makers. The *World Press Review* is compiled from clippings sent from missions abroad and is sent to government officials and offices; it may as well be available to members of the *sansad.* The XPS keeps in close touch with the Press Information Bureau (PIB) of the I and B Ministry, which shares some of XP's domestic workload. The I and B Ministry has one ISI officer assigned to each of the ministries (including MEA), who does informational work fielded to I and B rather than the respective ministry.

The last section, XPA, has a potpourri of tasks. Administration of course is handled here, as well as one-year advance budgetary planning. Liaison with the Press Trust of India (PTI) and the United News of India (UNI) is within XPA's purview, and the two large technical undertakings, the Overseas Communication Service (OCS) and Transmissions have XP liaison handled by XPA. Transmissions involve twice-daily teletype transmissions of current news from headquarters to missions abroad. This allows the production of newsletters and other materials for wide distribution. Transmissions also aid Indian spokesmen abroad in answering inquiries directed from their international audience. The OCS enables headquarters' secure telegraphic and telephonic contact with missions abroad, an important task. Most missions now have private lines which run through OCS, but up to the mid-1960s India was relying heavily upon commercial telegraphy, a remarkable fact considering the cost and insecurity of commercial lines.

Within many of the 135 overseas missions are small external publicity groups now called ISI Wings, though in the early 1960s named information units. The ISI Wings are named thus as several years previously external publicity was not handled by the IFS but by the ISI, assigned there from the I and B Ministry. There was considerable friction between the two services, and the division of labor was seen as unnatural and costly, leading to the reduction of the numbers of actual ISI officers in MEA to a handful. The ISI Wings became in this way ISI in name only. ISI Wings are found now in only a few of the larger embassies, such as in Washington, Moscow and Paris, and in the UN mission in New York. In most of the missions external publicity is handled by only one permanent officer, and in the small three to four man missions it is a group effort of the entire mission, not even of any one officer. In the larger missions, the ISI Wing is the charge of high-level officers; in Moscow, the Counselor has this duty. The best external publicity work is predictably the forte of the largest missions, due to the existence of ISI Wings and strong leadership, and conversely external publicity in the many countries with smaller missions is either weak or nonexistent. No concise figures exist for XP diplomatic mission manpower, due to the informal and fluid management of XP in most missions.

An interesting new development in Indian external publicity is the utilization of the Indian overseas community. Janata foreign minister A.B. Vajpayee claimed that besides the lack of funds, the major problem of Indian external publicity was that "[w]e have failed to utilize Indians residing abroad for projecting the image of the country."[6] During the Nehru period contacts with the communities were purposefully minimized to avoid the appearance of gathering an Indian "fifth column" in the many countries with large Indian populations. On the contrary, these communities were urged to integrate themselves into their host cultures as quickly as possible. This did not happen either in East African or Middle Eastern communities, where the Indian populations remained highly segregated, and so the "problem" of the Indian communities remained. Only very recently, since the Janata initiative, have the communities been seen not as a problem but as an asset, and only recently have attempts been made to fit the twelve million or so Indians living abroad somewhere into Indian foreign policy. This involves looking at the overseas Indians as a responsibility and a burden, but also as an important ally in educating the world about Indian culture. The Indians abroad have mostly retained their cultural identity, but have an intimate experience of the host culture which makes them better conveyors of Indian social values than any diplomatic mission. No detailed program has yet been operationalized on the role of the communities in external publicity and general foreign policy, but contacts are steadily increasing, and some XP projects have already been executed with the active involvement of Indians abroad,

---

[6] Louis and Chawla, "More Continuity than Change," *India Today*, January 16-31, 1979, p. 39.

such as the 1982 "Festival of India" in London.

9.2 PUBLIC RELATIONS

Much has been written on the need for the American foreign policy bureaucracy to remain open, open to the national public and instruments of the public (such as the Congress or citizens' groups). While India is also a democracy, this same goal of openness is not for MEA as meaningful an issue. In India, pluralistic institutions are not as powerful as in the United States, particularly in their ability to influence foreign policy formulation. The Indian parliament's attempts to influence foreign policy are, in the words of one official, "amateurish;" there are no foreign policy lobbies in India, and therefore no means for public opinion to influence foreign policy. The academic community is also fairly young and exercises only a diffuse influence.[7] Area studies programs are too poorly funded to compete with government analysts, even such as they sometimes are. For these reasons a program of bureaucratic openness in India would fall on deaf ears. There is, admittedly, a need to maintain a positive public image, but this has never been a problem for MEA. Public protests are never against institutions, as they frequently are in the U.S., but rather are against personalities. A protest against Indian foreign policy would use as object Indira Gandhi, the Congress(I) or Narasimha Rao, but would never have the MEA as object. Attacks on abstract institutions reflect a sophistication in popular protest to which the less literate Indian general public has yet to attain. Even if such a protest trend were to develop, it would adversely affect recruitment but not much else.

Inside MEA there is nothing like the Department of State's Bureau of Public Affairs, which maintains contact with the American public (though not to the degree that it might). The External Publicity Division inside MEA has contact with the Indian press, but ignores the universities, civic groups (such as the Arya Samaj) and Indian public forums. There are few speaking engagements and other public foreign affairs awareness activities. It will be argued that an illiterate public would probably not respond to such public programs.

---

[7] *Diplomacy for the '70's: A Program of Management Reform for the Department of State,* Department of State Publication 8551, Department and Foreign Service Series 143 (released December 1970), p. 386; personal interview, August 6, 1982.

For the small educated middle class, though, an audience would exist and a public affairs program would result probably in an IFS recruitment of increased size and quality. When Indian citizens are allowed to think of their sons and daughters as potential diplomats, and of diplomacy as enviable work, the manpower-shortage problem which has constantly plagued MEA might be alleviated.

9.3 CULTURAL RELATIONS

Establishment of a dialogue between nations and peoples has long been a popular quest of humanitarian private institutions and of nations founded on idealistic principles. Since all nations are founded on idealistic principles, organizations to promote the same can always be found. Cultural relations bodies, despite their usual idealistic bias, perform a number of objective tasks with immediate and local consequences. These bodies perform a valuable service by opening aesthetic and intellectual worlds to the public which would otherwise be closed, and these bodies also do a service to the state by acting as cognizant or unconscious propaganda outlets. In India, much of this is done by the Indian Council for Cultural Relations (ICCR), which operates out of Azad Bhavan, Indraprastha Estate, in New Delhi. The ICCR's parent body was the Indo-Iranian Cultural Committee, which seems to have come into existence during the British period. After independence the Education Minister and foreign policy confidant to Nehru, Maulana Azad, took an interest in the Committee and in 1950 refounded it as the ICCR. At that time it was formally constituted as an autonomous body but under the supervision and funding of the Government of India. Autonomous though it was, it was for a time closely tied to the Department of Culture in the Ministry of Education. Apparently up to 1967 activities of the ICCR were very limited.[8]

In 1967, foreign minister M.C. Chagla sought to expand the ICCR's activities after first bringing it under the MEA's wings, a move blocked by then-Education minister Dr. T. Sen. This stalemate was reversed in April 1970 when between education minister V.K.R.V. Rao and foreign minister Dinesh Singh agreement was reached to place the ICCR under MEA supervision. Then an IFS officer took over as secretary, the seniormost officer

---

[8] Jayantanuja Bandyopadhyaya, *The Making of India's Foreign Policy* (New Delhi: Allied Publishers, 1979), p. 230.

and administrative head of the ICCR (it is unclear as to whether this was stipulated within the original formal agreement between the MEA and the Ministry of Education).[9] Despite the ICCR's claim to autonomous operation, the top positions have been consistently staffed by IFS officers, and the annual report of the ICCR's activities is included in the MEA's *Annual Report* rather than in a separate publication. We might have expected a separate report from an autonomous body, so that the absence of such makes dubious the ICCR's claim of autonomy. The last two (in 1982) ICCR presidents have been foreign ministers Vajpayee and Narasimha Rao; before them the presidents were all retired IFS officers. In 1982 the only two IFS officers in the ICCR were the secretary Smt. Manorama Bhalla, and the deputy secretary Ram Lall, occupying ordinal positions one and two in the ICCR administration.

There does not seem to be any conflict with either the informational services of the MEA or the Ministry of Information and Broadcasting concerning the ICCR's activities. The information services handle inanimate, official culture--books, magazines, films, press releases--whereas the ICCR has jurisdiction over animate, popular culture. XP Division has more of an official life and is closer to the general mechanics of foreign policy, but the ICCR's partial autonomy gives it the liberty to represent Indian culture rather than the elite image of India. Both therefore have contrasting strengths with a degree of neutral overlap.

> The XP Division . . . carried out exhibition and cultural work through supply of photographs, paintings for arranging exhibitions abroad, coordinated the work regarding sending of cultural troupes, holding of exhibitions of Indian modern art and of philately exhibitions in various countries and coordinating the work regarding book exhibitions.[10]

It is peculiar that, given the scope of XP's activities which really fall more into the ICCR's realm, no clash of jurisdiction has occurred between the ICCR and XP Division. This anomaly is perhaps explained by the disjoint character of the XP's and ICCR's resource bases, due to the significant difference in the degree of

---

[9] Bandyopadhyaya(1979), p. 230; personal interview, May 3, 1982.

[10] *Report 1978-79,* p. 57.

autonomy associated with the two bodies. Because they are not fighting over slices from the same pie, they need not claim unique purview.

The ICCR's present activities are two-fold; it introduces talent from other nations to India and gives Indian artists, musicians, actors and writers opportunities to talk and perform outside of India. Artists from the outside are brought in through the intercession of the Indian missions, whose ambassadors and subordinate officers, upon receipt of advice from their host nations' government that a certain performing troupe might be sent to India, convey that message and their own recommendation to the ICCR headquarters. There special committees make the selections of artists to be invited to India, through the cultural exchange program which India has with that country. Going the other way, sponsoring Indian artists abroad, the ICCR takes advantage of six regional offices in Bombay, Calcutta (the largest regional office), Bangalore, Madras, Varanasi, and Chandrigarh, as well as a permanent representative in Trivandrum. The regional officers tour their jurisdictions (the Varanasi office has, for example, Uttar Pradesh and Haryana in its jurisdiction) searching for suitable artists and informing ICCR headquarters of selections.

Besides the recruitment of performing delegations, the regional office has also the more mundane function of advising foreign students and preparing for foreign delegations to visit their jurisdiction. Total ICCR regional office manpower was in 1982 at sixty-two, with the Calcutta office taking up almost a third of that personnel strength with twenty. The regional offices have an average staff strength of eight. In 1978-79 a certain amount of administrative reorganization was apparently taken within the ICCR, and more work was transferred from the Department of Culture in the Ministry of Education to the ICCR, with a view to making it more operationally independent. Work transferred in that year included the handling of all incoming and outgoing cultural delegations, all academic delegations and the organization of art exhibits. This was done on the recommendation of a committee headed by Ashok Mehta assembled the previous year.[11]

---

[11] *Report 1977-78*, p. 46; *Report 1978-79*, p. 58. Interestingly, not only are most visiting cultural delegations sponsored by the ICCR from other Third World nations, but most foreign students studying in India are from developing nations. Examination of the record shows that foreign students in India are overwhelmingly Nepalese, Nigerian, Mauritian and Kenyan, with other students tending to come from Africa, South Asia and

The ICCR also sponsors the annual Azad Memorial Lecture, the Jawaharlal Nehru Award for International Understanding, the publication of a number of books in several languages, and several periodicals such as the *ICCR Newsletter* (which is produced for foreign students living in India). This is accomplished through an annual budget (in 1982-83) of Rs. 24.035 million (an increase in one lakh [100,000] rupees over the 1981-82 budget) funding a large administrative apparatus. The president, for several years also the foreign minister, is only the formal head of the ICCR. Directly subordinate is the administrative head, the secretary, who leads a group of several joint secretaries. Under them are officers designated, in headquarters, deputy secretary, and, in the regional offices, regional director (both offices are of equal rank). Under the deputy secretary is an under-secretary rank. The ICCR has nine sections, shown in Table 9.1, each headed by an under-secretary.

What is generally important about the ICCR in our study is the extent to which the ICCR functions as a part of MEA without being administratively subordinate to it. It has been staffed by IFS, the MEA exercises considerable control over its budget and its report is placed within the MEA's *Annual Report*. Concurrently, it draws much of its production material from the Ministry of Education. The ICCR is the best example of foreign policy as a community effort, and illustrates the need to look beyond the MEA vista when studying the successes and failures in the implementation of Indian foreign policy.

---

the Middle East. Cultural relations is another success in the Indian achievement of better South-South relations.

Table 9.1: ICCR structure

E.C. 1 **student service unit**

E.C. 2 **chairs and visiting professors**
represents East Germany, Mauritius, Sri Lanka, Thailand, Trinidad.

E.C. 3 **publications**
books and periodicals regularly published by the ICCR.

E.C. 4 **libraries for cultural centres**
see E.C. 6.

E.C. 5 **Jawaharlal Nehru Award**

E.C. 6 **cultural centres**
in Fiji, Surinam (established November 1978), and Bulgaria, permanently established to sponsor the introduction of Indian culture, each equipped with a large library administered under E.C. 4. Cultural centres are the ICCR's most expensive program, one centre costing annually more than a million rupees. Each cultural centre has a staffing of about six instructors, with a total centres staffing of twenty-six (c. 1982).

E.C. 7 **professors on deputation**
these sponsored (before political turmoil struck the first two countries) in Afghanistan, Lebanon, Indonesia, Senegal.

E.C. 8 **preparation of source materials**
pre-publication production for E.C. 3.

E.C. 9 **cultural exchange program**
performing delegations. This section is under, not MEA, but Department of Culture jurisdiction.

9.4 PROTOCOL

Protocol is essentially a set of formalities, a set of symbols, which facilitate communications between diplomatic *corpora*. The importance of protocol for the larger process of foreign policy formulation is its role in the diplomatic optimalization of the impact of national power. Falling short of mastership in protocol can hamper negotiations and weaken unnecessarily one's position. Both the externalized process of diplomacy and the internalized process of policy formulation are linked in that more effective protocol expands the universe of possible operational policies, by removing constraints which force the diversion of resources from formulation into implementation, and thereby, relative to the decisional value system, makes better policy pragmatically conceivable. In South Block protocol is handled by the Protocol Division, which to fullfill its task apportionment is divided into three sections. First within Protocol is Privileges and Immunities, headed by a deputy chief (of deputy secretary rank). Privileges and Immunities, in 1982 the charge of Smt. Naurekha Sharma, is concerned with adherence to the Vienna Convention.[12] The head of Privileges and Immunities is also in charge of acquisition of gifts for visiting heads of government, for which she remains in close touch with a member of the prime minister's staff.[13] The second division within Protocol is that of Ceremonial, headed by a Deputy Chief (of under-secretary rank). Ceremonial is in charge of the symbolic communicative work of protocol, a very visible position which probably absorbs more external pressure than other MEA postings. The last section of MEA is that of Facilities, which makes all arrangements for facilities required in diplomatic functions.[14] Also under Facilities' control is

---

[12] The Convention tells diplomats what they may expect from their host government. It is in a sense a contract to protect the diplomatic community from the international environment. The Convention is revised regularly.

[13] The head of Privileges and Immunities was in 1982 Smt. Usha Bhagat. Gandhi takes a close personal interest in this mundane task, just as she takes part in other areas of protocol usually neglected by heads of state, such as meeting other heads of government at Palam International Airport (in New Delhi).

[14] The deputy chief (of under-secretary rank) in 1982 in charge of the section was outstanding because

Hospitality, which makes further arrangements for visiting guests.

Under the three deputy chiefs is a large group of section officers. The three deputies are supervised by the chief of protocol (with the rank of joint secretary). The manpower allocation of the division as a function of time has high variance, as large conferences or arrivals of VIPs can require much greater divisional manpower than during most periods. Additional staff at these times is temporarily coopted from other divisions. In the first months following the invasion of Afghanistan by the Soviet Union, India received her greatest influx ever of foreign officials, necessitating Protocol's establishment of a small office at Palam International Airport just to serve a steady diet of protocol to the visitors. Staffing requirements rose, but after a few months returned to normal. Similarly, when the 1983 nonaligned conference met in New Delhi, it probably required the establishment of a cell within Protocol for the duration of the conference. The manpower allocation of Protocol is kept low at most times by charging its staff to deal with the arrivals only of heads of government and foreign ministers; other foreign visitors are greeted by the staff of the related territorial division.[15]

Protocol, due to its human dimension, is more demanding than any other than CPV Division, but is very attractive to a few officers interested in mastering the art of protocol and dealing with this most graceful area of diplomacy. The section officer takes up a greater share of the responsible and non-clerical work than he does in other divisions, and the deputy chief in charge of Ceremonial is interestingly of IFS(B) cadre.

The disparate consular apparatus coalesced when in August 1951 a separate Consular Branch was formed. Shortly afterwards a Consular Division was formed of this Branch together with an extant branch which dealt with the recovery of advances made to evacuees of Burma, Malaya, etc. during World War II. This original Consular Division was staffed with personnel drawn from the territorial divisions. The old Passport and Emigration Division dealt not only with emigration, passports and visas, but also with the organization of paperwork for the Mecca Haj and other pilgrimages. Emigration and passport work was transferred in part in 1944 from the state governments and the remainder in 1953. The

---

of her long tenure, much longer than the standard three years, at the post.

[15] Personal interview, November 3, 1982.

responsibilities before 1959 of the Central Passport and Emigration Organization were managed by two bodies, the Central Passport Organization and the Emigration Organization. In 1963 Protocol Division was smaller than at present but organized similarly. The chief of protocol was assisted by only an additional chief and a deputy chief, both IFS officers. The assistant chief in 1963 was responsible to the Commonwealth secretary for some additional, non-protocol work.[16]

9.5 CONSULAR, PASSPORT AND VISA DIVISION

Consular operations are presently the responsibility of the Consular, Passport and Visa (CPV) Division. CPV Division is headed by a joint secretary, who is both joint secretary of the division and the chief passport officer. Under the joint secretary are three deputy secretaries, three under-secretaries, and five section officers. Each of the section officers is in charge of one of five branches within the CPV Division. The Division has jurisdiction over the grant of visas, consular work and passports. Over visas CPV Division has only the partial jurisdiction of diplomatic and official visas. CPV Division has full responsibility for consular work, the task of dealing with Indian nationals abroad. CPV functions as a clearinghouse for information on the overseas communities, but has little direct contact with Indian nationals and the overseas communities. The Indian ambassador and resident diplomats usually furnish this contact. CPV handles coordination of consular operations with its own staff, but in the grant and regulation of passports merely supervises another, much larger workhorse body, the Central Passport Organization (CPO).

The CPO is a MEA subordinate office, with eighteen Regional Passport Offices throughout India, with a total staff of 1,300. The CPO is staffed by non-IFS cadre personnel. The organization since the late seventies has been growing rapidly, in 1978 alone creating thirty-two additional officers and 334 additional supporting staff. The CPO is of high public visibility but its work is of low policy significance. It handles not only the purely mechanical process of passport and visa issue, but also the myriad problems arising in connection with the overseas Indians, repatriation of destitute Indians, the location of Indian nationals who have become lost, and cases of Indians dying while abroad. In recent years, with larger numbers of

---

[16] *Report 1951-52*, p. 1; Nair, pp. 282-83.

Indians accepting work in the Middle East, the CPO has been forced into the protective role of guarding Indians against the ". . . unscrupulous and unauthorized travel agents who sit on the edge of the massive emigration traffic."[17]

Closely related to the work of CPV Division is the Abducted Persons Unit. This function of MEA is an outgrowth of the communal disturbances of 1947-48, when during the mass migration across the Indo-Pakistani border many women and children were kidnapped by both Hindus and Muslims from the opposing community. The Unit's main task was to ensure the safe return of the women and children abducted in this manner. The Unit presently operates in all countries with Indian populations, dealing with isolated cases rather than the systemic national issue of 1947-48.

Other ministries play quite a role in CPV Division's work. Visas other than diplomatic and official are handled by the Home Ministry, which also handles immigration and is closely involved with the passport application process. The Ministry of Labor handles the emigration of work labor, chiefly to the Middle East. CPV Division has strong linkages not only with other ministries but with the general public. The need for passports brings many Indians annually to CPO offices, and the view which the Indian public has of MEA is largely of the MEA's passport officers. The public orientation of CPV Division's work is unique, and the officer in this division has probably a more personally-demanding job than any but of Protocol Division.

---

[17] *Report 1978-79*, pp. 63, 65.

X
Modern Leadership and the Bureaucracy

10.1 NEHRU AND THE BUREAUCRACY

On the bureau structure set forth above, a few embellishments have been added by successive modern Indian leaders.[1] The first prime minister, Jawaharlal Nehru, was in the control of foreign policy the strongest Indian prime minister. His prime ministership during the formative years of Indian government and polity made a deep impression both because of the uniqueness of Nehru's political environment and because of Nehru's mastery of the principles of charismatic practical leadership. Nehru, the very devout disciple of Mahatma Gandhi, stood in the afterglow of the Mahatma's charismatic presence. Gandhi's agitation campaign against the British had more than anything else earned the world's respect for Indian idealist political theory and democratic practice. Nehru had a need different from the Mahatma's to fullfill, that of leading a nation according to that political theory rather than of creating a nation by thus, as the Mahatma endeavored to do. Whether Nehru succeeded or failed, he would probably continue to be admired because of his proximity to the Mahatma, his participation in the class of symbols which Gandhi had developed.

As it was, he himself had a special understanding of the needs of leadership which made him independent of Gandhi's postcharismatic support. He used that political skill to gain an international position alongside Nasser and Tito, and held that status for over a decade. It was at that time that Nehru cast the

---

[1] This chapter will utilize methods on the idiosyncratic level-of-analysis, unless otherwise noted.

foreign policy counterpart to Gandhi's *satyagraha*, the doctrine of nonalignment, a doctrine which made a deep impression on the global psychology of the 1950s and continues to exert a wide ideological influence. In terms of the mere time spent in office Nehru's prime ministership was unique; he served longer in his office than any British prime minister for over a century and a half before him. In this time Nehru developed a remarkable political grasp over foreign policy, or over foreign policy as a domestic and rhetorical issue, but a dichotomy abided in Nehru as both politician and administrator.[2]

Nehru as the administrator had a characteristic style of leadership that showed up clearly in the operations of the bureaucracy and generated separate weaknesses and strengths in the Indian ability to both formulate and implement effective policy. Tharoor cites the difficulties of the Nehru MEA as

> . . . the scarcity of personnel and financial resources, inadequately developed language training and skills, the abdication of foreign economic policy to domestic ministries, the lack of a foreign policy planning body, and Nehru's typically impractical diffusion of India's scarce resources in a programme of rapid expansion of India's global presence . . .[3]

---

[2] N. Parameswaran Nair, *The Administration of Foreign Affairs in India with Comparative Reference to Britain* (New Delhi: School of International Studies, 1963), p. 198; there were a number of interesting dialectic pairs in Nehru's career. In the pre-independence struggle the important dyad was of Mahatma Gandhi and Nehru, who in their anti-colonial styles were respectively radical and moderate, but in setting the course for the newly-established nation were respectively moderate and radical. After Gandhi's death the appearance of the Panditji-Sardarji (Nehru and Sardar Vallabhbhai Patel) pair contrasted charismatic with machine politics, and since that time modern Indian government has been a combination of both styles of political leadership.

[3] Shashi Tharoor, *Reasons of State* (New Delhi: Vikas, 1982), p. 33. The expansion which Tharoor notes here brought the number of Indian missions up from twelve in 1947 to 129 in 1964. For another criticism of Nehru's bureaucracy, see M.O. Mathai, *My Days with Nehru* (New Delhi: Vikas, 1979), p. 129.

Nehru's political style could be seen in his *ex tempore* speech-making, his habit of personal intervention in crises (his actions during the post-partition communal riots were good examples), and his frequent contact with the Indian masses and with the international public. His administrative style had as its strongest feature Nehru's monopolization of decision-making.

Nehru's involvement in substantive government work was remarkable; he was never in possession of less than two government portfolios at a time, as prime minister and foreign minister. He was as well the minister-in-charge of the Atomic Energy Department, and since 1950 was chairman of the Planning Commission; was in 1951-54 the president of the Indian National Congress; was in 1953 holding the defence portfolio and in 1956 and 1958 holding the finance portfolio. In keeping with these many cabinet holdings Nehru kept in close personal contact with a wide political and governmental circle,

> . . . including members of Parliament, Central and State Ministers, important foreign visitors and many ordinary Congress workers . . . in spite of a very heavy schedule, he would not keep any visitor waiting, nor would any visitor leave him with a feeling of having been hustled.[4]

Nehru's massive involvement in government activities showed up in other additional ways. After Bajpai left the MEA post of secretary-general Nehru began to draft his own replies to a large proportion of the cable traffic that passed daily through the foreign ministry. In many such ways Nehru insisted upon being involved in many of the minute details of government, details that other leaders ordinarily leave to subordinates.

Nehru's close involvement with areas appearing extraneous to most heads of government served to weaken the efforts of his subordinates to establish their own work jurisdictions. He tried as much as was within his power to draw all the strings of policy to himself, to monopolize policy formulation, and to ignore or deny the important role of his subordinates.[5] That Nehru

---

[4] Michael Brecher, *Nehru: A Political Biography* (Boston: Beacon Press, 1961), p. 14; Subimal Dutt, *With Nehru in the Foreign Office* (Calcutta: Minerva Publications, 1977), pp. 23, 28.

[5] This was noticed by many of Nehru's contemporaries. See, for example, Walter R. Crocker, *Nehru: A*

had a tendency to monopolize policy does not carry the implication that success was complete (and we will in fact soon see that Nehru's power in the bureaucracy may have been lessened by this inflation of his responsibilities) or that he expanded in this way into all policy-areas. He seems to have left operations alone (he avoided detailed implementative decisions in the conduct of the 1962 Sino-Indian conflict, for example), centering his efforts on formulation, but in the formulative tasks of MEA no one below Nehru had a firm foothold.

In the analysis of Nehru's extraordinary interventionist approach to decision-making we should first examine Nehru's control of the foreign portfolio. The practice of executive control over and reserved jurisdiction in foreign policy is not uncommon. In most of the European nations and in the United States, the prime minister or president exercises a strong control over foreign policy. Because the Vienna Convention designates a general treaty signatories the Head of State, the Head of Government and the Foreign Minister, the strong interest of the executive in foreign policy is, in part at least, systemically determined. In Sri Lanka, the prime minister is by constitution placed in the seats of both External Affairs and Defence.[6] Executive control over Indian foreign policy is, in addition, a long viceroyal tradition. It is not Nehru's control over foreign policy that is remarkable but rather his tendency to occupy a great many levels in decision-making.

Nehru's interventionist policy leadership goes beyond tradition, to Nehru's own political personality and the special demands of the times in which he lived. The inexperienced early bureaucracy undoubtedly lacked some confidence, so that only an involved prime minister, with "his hands in the soup up to the elbows," so to speak, could have helped the IFS to gain the confidence that it needed in foreign policy. Due to the lack of a large class of senior officers, Nehru had to play surrogate senior officer to much of the early MEA bureaucracy. When more meaningful communication began to build laterally, between adjoining levels and between officers of equal rank, the strings that Nehru held would fall away. Nehru in fact did cease to play such an octopus-like part in the bureaucracy's life in 1959. By this time the bureaucracy was twelve years old, little more than a third of an IFS officer's usual

---

Contemporary's Estimate (London: George Allen and Unwin, 1966), pp. 84-85.

[6] Nair, p. 192.

thirty years of service. Though still no strong traditions had developed by that time, the IFS had developed confidence and a large class of senior officers. Nehru's tendency to take the reigns in almost any sector of government where the opportunity arose was a result not just of a young bureaucracy but of a weak political system, a weak cabinet and a Congress Party desperate for leadership. Both the weak cabinet and Congress arose from the presence of weak leadership in the upper echelons of the Congress (this power-vacuum disappeared before Shastri assumed the prime ministership). Finally, Nehru took control in this fashion for purely idiosyncratic causes, because it was simply the way that he did things.

Nehru's monopolistic style in administration had two immediate effects. Because so few careerists in the first ten years had the ability or confidence to take strong initiatives or to form strong leadership in their responsible section of the bureaucracy, those areas which received the personal attention of Nehru were the areas which developed.

> Policy areas in which Nehru was not interested--both geographic (South-East Asia, Latin America, even Africa) and thematic (economics and trade, bilateral as opposed to ecumenical relations)--were ignored. Meanwhile the MEA, its bureaucracy . . . proved incapable of effective or co-ordinated action on its own.[7]

Besides affecting structure in this way, Nehru's approach inhibited the growth of central career leadership. In addition to these other considerations must be added M.O. Mathai's observation that a great many, in fact too many, junior ministers under Nehru were too old to make effective deputies, and that most were chosen not purely for their abilities as junior ministers but because Nehru owed them certain political debts. Nehru's tendency to put "old men" into the important foreign policy political posts was joined by Nehru's role as promotion arbitrator in making the case of the junior officer very weak.

Nehru on one occasion asked his secretary in charge of the Commonwealth Department Subimal Dutt,

---

[7] Tharoor, p. 32.

> . . . why could he not promote a person [to a higher post in the Indian Foreign Service] about whose abilities he as Minister had no doubt? If rules stood in the way, he said, something must be wrong with them.[8]

This made promotion relatively high into the bureaucracy dependent on Nehru's will and eliminated the power of regular promotion processes in the emergence of strong and stable higher echelon career leadership. Nehru's unwillingness to accept certain restrictions in his own administrative authority led to unhealthy restrictions in the power of his subordinates. As was remarked of Nehru, "nothing would grow under a banyan tree."[9] This inhibited promotion process might have posed a serious problem to the successor Shastri leadership, had not Nehru's power lapsed in the 1958-64 period, allowing subordinates to regain normal control over their jurisdictions and rebuild the top career levels of MEA.

Nehru's arbitrary approach to the management of human resources over the entire bureaucracy was duplicated on a smaller scale in his relationship with the secretaries. Each of the secretaries, realizing that their only power flowed from their link with Nehru, ". . . went to Nehru, talked to him, got his consent for what he wanted and went his way."[10] This undoubtedly led to problems in the coordination of policy and perhaps led, as well, to distortions of policy. As Stanley Hoffman writes, in any situation of free bureaucratic enterprise (as existed between the secretaries),

> [t]here inevitably occurs a subtle (or not so subtle) shift from the specific foreign policy issues to be resolved, to the positions, claims and perspectives of the participants

---

[8] M.O. Mathai, *My Days with Nehru* (New Delhi: Vikas, 1979), p. 118; Dutt, p. 41.

[9] This remark was first uttered publicly by S.K. Patil in Bombay--date unknown--but authorship is claimed by M.O. Mathai. See Mathai (1979), p. 118. For other remarks on Nehru's irregular promotion procedures, see Crocker, p. 86.

[10] Durga Das, *India from Curzon to Nehru and after* (New York: John Day, 1970), p. 334, quoted in Tharoor, p. 33.

> in the policy machine. The demands of the issue and the merits of alternative choices are subordinated to the demands of the machine and the needs to keep it going. Administrative politics replaces foreign policy.

The situation in the Nehru era, though, may have been less a game of political competition than of "pin the tail on the donkey," where each secretary received his orders from Nehru effectively blindfolded as to what his colleagues were doing and necessarily acting only on his own limited information.[11]

Ironically, by retaining the policy-formulative potential in his own person, Nehru probably gave the lower levels of the bureaucracy a much broader policy autonomy than they would have enjoyed otherwise. Because the bureaucracy does have the power to interpret policy once it is released from the formulative stage, unless deputies of the central executive are placed at key positions in the upper, middle and lower ranks policy may be interpreted with a breadth that neither Nehru nor any other leader could afford.

Delegation of authority is necessary in running any large organization, since one can be personally involved in only a fraction of organization-wide activities at one time. Subordinates, in order to do their work effectively, must be able to make decisions and be assured that they will be supported with the confidence that the prime minister holds in them. As Destler remarks in connection with the Nixon-era of foreign policy organization in the U.S.,

> [u]nless . . . a system seeks to develop centers of strength at several hierarchical levels and to make them responsible to top level influence and priorities by the sharing of authority, communication and confidence with them . . . [t]op officials will lack "handles" for issues being dealt with at these levels because there seems no one with strong

---

[11] Stanley Hoffman, *Gulliver's Troubles, or the Setting of American Foreign Policy* (New York: McGraw Hill, 1968), p. 177, quoted in Destler, p. 75. Despite the lack of concert between the secretaries, Nehru was very close to all of them until the ascendence of Krishna Menon as Nehru's policy advisor in 1956-62. See Escott Reid, *Envoy to Nehru* (New Delhi: Oxford University Press, 1981), pp. 186-87.

influence with whom they can deal.

In Nehru's constant attention to the details of formulation, the keys to operations were left unguarded and, as Mathai writes, Nehru's "policies could be largely defeated at the level of details by scheming men" through their knowledge of implementation.[12] Not only Nehru's concentration of power in his own person but also his neglect of the operational field led to the decline in his authority and to the stagnation of the career executive group. Assignment of greater responsibility to his career subordinates might have reduced Nehru's immediate authority but would have strengthened it in the long run by incrasing the number of "eyes and ears" capable of noting and reporting to Nehru the degree of effectiveness of government in carrying out his programs. Nehru, no matter how powerful or active, could not be in more than one place at a time.

It was not, however, true ". . . that the Indian foreign policy elite was, in fact, one man [Nehru]."[13] The final authority, as it had to be, was always Nehru, but on many occasions he gave considerable representative license to non-career deputies. Usually, these individuals were given special powers only when they were outside New Delhi, such as K.M. Panikkar in Beixhing, Krishna Menon in New York, or V. Pandit in Moscow. Perhaps the best known of such Indian confidants was Krishna Menon, the most powerful of Nehru's advisors and also the most controversial. Menon was not only responsible for India's presentation of its national policy, largely in the UN, but also was in charge of operations in the takeover of Goa (1961) and was the man responsible for India's unequal, non-non-aligned treatment of the Hungary and Suez events. Menon was not in any sense simply a mouthpiece for policy, a puppet with Nehru pulling the strings, but was pulling a few strings himself, with some control over both the diplomatic and military machineries of the era.

The case of Krishna Menon sheds some light on the motivation behind Nehru's selection of these special confidants. In order for a subordinate to function effectively as a deputy, he must have a good executive reputation and should be able to stand on his own, soliciting his leader's grace as little as possible. He should also be, as the conduct of the deputy

---

[12] I.M. Destler, *Presidents, Bureaucrats and Foreign Policy* (Princeton: Princeton University Press, 1974), p. 151; Mathai (1979), p. 118.

[13] Tharoor, p. 23.

reflects on the leader, as respectable and "clean" as possible. Krishna Menon went against the grain of all these principles of political purity, and was from the very beginning a controversial figure. His reputation as a cryptocommunist was bound to be unsettling to conservatives in the Indian National Congress and the opposition, and his reputation as a single-minded, hard-driving, temperamental individual would not help him to serve people whose positions demanded a certain amount of respect and forebearance, even from men as powerful and highly placed as Krishna Menon. From the example of Krishna Menon we learn that Nehru did not choose all of his deputies with thought to spreading and utilizing influence, but rather for reasons of friendship without critical assessment of their leadership abilities in a critical political environment.[14] Krishna Menon, unsuitable as a deputy in Nehru's administration, became less the man whose advice and approval was solicited in planning, and fell into the dangerous position of a proxy target at whom attacks were aimed with the failure of Nehru's foreign policy objectives. This was especially true during the 1962 war, in which critiques of Nehru's policy became a vitriolic assault on Krishna Menon, known of course to enjoy Nehru's favor.

A small group of individuals have exercised influence over Nehru's decisions in the foreign policy sphere, such as Muslim divine Maulana Azad, and the first Indian ambassador to China, Sardar Panikkar. However, these individuals functioned as advisors, not deputies, and their advice tended to reflect Nehru's own foreign policy paradigm.[15] Nehru still had no consistent idea of how far down on the bureaucratic ladder he would reach on the problems that greeted him in foreign policy. While he did on occasion allot policy freedom to certain people as deputies, it seems that this was not a bureau-utilitarian decision.

The last three years of Nehru's regime, like the two or so years of Janata, were years in which MEA's power grew disproportionately. The reason for this in both cases was a weak political leadership, either lacking the ability or the confidence to wield power.

---

[14] Nehru appointed another person, Sardar Kavalani Madhava Panikkar (1896-1963) to his post because of his friendship with Panikkar as another historian rather than because of his respect for Panikkar's skill as a diplomat. See Reid, p. 34.

[15] Brecher, p. 219 J. Bandyopadhyaya, *The Making of India's Foreign Policy* (New Delhi: Allied Publishers, 1979), pp. 211-12.

M.O. Mathai asks

> . . . how Nehru managed after I left government in 1959. All except him know that it was not much of a management. It was a sorry spectacle of slow but steady deterioration, both mental and physical, and final collapse of the man I knew. I would like the reviewer to find out how many public statements of Nehru during this period had to be 'clarified' by the officials of the External Affairs Ministry.[16]

MEA was forced to take power in that period because of the relative vacuum left by the absence of Nehru's active leadership. Ordinarily Indian foreign policy leadership has not fallen on the careerists. Political leadership has been dominant through most of the modern period. Political leadership has maintained a close control over foreign policy chiefly due to the importance of foreign policy as a political symbol in India. The author surmises that no other Third World political party has had to defend its stance in foreign policy as vigorously as Congress, and has taken as great an effort to project a particular image in this sphere at home and abroad. In Lok Sabha debates the accusation that one or another party has "foreign backers" is prolific. Most of the interviews that Gandhi gives are to foreign journalists, and the topic is generally India's foreign policy (by her choice).

A large portion of Indian political energies is directed outside of India, and contrary to certain nations (such as Iran) which exhibit definate xenophobic tendencies, India may be said in a national character analysis to exhibit xenophilia or a strong attraction to things foreign.[17] It is probable that the

---

[16] Mathai (1979), p. viii.

[17] Our discussion at this point takes place on the domestic level-of-analysis. This reference to national character should not be taken to mean that xenophilia is a manifestation of a national personality. Nations do not have personalities; individuals do. However, certain types of group behavior resemble individual behavior sufficiently that certain similes drawn from individual psychology can be applied to the group. The xenophiliac behavior (more common among Third World national societies than both xenophobia and neutrality) may be explained by more basic and objective economic

desire (above a base level determined from the population of all Third World national societies) of the average Indian to form relationships outside of the country is proportional to the degree of frustration of those desires, rather than the result of any Indian inherent conditions. Above a certain level of frustration a frustration-xenophilia positive feedback spiral may be initiated. Exceptionally strong xenophilia is, probably in many cases, an elite-generated condition. Due to this xenophilia, MEA and the foreign policy have become strong political factors and elements in a political party's domestic strength. Indian diplomacy will probably never devolve into a technology in which the practitioners of diplomacy are able to perform their duty in cool objectivity. MEA has become a passive political symbol, part of the spoils of fortune in good times and a factor threatening political damage to the party in bad times. MEA is a passive tool because control of it will never by itself lead to a change in the political climate, but if it is not operating in complete harmony with the governing party's objectives criticism of MEA by outsiders becomes criticism of the party. In the same way, if it is closely identified with the party and is functioning well, praise of MEA becomes kudos for the governing party. Foreign policy, undoubtedly due to Nehruvian leadership precedents (but probably fully explicable only by a hypothesis of multiple causation) has become a powerful political symbol. MEA has, in this way, become strongly related to the domestic political process.

Nehru's choice of subordinates follows a clear pattern.[18] Many involved in foreign policy leadership were members of Nehru's family, three examples being B.K. Nehru, cousin to prime minister Nehru and the Indian ambassador in Washington during the 1962 war; R.K. Nehru, another cousin of the prime minister and secretary-general of MEA, again at the time of the

---

and cultural factors.

Penetration refers to the average strength of an individual's relationship with individuals or groups outside of the national society. Xenophilia refers to the average desired strength of an individual's relationship with individuals or groups outside of the national society. Frustration is defined as the difference between national xenophilia and penetration. Xenophilia and penetration both could be measured by the number of letters sent and received to and from abroad, expenditures on processed imports, etc.

[18] The following will draw heavily upon the decision-making or small-group level-of-analysis.

China war; and Vijayalakshmi Pandit, Nehru's sister and first Indian ambassador to the Soviet Union.[19] A fourth and more important example might be Nehru's daughter, Indira Gandhi. Nehru's preference for family members in positions of power is the sociological result of the primacy of the family as a unit in Indian society. Nehru was in debt to his father--and thereby to his family--a number of times during his years in England and later during his pre-Independence political career. The appointment of family members probably had as its main motive Nehru's sense of responsibility to his family for his position of authority and worldly success. Not to have appointed family members to positions of power would have been a betrayal of those people whose approval for his emotional well-being Nehru deeply needed.

The appointment of family members might have had two additional motives. In a political environment where distrust of subordinates is rampant, appointment of family members might be considered when the allegiance of no one else is guaranteed. This seems an important cause of political nepotism in certain Latin American dictatorships, but is not a useful explanation in the Indian polity; Nehru generally trusted the people who surrounded him and those who solicited positions without seriously questioning their motives or real qualifications. Caste is also a strong influence in gaining entrance to and power within government and business, and Nehru was probably influenced by this sociological element. Finally, we see a very strong family connection in the way in which prime ministerial succession has transpired, the first, third and quite possibly the sixth prime ministers being successive generations in the same blood line. Altogether, the Nehru family has ruled for eight-ninths of the span of modern Indian history.

Brecher notes also that Kashmiri Brahmans enjoyed a high representation in Nehru's list of appointments. This group was well-represented even after the Nehru period, and RAW's first director in 1969 was a Kashmiri Brahman related to the Nehru family. Though Nehru probably had no conscious caste bias, many of Nehru's friends and acquaintances would have been Kashmiri Brahmans, and it would have been only natural for Nehru

---

[19] Neville Maxwell, *India's China War* (New York: Doubleday and Co., 1972), pp. 227, 253; Dutt, p. 190; Pandit was said to be one of India's most pro-American diplomats, and her appointment to Moscow was thus a bit inexplicable to many observers. For further comments on Nehru and nepotism, see M.O. Mathai, *Reminiscences of the Nehru Age* (New Delhi: Vikas, 1978), p. 12.

to put those people whom he knew into important government positions. To Nehru, the fact that his friends also happened to be of a certain *jati* would have seemed irrelevant. Caste affected Nehru's decisions by determining the people whom he had as close friends. Caste is still very important, even in the lives of extremely Westernized people such as Nehru, and Westernized institutions as, for example, MEA.

In the way in which Nehru built up the bureaucratic leadership we see an absence of political motivation. Members of the ICS who had earlier happily served the British were not castigated but were instead retained in positions of power. Sandhurst-trained officers in the Indian military maintained their positions and were not replaced by officers who had not been so closely associated with the British. The only appointments made on the basis of participation in the Congress resistance movement were those of members of the defunct Indian National Army (INA), who had fought for the Japanese against the British in World War II. The INA soldiers had been shut out of many government positions due to their involvement in the INA, an ostracism that persisted long after independence. Nehru insisted that a certain number of INA soldiers be inducted into both the IFS and IAS to help correct what Nehru saw as a great injustice.

Nehru did not seem to have a set of exacting standards by which he evaluated applicants or a precise idea of what he wanted from an applicant according to which he (the applicant) would either pass or fail. Instead, Nehru seemed to rely on first impressions, making his selections according to personalistic rather than bureau-utilitarian standards. In this way, Nehru's personnel evaluations resembled his manner of making speeches: impromptu, to the inclinations of the moment, rather than according to script. This reliance upon feeling a person out rather than cold evaluation of a person's strengths and weaknesses also resembles Mahatma Gandhi's approach to political activism. Gandhi emphasized the need for intuitive self-reliance in decision-making and that situations should be first felt and then dealt with according to the initial impressions.[20] Nehru, who adored the Mahatma, was

---

[20] This is distinct from both the reliance upon "rationality" and "self-interest" unique to the cognitive maps of Western decision-makers, and the intricate decisional system implied by Marxism-Leninism and followed by the Eastern communist national elites. Analysts sometimes shrink from the acceptance of nonalignment and other allied views of the world as valid policy bases. The same may deny the strength of

probably deeply impressed by this political strategy or philosophy and continued to follow this approach in his work with the bureaucracy.[21]

Much of Nehru's energy and magnetism probably flowed from his reliance on intuition and spontaneity. But this spontaneity also gained him the reputation of a person who could easily be taken in by skilled actors who lacked strong qualifications for the tasks which they were hired for.[22] This should not be, as it has been, interpreted as gullibility, but is rather a sign of Nehru's strong faith in the value of impressions in decision-making. Once such a decision based on intuition had been made by him, he regarded it as quite final. This made cold evaluation of information difficult and infrequent.

Nehru's administrative efforts were dominated by his immense drive. Nehru was a fast-paced man who expected his subordinates to follow his pace closely.

> Reports of ceaseless activity of the Prime Minister were circulating in Delhi--how he retired to bed long after midnight and was up again in the early hours of the morning fresh for another day's work. In later years I was an eye-witness to his unrelenting daily schedule. Not unoften would he send for the

---

Marxism-Leninism in determing Soviet international behavior, presumably because thoughts without a material investment of some sort are held to be indeterminate with respect to behavior. However, it has been shown that obsessive and some other psychotic behavior substitutes internal subjective for external objective stimuli. To a lesser degree, internal subjective stimuli determine behavior for normal introspective personalities to a degree which is often difficult for the non-empathic extroverted personality to appreciate. It is probable that the same lack of empathy for a completely valid, obverse and largely determinate Indian cognitive map and perceptual framework is the central villain in some political scientists' distrust of nonalignment theory (leading to conclusions that nonalignment is "merely rhetoric," or speculations on "what do they *really* want?"). Kremlinologists are frequently required to place themselves in the role of the party official, and temporarily believe in and completely accept the conclusions of Marxism-Leninism. Obviously, that does not make them Marxists. South Asian scholars might not choose nonalignment policy were they leaders in that region, but they are not those leaders. Temporary suspension of disbelief is an essential ingredient

> senior officials of the Foreign Office at midnight and discuss international issues at an hour when ordinarily most persons' physical and mental capacity would be at the lowest ebb. And whether or not the Prime Minister was available for personal guidance, he would not keep any matter pending with him for more than a few hours. All papers which reached him by late evening came back the following morning with clear decisions recorded on them.

Nehru's drive plainly impressed his subordinates, and kept MEA and the related ministries moving at a fast clip.[23] As Nehru's age began to slow his pace, new leaders such as Krishna Menon came to the fore in the late fifties and maintained the pace by continuing to make large demands on the apparatus. This kind of energy and drive is found among many national executives, such as Stalin who kept his Ministry of Foreign Affairs opened and staffed almost twenty-four hours a day, or the American presidents, of whom stories of long hours and wearing work abound.[24]

Nehru's energy was essential in the first years of Indian independence, and was a very positive element in the operation of the government at that time. However,

---

in accurate analysis.
A cognitive map, on the other hand, could not be inferred wholly from a leader's public statements; in some cases very few such statements may correspond to a leader's cognitive structure. Nehru, it may be posited, was more incomplete in public statements than deceptive, relative to his cognitive structure. See Robert Axelrod, ed., *Structure of Decision: The Cognitive Maps of Political Elites* (Princeton: Princeton University Press, 1976); Nathan Leites, *The Operational Code of the Politburo* (New York: McGraw Hill, 1951); "Puzzle: What Does Nehru Really Want?" *United States News* (New York) 30: 35-36, February 9, 1951.

[21] In a letter dated June 3, 1942, addressed to Rajkumari Amrit Kaw, Nehru wrote of Mahatma Gandhi,

> I find his approach to events is rather feminine, if I may say so. That is to say it is intuitive and is more of a reaction than the business of logical reasoning. Much can be said for this, but it is a risky business sometimes.

his demands on junior officers might have been too great, as the work of Nehru's subordinates was very different in content and emotional requirements than his own work, and it would have been quite a different thing for them to clear a workload comparable to Nehru's. Nehru's demands of his close subordinates created an "inverted pyramid" of work allocation, which, as Dutt wrote, did ". . . not make for efficient and ordinary disposal of Foreign Office business."[25] The inverted division of MEA labor suggests Nehru thought that the strength of the lower ranks of the bureaucracy was largely dependent on top leadership, rather than the other way around.

That there was some dissatisfaction with MEA during the Nehru period is obvious; witness Mathai's comment that "[t]he administration of the External Affairs Ministry and its missions abroad were nothing short of lousy. The Air India offices abroad were better and more useful than many of India's missions abroad" or Crocker's critique of MEA that "[t]here was not enough training or professional competence, not enough *esprit de corps,* and too much eagerness to please the boss." The problems affecting the MEA of that era cannot be localized in any one division or service cadre. We cannot lump all blame on an ICS or Sandhurst "generation," though the British inheritance gave the Indian leadership problems.[26] Throughout the Nehru era men who had earlier been members of the ICS were in positions of power and influence, and the inefficiencies of the administration impinged upon their work. The indictments of their work in the Nehru period seem

---

Though Nehru showed every evidence of following a more intuitive style of decision-making, even in his impressionistic use of history, this fragment shows that he was not fully aware or forthright with colleagues concerning this dependence. See Mathai (1978), p. 30.

[22] Dutt, pp. 288-90 Brecher, p. 244.

[23] Dutt, pp. 10, 28 T.N. Kaul, *Diplomacy in Peace and War* (New Delhi: Vikas, 1979), p. 83; Crocker, pp. 135-36; B.N. Mullik, *My Years with Nehru,* -16 (New Delhi: Allied Publishers, 1972), p. 207.

[24] Aleksandr Solzhenitzen, *The First Circle* (New York: Harper and Row, 1968), p. 1.

[25] Dutt, p. 27 Brecher, p. 241.

[26] Mathai (1979), p. 129 Crocker, p. 87; Bandyopadhyaya (1971 edition), p. 182.

actually to be in disapprobation of their extravagant lifestyle, haughty demeanor and discordant service attitudes rather than their inefficiency as administrators. There seems to be no direct link between the background of the three dozen ICS officers and the administrative difficulties experienced by MEA in this period. Indeed, the original cadre group of thirty-six officers was selected for bureaucratic and administrative prowess, so that animadversion of the original ICS recruits would seem more a critique of the IFS selection process than of the ICS itself. Most attempts to find the roots of the problems of the early MEA in the ICS cadre group have their own roots in the friction of personalities in the early years of Indian diplomacy.

Inefficiencies in MEA administration were less the fault of any cadre than of ministerial and secretarial leadership. Top leadership was very unstable during much of the Nehru period (particularly 1950-55), authority shifting at random intervals between Krishna Menon, Vijayalakshmi Pandit, R.K. Nehru and N.R. Pillai. The situation is best set out in a letter written by the Canadian ambassador to India (1952-55) Escott Reid to the Canadian prime minister Lester Pearson in 1952:

> So far as I can make out, the situation is simple. Krishna Menon has no use for Pillai and R.K. Nehru. Pillai has little use for Menon and considers that his anti-American speeches in the United States were stupid. Mrs. Pandit has no use for Krishna Menon. The relations between Pillai and R.K. Nehru are strained. I am not certain what Pillai and R.K. Nehru think of Mrs. Pandit and she of them, except that Pillai and R.K. Nehru undoubtedly consider that she is a lesser evil than Krishna Menon. Mrs. Pandit and Krishna Menon compete for the Prime Minister's favour. According to Alec Clutterbuck [Sir Alexander Clutterbuck, the British High Commissioner to India], Mrs. Pandit has tried to persuade her brother to make her Foreign Minister. This her brother has refused for two reasons: the Congress Party would object and she would argue with him on foreign affairs. In order to stop her from arguing with him face to face, he sends her off to international conferences. When I get an explanation of why he sends Krishna Menon to the same conferences, I'll let you know. Perhaps he doesn't want his sister to get a

swollen head from too much limelight.[27]

While Menon was the prime minister's principal advisor on foreign policy, Pandit held the official position of authority in UN policy. There was a bitter struggle at that time between Menon and Pandit for control of UN policy and for greater influence in the policy process. Pandit in her position as ambassador to the UN was a mainstream policy contributor and no great threat to Menon, but as long as she continued to take advantage of her special relationship with Nehru to protect her influence as ambassador, Krishna Menon's power, drawing from the same base, would suffer. Menon, of course, would never relinquish his role as principal foreign policy advisor to Nehru. Below the warring giants sat the implementors of policy, R.K. Nehru and N.R. Pillai. We find no major dispute separating them, but only a degree of tension from the somewhat convergent roles of the secretary-general and foreign secretary.[28]

Menon and Pandit were acting on the political stage in a struggle quite similar to that which has been enacted in most recent American administrations between the national security advisor and the secretary of state. In both cases the individuals involved were seeking identical "vicarships" in their country's foreign policy, though the Menon-Pandit dispute was much shorter and more vicious than the American infighting. For five years the Menon-Pandit dispute left India without firm middle-level foreign policy elite leadership, resulting in embarassment in the UN, India's principal interest during this period, and retarding the progress of Indian diplomacy at the lower levels in MEA at a time when the efforts of top leadership should have been devoted to the most rapid possible development of the IFS and division administration. Control could not shift to the lower secretarial level (as could happen in the case of a weak and vacillating top-echelon leadership), as the interference of Menon and Pandit was too great, however ineffectually divided.

---

[27] Reid, pp. 37-38. For further illuminating observations on the relationships of power between Menon, Pandit, Pillai, Nehru and others in the 1952-55 period, see Escott Reid, pp. 37-38, 183-84, 186-87, 193. Reid's book is written with a degree of political insight into the Indian scene far surpassing that of the "India memoirs" of Crocker, or of U.S. ambassadors Galbraith or Bowles.

[28] Possibly another factor was the tension between the wives of the two men. See Reid, p. 12.

Though great weakness in Nehru's policy did not set in before 1956, it is possible that the divided leadership of 1950-55 exaggerated the later mistakes and difficulties.

Pandit tried to end the struggle in the only way she could, by gaining the foreign ministership from her brother. To become foreign minister would have been to gain everything that Menon had at that time, crowned by an authoritative cabinet position. Unfortunately for Pandit, the same constitutional finality which would have given her supremacy through the ministership also made it impossible for her to gain such a position, due to the disinclination of Nehru to the creation of a post which would in any way appear to challenge his own potent foreign policy leadership. Fortunately for Menon, he had chosen the ideal path for entrance into policy dominance at such a level, that of the unofficial advisor to Nehru on foreign policy. By 1955 he was unchallenged in his position, with his opponents Pandit in London as the Indian high commissioner, an uncooperative R.K. Nehru in China and Panikkar in New Delhi but easily eclipsed by Menon. In February 1956 Menon became a cabinet member without portfolio, through this cementing his authority in a way that would not have threatened Nehru as much as an independent foreign minister would have, but retaining his office in South Block as well as his unofficial position in the foreign policy community. With the new portfolio Menon was empowered to take control of all MEA and Indian foreign policy operations relating to Kashmir, Goa, Suez and the United Nations, really the entire range of Indian foreign policy at that time. Certainly, by the beginning of 1956 any ambiguity which might have existed about Menon's preeminence had completely dissolved.

Menon's position had been further strengthened when he was granted the defence portfolio in March 1957 after his presentation before the UN Security Council of the Indian position on Kashmir. At this point Menon was very strong, but had the quality of leadership improved? Strong, unchallenged policy did not guarantee good policy. In fact, conflict between points on the elite plane did not decrease, but the expression of the conflict only underwent a ninety degree shift. No longer was it a horizontal conflict between two equals, Menon and Pandit, but was now rather a vertical discord between Menon and his subordinates. N.R. Pillai, no friend of Menon, was at the time secretary-general. Cut off from Nehru by Menon's monopolization of Nehru's attention and lacking any kind of close contact with Menon, Pillai could do little to improve MEA's operations. He had no information on the top echelons' detailed operational goals.

An organization cannot improve its operations until it has an idea of what would be considered improvement. Foreign policy organization in 1950-55 was divided and weakened; in the period 1956-62 cabinet-level leadership was strong but ignored the body of MEA. After 1962 until Nehru's death there seems to have been little anyone could do but wait for the change in leadership. In summary, the debility which inflicted MEA during much of the Nehru period may have had its causes in what was happening at the highest levels (and was not just a problem of inadequate infrastructure). The presence of strong leadership at some level of the bureaucracy (a sharp, well-defined locus of power) is necessary to the correct guidance and motivation of the organization. Without such, requisite input may be missing and the lower implementative levels of the organization will find themselves without a mission.

10.2 AFTER NEHRU

After Nehru's death Lal Bahadur Shastri, through Congress and Kamaraj Syndicate machinations, gained the prime ministership. He did not think of himself as an expert in foreign policy and did not launch into a very energetic involvement in foreign policy upon assuming office. The ITEC program owed its establishment to Shastri, as well as the Office of the Prime Minister (Office), in its early form as the Prime Minister's Secretariat (PMS), perhaps the highest body of officers in Indian government to be concerned with foreign policy organization.[29] The PMS was instituted at the recommendation of two senior civil servants in the government, Dharam Vira and L.K. Jha, when Shastri was recovering from his first heart attack (July 1964). The philosophy behind the creation of the PMS was one which assumed the prime minister's role not only as political head of the cabinet but also as the central government executive. In other words, the prime minister controls the government not only through leadership in the cabinet but also through direct contact with the career leadership of the bureaucracy, the secretaries and whoever else the PM finds essential in getting

---

[29] In its original conception foreign policy was a secondary topic of the PMS, but it soon became a high-priority concern of the officer in charge of the PMS. Most of the total PMS staff was concerned with domestic issues. See Michael Brecher, *Succession in India* (London: Oxford University Press, 1966), pp. 119-20.

things done. When the prime minister is viewed as the head of government in this much deeper sense he acquires the capabilities and responsibilities of a "government within a government." By himself, though, at least in the Shastri period, he is not able to make the many secretarial and sub-secretarial contacts which he must make in such a role (though Nehru, in that less complicated era of Indian government, seemed quite willing and able to fullfill this intense executive role). It was to furnish the prime minister with deeper contacts in the government that the PMS was created.

As Brecher notes, the PMS did not at first seem so important a Shastri innovation. Shastri wanted no more than a small personal staff to help him handle the problems which came to his attention; he was both unwilling and unable to make the heavy personal investment of time and energy that Nehru had made to the routine task of coordination of the career bureaucracy. As Brecher elaborates, based on an interview with Jha,

> [w]henever a proposal was put to Nehru, outside the sphere of external affairs, he would answer promptly, 'yes, I agree' or 'no, I have doubts,' and he would pass the matter on to the appropriate Ministry for detailed consideration; later, when the issue came before Cabinet he would put his mind to it; and, not infrequently, at that late stage Nehru would reject the proposal, with the result that the effort in preparing material would be wasted. By unconcealed interference, the new Secretariat was designed to prevent this 'inefficient' way of conducting Government business, by keeping the Prime Minister advised throughout. Stated somewhat differently, Jha remarked that Nehru took decisions quickly and Shastri acts slowly.[30]

Shastri recognized that coordination *au Nehru* would in any case probably not have been possible in the more specialized foreign policy world of the sixties; possibly he saw the staff as simply a better and more modern way of doing business (the staff, originally a military administrative tool, was used by American leadership with increasing frequency in the 1960s, with president Kennedy giving it the personalistic form which it has held through the past two decades). Shastri originally

---

[30] Brecher (1966), pp. 115-16. The early domestic orientation of the PMS is clear in this reference.

intended that his staff be headed by two secretaries; by L.K. Jha, a former finance secretary, for economic affairs and by L.P. Singh for general administration. Interestingly, in the original conception external affairs would be handled, not by a secretary, but by a deputy to one of the two secretaries. This tells us something of Shastri's low valuation of foreign policy; such a downgrading of foreign policy management would have been unthinkable in even the weak years of the Nehru period.

Another revealing detail of the original PMS plan was Shastri's determination of the formal institutional structure only after selecting Singh and Jha as the principals of the staff. He was an executive concerned primarily not with institutions, as was president Eisenhower, but rather more, like president Kennedy, with people and personalities. PMS was established to place Jha and Singh; Jha and Singh were not selected for predetermined positions. As it happened, this personalistic approach to the formation of the original PMS gave the PM's secretary close to full control over the placement of resources within PMS. Though Shastri expressly wanted L.P. Singh in the PMS, Singh was at that time secretary(special) (soon to be promoted, probably as incentive to stay in Home, to home secretary) of the Home Ministry, and home minister Nanda would not release this exceptional administrative officer from his Home posting. As Shastri wanted Singh and Singh only for the PMS administrative post, upon failing to get Singh he dropped the position altogether. Thus was born a tradition of the placement of only one secretary in charge of PMS, the first such officer being L.K. Jha, with two officers under him, S. Bannerji and a Shri Shrivastava, in charge of the two divisions in the early PMS (the same structure as in the original conception, but administered differently).

The PMS, a piece of progressive administration, also had in it, through L.K. Jha's and L.P. Singh's ICS backgrounds, a mark of reaction. While Jha's ICS heritage did not affect his abilities in strict administration, at a later date his British administrative background was held against him. While Jha's personal history lent some continuity to bureaucratic practice in the 1960s, the PMS was a radical break from traditional government practice, and the zealous fullfillment of his very liberally defined responsibilities soon aroused resentment in many sections of the bureaucracy. Jha, who as the singular and appointed head of PMS controlled the full range of PMS's vaguely defined responsibilities, was exempt from many of the pressures which government officials played ordinarily against each other. As well, with the advent of PMS the line secretaries lost some of their consequence with the prime minister personally (though considering the type of leader Shastri was, it is doubtful that they would have been able to keep up this contact whether the PMS had come about or not). This naturally led to some hostility on the part of line bureaucrats, but Jha may also have been more passionately devoted to building up a powerful extragovernmental power base in the PMS than he need have been.

Though not used aggressively until Gandhi came to power, PMS was built up rapidly throughout Jha's posting. Three joint Secretaries with a small auxiliary staff were gradually transferred to the PMS and integrated into a new centrally coordinated organism. The new prime ministerial staff presented a unified face to the world, not at all like Nehru, who

> . . . had a multiple staff: a personal secretariat, headed by a Principle Private Secretary, to assist him with routine papers; a Secretary-General of External Affairs; a Private Secretary(Plannning) to maintain liaison with the Planning Commission, and others.[31]

This staffing pluralism was dispensed with by Shastri, which in itself may be enough to explain the unprecedented development of the PMS as a power center.

When Soviet deputy minister Kosygin made, in 1969, a questionable remark at Dr. Zakir Hussain's funeral, it was the PMS which asked for clarification from the Soviets, just as the White House might ask for clarification on behalf of the president of the United States. The relationship between the two executives and their staffs are similar. The purpose, publicly ennunciated, of PMS is the preparation of "drafts of important speeches, statements and letters."[32] This alone gives the PMS potential policy-formulative powers in almost any area, subject to the amount of supervision and revision made at the crucial drafting stage. But the power of the PMS, or more precisely of the PM's principal private secretary (PMPPS), extends beyond drafting authority. Not only was Jha in control of the PMS, but he also coordinated the activities of the cabinet secretariat and was a member of many secretary-level committees in the government.

---

[31] Brecher (1966), pp. 116-17.

[32] Kuldip Nayar, *Between the Lines* (Bombay: Allied Publishers, 1969), pp. 119-20; Brecher (1966), p. 117.

In the foreign policy realm perhaps the most forceful expression of Jha's growing influence was the establishment in the spring of 1965 of the committee of secretaries. Created with foreign policy in mind, the committee (in lower-case letters due to the uncertain officiality of the committee's name) consisted of the secretaries of the ministries of Finance, Commerce, the cabinet secretariat, Defence, external affairs (then C.S. Jha) and included the PMPPS L.K. Jha.[33] L.K. Jha was *primus inter pares* on this committee, which served as both an evaluative and control group. All secretaries on the committee participated in evaluation, and Jha largely implemented control. The establishment of the committee became a serious point of dispute between the PMS and MEA. There is today a fairly constant friction between MEA and the Office; the Office, for example, recently blamed the Tarapur nuclear fuel dispute with the United States on MEA (as it was handled by a past foreign secretary Eric Gonsalves) and on the Department of Atomic Energy of H.N. Sethna.[34] The committee of secretaries, however, was subjected to an open assault by foreign policy professionals, rather than the low-key criticism which generally greets Office or PMS initiatives. This is important evidence for the perceived power of the committee and perhaps indirectly for the perceived influence of the PMS.[35]

---

[33] Brecher finds it odd that the other two MEA secretaries and the home secretary were not invited, but the other two secretaries do no have the broad responsibilities that the foreign secretary does, nor does the home secretary deal much with foreign policy.

[34] Personal interview, September 7, 1982.

[35] There is no reason to regard the committee of secretaries, as Brecher does, as a "slight to the professionals of the Ministry of External Affairs," as the committee in now way interfered with or was a substitute for the specialized line functions of MEA. L.K. Jha was made somewhat more powerful through the committee, but the other secretaries were made more powerful as well in policy circles. In any case, the committee was only a tool of Jha's rise in influence, and not a primary cause of that ascension. There is not reason, also, to ascribe the committee of secretaries' formation, as Levi does, to underhanded influences,

> . . . that the intention behind the creation of this committee had been to undercut the

Of course, the PMS during the emergency period became very powerful and criticism, for political reasons, waned. The cabinet secretariat (Cab Sec), which was itself controlled by PMS, was in charge of general programming for both RAW and MEA's PPRD. Cab Sec was also in charge of the strong-arm Department of Revenue Intelligence (DRI) and the Department of Enforcement (which before the emergency were both Ministry of Finance departments). After Gandhi's fall from power the DRI, the Department of Enforcement and the PPRD were all returned to the control of their respective ministries.[36] As the PMS's power grew in the extraordinary manner of emergency organizations, that growth tended to enhance the power of the PMPPS rather than the PMS as an institution. PMS was headed by Jha in 1964-69, followed by P.N. Haksar (1969-73), undoubtedly the most administratively competent and energetic of the secretaries, as well as the most politically radical. P.N. Haksar has an IFS background, having held a senior position in MEA before becoming the PMPPS. Haksar was followed by the Kashmiri P.N. Dhar (not to be confused with D.P. Dhar), now a senior economist for the government (and presently in policy "exile" at the UN). After P.N. Dhar came the two emergency secretaries R.K. Dhawan and Yashpal Kapur, whose administrations were, at best, regarded as lackluster.[37] In reaction to emergency over-centralization, Morarji Desai's Janata government changed the name of the PMS to that of the Office of the Prime Minister, diminished its role in policy-making, and replaced Yashpal Kapur

---

> foreign policy attitudes *[sic]* of the Ministry, considered too unfriendly to the west, that the economic and planning agencies of the government wanted policies more pleasing to the United States which they could not get from the professionals of the External Affairs Ministry.

The committee was only an IG similar to those found in the American bureaucracy (see chapter 5, "Community Coordination"), and is today a common Indian practice. See Brecher (1966), p. 120; Werner Levi, "Foreign Policy: The Shastri Era," in K.P. Misra, ed., *Studies in Indian Foreign Policy* (New Delhi: Vikas, 1969), p. 194.

[36] See "Cutting the 'Cab. Sec.' to Size," *India Today*, June 1-15, 1977, p. 16.

[37] Personal interview, August 6, 1982; see discussion, Tharoor, pp. 143-46.

with V. Shankar as PMPPS.³⁸ When the Lok Dal's Charan Singh became prime minister, V. Shankar was replaced with Rao Sahib, who held that post for roughly one year after Gandhi's return to power. Rao Sahib, probably in 1981, was replaced by P.C. Alexander, who is the PMPPS at present. The Office has retained this Janata appellation, despite the return of the Office to Indira Gandhi's hands.

G. Parthasarathi (known in Indian ruling circles as "GP") has been in the post-Janata period Gandhi's most important advisor. Parthasarathi, like Haksar, has an IFS background; he was at different times permanent representative to the UN and foreign secretary, and is well-versed in foreign affairs. Parthasarathi's influence in policy is established, but his status in the decision-making elite is complex. He is, as Dr. Bhabani Sen Gupta has suggested to the author, a bureaucratic trouble-shooter and not a regular decision-maker with regular responsibilities. Despite chairmanships in the Council of Scientific and Industrial Research and in such bodies as the Indo-U.S. commission, Parthasarathi is denied a strong institutional role; the PMPPS P.C. Alexander is now occupying the official position closest to Gandhi.³⁹ However, Alexander's responsibilities inside the Office are no more clear than those of Parthasarathi, outside of the government. It is probable that Parthasarathi wields far greater influence than does Alexander, because of Parthasarathi's close friendship with Gandhi but also because of his position at the apex of a very important informal policy advisory triangle. It is said that not a day passes without three men, Parthasarathi, P.N. Haksar and T.N. Kaul, consulting between themselves and being consulted in turn by others in making important government decisions. The group leans quite far to the left, but they are much less radical as a group than P.N. Haksar, a dedicated "anti-imperialist," is as an individual.⁴⁰ Through his membership in this informal

---

³⁸ V. Shankar is the author of *My Reminiscences of Sardar Patel* (Delhi: Macmillan Co., 1974), two volumes.

³⁹ Parthasarathi sits, *inter alia*, on the Indo-U.S. subcommission on education and culture as co-chairman, with an American. The commission is the product of Henry Kissinger's effort around 1974 to repair Indo-U.S. relations. Thanks to Lloyd Rudolph for guidance on this point.

⁴⁰ P.N. Haksar lost his PMS post in 1973 due to loss of prime ministerial favor; he is thought presently to be once again on the rise in this regard. Tri-

policy club Parthasarathi more than makes up for any formal primacy which Alexander may have over him.

The Office is the result of a triphasal power evolution. The power of Jha's nascent PMS was power inherent in the PMS as a formal body. At that early stage, the PMS was evolving in internal clout and potential, but its actual use remained limited and internalized. The second stage of the PMS's development began in 1969 when it, with the Cab Sec, began to be used aggressively by Gandhi in a rise to power which culminated in the emergency. In the third phase, that of the Janata and post-Janata period, the power of the Office as an institution has not increased, but the prominence of the PMPPS and of informal advisors close to the Office (such as Parthasarathi) in decision-making circles has increased markedly.

Under the PMPPS (a large number of whom were previous Commerce Secretaries) are four senior officers in charge of the separate fields of foreign, defense, science and economic policies. These officers (any one of whom might deal with foreign policy) are, with the secretary, Gandhi's eyes and ears within the bureaucracy. The Office plays, therefore, an important informational as well as formulative role. Her present information advisor H.Y. Sharada Prashad (her first was George Verghese, now a part of the "Opposition Forces"), closely tied into the general elite system of which the Office is a part, drafts all of Gandhi's speeches; she generally makes only minor corrections in this material. In addition, a great many of the communications which MEA receives from "Smt. Gandhi" have really been sent by her Office officials. The contact which she has with MEA is sometimes directly with the MEA secretaries but more frequently with her Office people, who sit on all interdepartmental groups concerned with foreign policy. On all of Gandhi's trips abroad a senior official from her Office and from MEA seem to have accompanied her. Arjun Sen Gupta, presently additional secretary in the Office, was one of those who accompanied Gandhi on her July 1982 visit to America; foreign secretary M.K. Rasgotre also went along.

Communications between India and other governments frequently take place through the Office, circumventing MEA in its traditional interest in international communications.[41] In all these ways, and perhaps in some

---

loki Nath Kaul is a senior Indian diplomat, a former secretary-general and ambassador to the U.S. He has written several works on diplomacy, one of which, *Diplomacy in Peace and War,* was published with ICCR involvement.

not understood at present, the Office has become a powerful influence in foreign policy, and is an important political support for prime minister Gandhi. She has, in part through the instrumentation of the Office, lifted the parliamentary executive to a place of at least as much power as is exerted by the American presidential executive. The closest thing to the U.S. National Security Council (NSC) in India is the Office; both supply the executive with high-powered deputies for action in high policy. The Indian bureaucracy is small enough so that anything so elaborate as the NSC is unnecessary (and the Office wields an arbitrary power which gives it very little resemblance to the more institutionalized American bodies).

The staff, a group tied down to no formal service but only to a central executive executive, is a very American (and in its earliest gestation, German) idea. In the United States one observes the development of a modular diplomacy (following Alvin Toffler) with ambassadors-at-large, special envoys such as Phillip Habib in the Middle East, and many variants of shuttle diplomacy. This style of diplomacy, in which diplomats are "plugged" into global situations as they arise has been criticized as inappropriate for India (adding that the British diplomatic model is far more useful a guide for Indian diplomacy). But because the Office provides Gandhi with more data and control over the bureaucracy than she might obtain only through the line bureaux, she is likely to maintain the Office until it is superceded by other more effective staff forms.

The cabinet secretariat, like the ministries, is directed by the Office. Cab Sec (with the help of the committee of secretaries, which is informally inside Cab Sec) has as its major responsibility the coordination of the governmental community. Its efforts, then, are directed down into the bureaucracy rather than, like the Office, up to the prime minister. Ideally Cab Sec acts as a superministry, a court of last appeals in the procurement for the ministries of requisite resources. Cab Sec views the ministries not as a collection of diverse concerns but as a single organization. It is perhaps because of this that Cab Sec's relations with MEA have been less than optimal. Cab Sec, in the coordination of the government community as a rather homogenous whole, has failed to recognize the special needs of the MEA. This is obfuscated by MEA's perverse unwillingness to be subjected to extraministerial coordination of this sort.

---

[41] Nayar, pp. 119-20.

Cab Sec, the recipient of much executive attention, has had three major reorganizations, the first in 1950 as part of an early course setting. After 1969 Gandhi arranged in stages the transfer to Cab Sec supervision of sixty of the Home Ministry's one hundred divisions, which included the IB and CBI.[42] The Cab Sec was by then (through the Office) very much under prime minister Gandhi's control, and both the Office and Cab Sec became a joint emergency institution. Of course, it was because of the misuse of the Office during the emergency that the third general set of changes came about, the effective dismemberment of Cab Sec during Janata. Even though, as stated above, certain individuals in the PMS have become in the post-Janata period quite powerful, the power of the more institutionalized Cab Sec does not seem to have been restored. Disruption of formal lines of communication is very effective in reducing the power of the institutionalized group (utilizing a bureaucratic decision-making system), but almost completely ineffective in reducing the power of the personalistic group (which follows a predominately collegial decision-making system). However, because of the close coordinative interconnections between the two groups, the fortunes of one are communicated to some degree to the other. Unlike its relationship with most of the foreign policy bureaucracy, the Office is allied with the Cab Sec and cooperates in net effect with the Cab Sec. Resource pools, capabilities and the set of lines of communications of the two bodies with points external to the two bodies are largely disjoint. The goals of the two bodies are similar, though, and the Office has strong control over the Cab Sec, overruling potential dissent.

10.3 JANATA AND THE BUREAUCRACY

Janata at least in foreign policy was not, despite certain impressions to the contrary, the rule of the bureaucrats. A.B. Vajpayee maintained a very fine political control, and at no other time in modern India have more non-careerists been appointed to ambassadorships.[43] If we are to ascribe to the bureaucracy a

___

[42] Personal interview, August 6, 1982 Tharoor, p. 117.

[43] It is true that during the emergency a comparable number of non-careerists were used as diplomatic envoys. They were, however, denied the formal ambassadorial rank. See Louis and Chawla, "More Continuity

more than usual influence, it must be in recognition of Jagat Subha Mehta's skill as foreign secretary rather than any laxity on the part of the central executive. If anything, political involvement during Janata in the bureaucracy was excessive. A notorious case concerned then-diplomat Nirmala Prasad, who became a favorite of Congress(U) president Devraj Urs and ended up resigning under Indira Gandhi's regime because of her political involvement.[44] Janata political openness perhaps encouraged a spirit of party machine participation to which MEA had some difficulty in remaining immune.

In a related area, Janata's relations with the intelligence community were quite bad, due to probably dubious information that the RAW had engaged in political sabotage during the emergency. Not only was RAW's N.F. Suntook pushed down to additional secretary rank, making three officers in MEA his senior officers, but Suntook only met with prime minister Desai three times (with the first meeting less than three minutes long). The PPRC (but not the PPRD) took over many compilatory intelligence operations in this period. MEA thus faced none of the competition from RAW which it may have encountered during the emergency.[45]

The divergent MEA policies of the Janata and post-Janata Gandhi periods can be to some extent deduced from the varied complexions of foreign delegations sent by the two governments. Choosing the years 1975-76 and 1977-78, the first years of the emergency and of Janata respectively, as points of reference, we find that:

- the number of official and unofficial delegations sent by the emergency government was almost quadruple that sent by Janata, approximately eighty as opposed to twenty-one for Janata;

- The percentage of delegations represented or headed by a MEA official was for the emergency regime twenty-five percent as opposed, for Janata, to fifty-seven percent;

- the percentage of delegations represented or headed by a cabinet minister outside of the MEA hierarchy was approximately equal for both regimes, thirty percent of emergency delegations and thirty-three percent of Janata regime delegations;

---

than Change," *India Today*, January 16-31, 1979, p. 39.

[44] *India Today*, August 1-15, 1980, p. 7.

[45] Asoka Raina, "Touching a RAW Nerve," *India Today*, June 16-30, 1980, p. 29.

- the percentage of delegations represented or headed by an official not belonging to either the cabinet or MEA proper was forty-five percent for the emergency regime as opposed to only ten percent for Janata.'⁶

That the Gandhi post-Janata government could sponsor almost eighty delegations in the first year of the emergency says much in favor of prime minister Gandhi's ability to organize, even in that crisis period (though it was largely precisely because of that crisis that the delegations were sent abroad, to stir up international support during the emergency for the Gandhi government, as she had done during the Bangladesh intervention). The higher fraction of delegations led by IFS officers is indicative of the broader experience allowed careerists during Janata. On the other hand, the high fraction during the emergency of nongovernmental delegate heads may be a mark of Gandhi's distrust of the politically-independent careerists. A large proportion of this nongovernmental group were men such as the All-India Congress Committee's general secretary, the Congress(I) president, and among other politicians a large number of members of parliament. Congress(I) management during the emergency may have been using foreign policy as a safety valve for the party, or Indira Gandhi may have been using consciously the politically symbolic force of foreign policy to strengthen her position in the Congress hierarchy. This practice largely ended with Janata, and during Janata a larger number of bilateral talks on international economic and political issues began to be handled by the foreign minister himself, the MEA minister of state, the foreign secretary and occasionally the other secretaries, a phenomenon of the direct substitution of career for political talent. This certainly is indicative of greater faith in the bureaucracy, though Janata may have felt also that its talent was more needed at home than abroad. The stability of the Janata coalition probably would have been eroded by the absence abroad of too many key figures.

There were no important administrative changes within the space of the Janata-Lok Dal coalition. Other than foreign secretary Mehta's removal due to the disastrous Lusaka Conference of the Non-aligned (this during the generally unfortunate Lok Dal period), the

---

⁴⁶ These figures are a collation of the MEA *Annual Reports* for 1975-76 and 1977-78, and are subject to omissions of mention of delegations which the drafters of the *Annual Report* may have thought not really within MEA jurisdiction, e.g., defense delegations.

interesting changes all took place at higher political levels. During Morarji Desai's leadership foreign policy was left largely to Vajpayee, and on a few occasions Vajpayee even contradicted Desai's judgement in foreign policy, a previously unseen manifestation of pluralism in India.[47]

10.4 AFTER JANATA

Prime minister Gandhi, while remaining in "close overall touch" with the bureaucracy, has not viewed the bureaucracy, as Nehru did, as an extension of her power or of her responsibilities. She does not seem to have any plans to turn MEA into, as S. Nihal Singh writes, an "Indiracracy."[48] There has been actually less political involvement in career compositions in the post-Janata period than during Janata. She has instead tended to look at MEA as a separate agency functioning independently of herself, a partner rather than servant. Accompanying this is her relative lack of interest in the administrative details of the bureaucracy, the effect of her lack, relative to her father, of conceptual dexterity. She does not seem to interfere much with the flow of policy at subsecretarial decision-making levels. All of the important initiatives taken in the reform or expansion of the apparatus were initiated by the Shastri or Nehru governments, never by Indira Gandhi. The PPRD, JIC, ITEC program, Pillai committee report, the Cab Sec and Office, were all brought about before she came to power. Not a single foreign policy organizational initiative seems to be owed to her regime.

Even the RAW, while it achieved maturity under Gandhi, was the brainchild of Shastri's administration, and its basic structure, philosophy and staff composition had been decided upon before Gandhi's emergence as the Indian leader. Under Gandhi relations with the intelligence community have been much better. She has been unhappy with the quality of intelligence, though, and the waters have been disturbed more than once by high-level purges. In May 1980, for example, the

---

[47] A good account of Lusaka, Lok Dal and the Desai-Vajpayee relationship can be found in Tharoor, pp. 397-403.

[48] Personal interview, September 8, 14, 1982; "Indiracracy" is a takeoff on *Le Monde's* "Giscardocracy;" see S. Nihal Singh, "The New Indiracracy," *India Today*, April 1-15, 1980, p. 10.

number two and three ranked officers in the RAW were told to leave, and other dismissals considered.[49] There are two reasons for Gandhi's post-Janata purges of top RAW leadership: (a) intelligence products were of insufficient quality; (b) factionalism within the RAW has created an embarassing and insecure situation, and she has assessed that the purges will, by removing the elements responsible for the factionalism, eliminate the fragmentalization. It has not had this effect, though, a fact for which MEA should be grateful. So long as the intelligence community's effectiveness is impaired, Gandhi will be forced to depend to a greater extent on MEA for external intelligence.

The overseas Indians initiative was taken by foreign minister Vajpayee under Janata, and is only being continued by the Gandhi government.[50] The present shift in manpower in the Indian missions abroad seems to be Gandhi's idea, though the decision-making behind the policy is unclear.[51] In the summer of 1980 the decision was made to cut the staffing of many missions abroad, and to increase the size of certain missions, particularly in the Indian Ocean area, which had been neglected. As Table 10.1 shows, there was strong representation in the South Asian region, and in Europe, but most of the Eastern hemispheric developing nations were underrepresented. Five missions, namely India House in London, Washington, Moscow, Kathmandu and Rangoon, would be cut twenty to forty percent (the strong representation in these missions was the result of both

---

[49] Asoka Raina, "Touching a RAW Nerve," p. 29.

[50] The "White Paper on Punjab Agitation" underscores the new Indian awareness of the potential political impact of the overseas communities, by claiming support of the Khalistan movement by Sikhs in the U.S., Canada, Britain and West Germany:

> A sensitive border state with a dynamic record of agricultural and industrial development would be an obvious target for subversion. In this context the activities of groups based abroad acquire a special significance.

Christian Science Monitor, July 11, 1984, p. 2.

[51] The first open mention of the manpower shift came in the fall of 1980. Prabhu Chawla, "Trimming the Fat," *India Today*, September 1-15, 1980, p. 89.

vestigial British imperial priorities and acute Indian elite fascination with the superpowers). This was a test for both Gandhi and the bureaucracy.

> Predictably, pressure is mounting on the ministry to abort the programme. Those who have been ordered to move are pulling all kinds of strings to stay put. Some of them are related to senior bureaucrats and politicians and have established business contacts abroad. Moreover, the Indian Foreign Service Association (B) has reportedly objected to the cuts because their members are likely to be the worst sufferers.
> Though the ministry has been able to brave all kinds of pressures and pulls so far, officials fear political pressures might compel them to opt eventually for a less ambitious plan.

The redirection of Indian attention toward the South is one of the most important Indian projects undertaken, and yet is resisted by much of the bureaucracy.

There are, however, exceptions to the resistance. The about-face toward the South has had the active support of Economic Division, that having been the focus of their work for many years. The conclusion of much of UN Division's efforts in New York has been a UN increasingly South-South oriented, a strong voice in support of nations with strong Southern priorities. The territorial divisions (staffed by the more conservative IFS[A]) are not supporting the manpower policy, however. Officials in the America and Europe Divisions have never felt that their staffing was sufficient; a move to cut staff strength would not be greeted by appreciation of the foresight shown by Gandhi's restructuring of South-South priorities.

We should give credit for the new Southern restructuring of manpower to the Gandhi government, but it is still not a good track record. Gandhi has been very resourceful in the use of the existing machinery, but she has not exercised much bureaucratic creativity. The problem is not systemic, as her strength is such that any initiatives she might take would have no trouble gaining acceptance. The relatively few new bureaucratic ideas of the Gandhi leadership seem to have resulted from the belief that the organization of foreign policy does not greatly affect the execution of foreign policy. Because she does not take much interest in the details of the bureaucracy, Gandhi is dependent upon the bureaucrats. When going abroad she usually has at least one senior MEA official with her; when she has not she has occasionally "slipped up" in the broad tasks of diplomacy. When she made her 1982 trip to the island of Mauritius, a left-leaning Indian satellite nation, no MEA officials came with her. It was during that trip that she made the comment that the next non-aligned conference in 1983 would be held in New Delhi. This had, in fact, not been decided, and the announcement caused embarassment in New Delhi and had to be quickly "explained" by MEA spokesmen (as noted, this was a common task of MEA spokesmen during the late Nehru period as well). It would seem that despite the difference in breadth and the nature of responsibilities, a close relationship is required and exists between the bureaucracy and political leadership. This is a way of avoiding the weakening combination of the political sin of not paying sufficient attention to the fine print, and the bureaucratic vice of assuming that "we can do it all by ourselves."

Table 10.1: Regional Indian diplomatic representation

	missions	employees	expenditure[a]
Europe	29	728	31.33
America, Canada	20	384	16.64
Middle East, Gulf area	18	483	16.22
Africa	25	469	12.99
South East Asia, Far East	20	454	13.55
neighboring countries	16	854	9.27

[a] as percentage of total
source: Prabhu Chawla, "Trimming the Fat," *India Today*, September 1-15, 1980, p. 89.

Table 10.2: A chronology of political control

1947-56 strong political control.

1956-62 Nehru somewhat shaken by death of close colleagues; political hold weakened. Numerous crises and policy set-backs: Hungary, Tibet, Sino-Indian war. Krishna Menon rises in authority, only to enfeeble position further.

1962-64 Nehru demoralized by China defeat; very weak and uncertain political control over bureaucracy.

1964-66 Shastri exercises some administrative reforms and thereby improves political control over bureaucracy.

1966-69 Early Gandhi period; position in relation to bureaucracy unclear.

1969-71 Rapid growth of Gandhi's power after defeat of Kamaraj Syndicate.

1971-75 Political control strong after Bangladesh intervention; stable plateau.

1975-77 After short period of instability, Gandhi's position restabilized through Emergency. Pluralism dissolved; puppet bureaucratic leadership installed.

1977-79 Political control during Janata highly variable; bureaucratic pluralism during this period more highly developed than at any other time in modern Indian history.

1979-82 Political control comparable to 1971-75 though relatively less stable.

Appendix A:
Neo-Reductionism

The operation of the international system through the formulation and implementation of foreign policies, through national actions and in all single events and event nexuses, can be thoroughly understood through the application of a five-leveled qualitative methodology.[1] All foreign policies, actions and events (single or nexus) are the result of laws peculiar to or social or individual actions expressed through one of these five circles of involvement:

- LEVEL-ONE. *Idiosyncratic or psychological*. The behavior of powerful (relative to the international system) individuals when not bound by larger

---

[1] A policy is a large set of decisions, related through some independent organizing principle. A foreign policy is a policy which will affect members of other national groupings if implemented. An international policy is an external policy of an international organization. Transnational actors, being based in some nation, can have a foreign policy. In my interpretation, any individual can have a policy, so that speaking of "U.S. foreign policy," for example, is impermissable. The level depth of the policy must be specified, and competing policies specified if they exist.

An action is the implementation of a decision, but does not imply or preclude a policy. An event is a complex nexus of actions.

Foreign policy analysis, because it allows the study of phenomena the result only of policy, ignores the large class of individual decisions not the part of any policy. Crisis environments, as one example, often give rise to such decision-making. International relations theory, then, differs from foreign policy analysis chiefly in the inclusion of non-policy decisions.

groups. This typically refers to top national executives, but also includes the leadership of many transnational corporations (and other transnational bodies, such as the CIA), leaders of some international organizations, and a diverse group of other individuals who, while ordinarily of insignificant influence, at the proper place and time, and under selected conditions, experience a multiplication of influence while retaining independence of action. Such may include battlefield commanders, terrorists, assassins, private citizens acting as unofficial diplomatic envoys, etc.

Because at this level individuals are not bound by larger groups or systems, analysis must utilize psychological and perceptual methodologies.

- LEVEL-TWO. *Decision-making or small-group*. This circle typically includes Cabinet-level individuals, individuals of ministerial rank, and all individuals capable of behaving as level-one influences within national, international and transnational bodies, or alone, but only in lateral cooperation with others of like status. Because lateral cooperation tends, for combinatorial reasons, to be impractical for groups of larger than twelve to twenty people, decision-making tends to follow small-group principles. Allison refers to this analysis as the governmental politics "model."[2]

  Game theory, sociological methodologies and all research into small-group dynamics tend to have utility here.

- LEVEL-THREE. *Bureaucratic*. This circle includes all individuals capable of exerting level-one influence but only as members of large organizations, typically government bureaux. Such organizations may be, again, national, transnational or international in orientation, but must be organizations as defined by Downs.[3]

  Organizational research, such as that pioneered by Herbert Simons, is most helpful in research into effects at this level. Richard Snyder's decision-making system of analysis incorporates primarily level-two and level-three factors.[4]

---

[2] Graham T. Allison, *Essence of Decision* (Boston: Little, Brown and Company, 1971), p. 144.

[3] Anthony Downs, *Inside Bureaucracy* (Boston: Little, Brown and Company, 1967), pp. 24-25.

[4] Richard C. Snyder, H.W. Bruck, and Burton Sapin,

- LEVEL-FOUR. *National or domestic*. This includes all foreign policies, actions or events involving the unorganized national or international public or its generalized organs. All macroeconomic phenomena originate here, as well as electoral and classical political phenomena. Because of its internal complexity, it is very difficult to trace causality with domestic conditionality, so correlative studies predominate.[5]

  Macroeconomic and mainstream political methodology are employed at this level.

- LEVEL-FIVE. *Systemic*. This final circle includes all of humanity. Because of the proliferation of different methods of government, different means of production and distribution, different means of communication (e.g., language), unequal resource endowments, and other compounding effects, humanity is presently organized into nation-states with, ideally, complete individual freedom of internal collective action. The geographic, demographic, economic, technological and other conditions of this system impose, however, a large universe of behavioral boundaries upon the nation-states. Therefore, while no supranational government exists, objective conditions make certain events impossible, certain policies irrational, and the consequences of certain actions easily predictable. Some transnational and international organizations are affected similarly by the system. Until supranational government exists, the system is entirely passive and restrictive. Once limited regional supranational political-economic communities become active, we will have to develop a sixth subsystemic level-of-analysis, since a subset of the system will then assume active character.

  Study of this system falls within the classical realist school of international relations, the neo-realist school, most peace research, and political economy/interdependence research. It is most easily subject to a general systems analysis approach, such as is offered by Morton Kaplan.[6]

---

editors, *Foreign Policy Decision-Making* (New York: Free Press, 1962)

[5] J. David Singer, "The Level of Analysis Problem in International Relations," in Klaus Knorr, Sidney Verba, editors, *The International System: Theoretical Essays* (Princeton: Princeton University Press, 1961), p. 82.

This is a jurisdictional methodology, in that it breaks complex international problems down into sub-problems by analytic jurisdiction, solved by existing methodologies. Only such an approach can produce can produce a unified theory in international relations research, by acknowledging the large number of epistemological discontinuities inherent in the research. I see no way to resolve large-scale human behavior into parallels to the micro- and macroeconomic methodological divisions, neither is it possible to topically separate the political from the economic, as we can do if we are concerned only with a type of relationship. Instead of defining itself as the study of a type of relationship, as does economics and political science, international relations research is defined as the study of a system of relationships expressed at a given scale of human interaction. International relations research is concerned with all problems relating to very large-scale human behavior, which has been the source of difficulties in unifying theory and resolving disputes between schools. We cannot have a unified methodology as the other social sciences do, since we are studying system and not relata categories. We can however develop a jurisdictional methodology which unfailingly breaks down international policy, action or event for analysis by other existing topically defined methodologies.

This methodology, which the author calls neo-reductionism, has limitations. One important stimulus in the international system lies in natural phenomena. Droughts, earthquakes, communications-disruptive solar flares, all have effects and are unpredicted by any methodology invoked by neo-reductionism. Neo-reductionism allows only for the prediction of phenomena at least the partial effect of human behavior. Models developed within the neo-reductionist methodological framework must treat natural phenomena as exogenous variables. Second, neo-reductionism only predicts behavioral ranges, which might be quite wide. Individuals immersed in any of the five circles of involvement are subject to a great many conscious and unconscious behavioral boundaries, which may nevertheless be insufficient to facilitate prediction and explanation to an acceptable degree.

Neo-reductionism's level-factoring is nothing new; it is simply an appellation and systematization of an old international relations problem.[7] Acknowledgement

---

[6] Morton Kaplan, *Systems and Process in International Politics* (New York: Krieger, 1975)

[7] See Singer also, Robert Jervis, *Perception and*

that there is more than one level of analysis necessitates this systematization, due to the failure of the older "schools" to acknowledge the problems posed by theoretical discontinuity in a science of scale. It differs from a mind-of-man or reductionist methodology in that it proposes the existence of theoretical discontinuities with the variation in system extent (number of people potentially involved), as practical theoretical discontinuities exist in the movement from the study of atoms to molecules, to gaseous systems. Phenomena are seen as the result entirely of the operation of objective processes within objectively-determined parameters, rather than as the interaction of subjective entity and objective conditions (the realist, neorealist schools) or of subjective entity and subjective conditions (the idealist or liberal schools).

Neo-reductionism, as a jurisdictional methodology, might appear at first glance the dependent creature of the established level-methodologies. But its implicit guidance has inspired methodology research which in the context purely of the level-specific methodology might have been supernumerary (for example, foreign policy bureaucratic research; works on military sociology; psychological aggression research in the study of international terrorism; crisis decision-making research). Jurisdictional methodology is a very different type of epistemological organizer, but hardly

---

Misperception in International Politics (Princeton, N.J.: Princeton University Press, 1976), pp. 15-17; Robert Axelrod, ed., *Structure of Decision: The Cognitive Maps of Political Elites* (Princeton, N.J.: Princeton University Press, 1976), pp. 27-29; Arnold Wolfers, *Discord and Collaboration: Essays on International Politics* (Baltimore, Md.: Johns Hopkins University Press, 1962), pp. 2-24; John Spanier, *Games Nations Play: Analyzing International Politics* (New York: Praeger, c. 1972), pp. 9-50; Kenneth Waltz, *Man, the State, and War* (New York: Columbia University Press, 1959); James Rosenau, "Pre-Theories and Theories of Foreign Policy," in R. Barry Farrell, ed., *Approaches to Comparative and International Politics* (Evanston, Ill.: Northwestern University Press, 1966), pp. 29-92.

Some indication that certain behavioral variables are invariant over a group size class but are a partial function of group size (giving rise to "theoretical discontinuities") can be found in Maurice A. East, "Size and Foreign Policy Behavior: a Test of Two Models," *World Politics* 25, 4, pp. 556-76, and R.C. Ziller, "Group Size: a Determinant of the Quality and Stability of Group Decisions," *Sociometry*, 1957, 20, pp. 165-73.

just a rationalization of a discipline, due to its manifestly active effect upon component methodologies.

The introduction of the neo-reductionist methodology into this study qualifies my use of organizational analysis as a jurisdictionally limited though indispensable international relations research tool. Neo-reductionism underscores its importance and defensibility within a certain class of phenomena, and justifies the introduction of level-one and level-two factors into what is fundamentally a level-three analysis.[8]

---

[8] A book by the author fully detailing the technique of neo-reductionist analysis of international phenomena is forthcoming.

Abbreviations

ARC	Aviation Research Centre
BHU	Benares Hindu University
Cab Sec	Cabinet Secretariat
CBI	Central Bureau of Investigations
CCB	Central Cypher Bureau
CCPA	Cabinet Committee on Political Affairs
DAI	Directorate of Air Intelligence
DG(S)	Directorate-General of Security
DMI	Directorate of Military Intelligence
DNI	Directorate of Naval Intelligence
ED	Economic Division
EPO	External Publicity Organization
FPSC	Federal Public Service Commission
F and P	Foreign and Political Department
HD	Historical Division
IAS	Indian Administrative Service
I and B	Information and Broadcasting
IB	Intelligence Bureau
ICCR	Indian Council for Cultural Relations
ICS	Indian Civil Service
IDSA	Institute for Defence Studies and Analyses
IFS	Indian Foreign Service (generally A branch)
IFS(B)	Indian Foreign Service (B branch)
IG	interdepartmental group
INA	Indian National Army
IPS	Indian Political Service
ISI	Information Service of India
ITEC	Indian Technical and Economic Cooperation
JIC	Joint Intelligence Committee
JIO	Joint Intelligence Organization
JNU	Jawaharlal Nehru University
L and T	Legal and Treaties
MEA	Ministry of External Affairs
NEFA	North-East Frontier Agency
NSC	National Security Council
NWFP	North-West Frontier Province
OCS	Overseas Communication Service
Office	Office of the Prime Minister
O and M	Organization and Methods

PCV . . . . Passport, Emigration and Consular
PMPPS . . .prime minister's principal private secretary
PMS . . . . .Prime Minister's Secretariat
PPRC. . . . . . . .Policy Planning and Review Committee
PPRD. . . . . Policy Planning and Review Division
R and I . . . . .Recording and Indexing
RAW . . . . .Research and Analysis Wing
SCST. . . . . Scheduled Castes/Scheduled Tribes
S/PC. . . . . Planning and Coordination Staff
SSB . . . . Special Services Bureau
UN. .United Nations
UPSC. . . . . Union Public Service Commission
XP. . . . . .External Publicity

Bibliography

FOREIGN POLICY BUREAUCRATIC ANALYSIS

Albinski, Henry Stephen, *Australian External Policy under Labor* (St. Lucia: University of Queensland Press, 1977)

Alger, C.F., S.J. Brams, "Patterns of Representation in National Capitals and Intergovernmental Organizations," *World Politics* 19 (4), July 1967, pp. 646-663.

Allison, Graham T., "Conceptual Models and the Cuban Missile Crisis," *American Political Science Review* 63 (3), September 1969, pp. 689-718.

_____, *Essence of Decision: Explaining the Cuban Missile Crisis* (Boston: Little, Brown and Company, 1971)

_____, Morton Halperin, "Bureaucratic Politics: A Paradigm and some Policy Implications," *World Politics* 24, 1972, pp. 40-79 (supplement). Also in R. Tanter, R. Ullman, eds., *Theory and Policy in International Relations* (Princeton, N.J.: Princeton University Press, 1972).

_____, Peter Szanton, *Remaking Foreign Policy* (New York: Basic Books, 1976)

Alsop, Stewart, "Let the Poor Old Foreign Service Alone," *Saturday Evening Post*, 240 (5), March 11, 1967, pp. 14-15.

Altshuler, Alan A., ed., *The Politics of the Federal Bureaucracy* (New York: Dodd, Mead and Co., 1968)

American Foreign Service Association, Committee on Career Principles, *Toward a Modern Diplomacy* (Washington, D.C.: American Foreign Service Association, 1968)

Andersen, Walter K., "India in 1982: Domestic Challenges and Foreign Policy Successes," *Asian Survey* 23 (2), February 1983, pp. 111-122.

Argyris, Chris, *Some Causes of Organizational Ineffectiveness within the Department of State* (Washington, D.C.: Department of State, 1967)

Arkes, Hadley, *Bureaucracy, the Marshall Plan, and the National Interest* (Princeton, N.J.: Princeton University Press, 1972)

Armstrong, J.D., *Revolutionary Diplomacy* (Berkeley: University of California Press, 1977)

Art, Robert J., "Bureaucratic Politics and American Foreign Policy: A Critique," *Policy Sciences* 4 (4), December 1973, pp. 467-490.

Ashton-Gwatkin, Frank T.A., *The British Foreign Service: A Discussion of the Development and Function of the British Foreign Service* (Syracuse, N.Y.: Syracuse University Press, 1950)

Attwood, William, "The Labyrinth in Foggy Bottom," *Atlantic Monthly*, 219 (2), February 1967, pp. 45-50.

Atwater, Elton, "The American Foreign Service since 1939," *American Journal of International Law* 4, January 1947, pp. 73-102.

Australia, Government of, Department of Foreign Affairs, "Australia's Property Overseas," *Australian Foreign Affairs Record* 45 (7), 1974, 426-430.

_____, "Organization of the Department of Foreign Affairs," *Current Notes on International Affairs* 43 (3), 1972, pp. 93-98.

_____, R.G. Neale, ed., *Documents on Australian Foreign Policy 1937-1949, 1, 1937-1938*(Canberra: Australian Government Publishing Service, 1975)

Australia, Government of, Department of Foreign Affairs, A.P. Renouf, "Foreign Affairs and the Challenge of the Seventies," *Australian Foreign Affairs Record* 45 (1), pp. 24-31.

Aziz, Raja Ehsan, "India's Change in Government and Foreign Policy," *Strategic Studies* (Islamabad), October-December 1977, pp. 37-49.

Bacchus, William I., "Diplomacy for the 70s: An Afterview and Appraisal," *American Political Science Review* 68 (2), June 1974, pp. 736-748.

_____, *Inside the Legislative Process: The Passage of the Foreign Service Act of 1980* (Boulder, Colo.: Westview Press, 1983)

_____, "Obstacles to Reform in Foreign Affairs: The Case of NSAM 341," *Orbis* 18, 1974, pp. 266-276.

Bailey, Sydney D., *The Secretariat of the United Nations* (New York: Praeger, 1962)

Ball, Desmond J., "The Blind Men and the Elephant: A Critique of Bureaucratic Politics Theory," *Australian Outlook* 28 (1), April 1974, pp. 71-92.

Bandyopadhyaya, Jayantanuja, *The Making of India's Foreign Policy*, two editions (New Delhi: Allied Publishers, 1971, 1979)

Banerji, Arun Kumar, "Role of the Diplomat in the Decision-Making Process: Some Case Studies," *India Quarterly*, April-June 1979, pp. 207-222.

Banks, Michael, "Professionalism in the Conduct of Foreign Policy," *International Affairs*, October 1968, pp. 720-734.

Barnes, William, John Heath Morgan, for Historical Office, Bureau of Public Affairs, Department of State, *The Foreign Service of the United States: Origins, Development, and Functions* (Washington, D.C.: U.S. Government Printing Office, 1961)

Barnett, Vincent M., Jr., "Changing Problems of United States Representation Abroad," *Public Administration Review* 17 (1), Winter 1957, pp. 20-30.

_____, ed., for the American Assembly, *The Representation of the United States Abroad* (New York: Praeger, 1965)

B'Crat, A.N. (pseudonym), "The Uncivil Masters who Rule India," *Perspective* 1, September 1977, pp. 20-33.

Beaglehole, T.H., "From Rulers to Servants: The I.C.S. and the British Demission of Power in India," *Modern Asian Studies* 11 (2), 1977, pp. 237-255.

Beaulac, Willard Leon, *Career Diplomat: A Career in the Foreign Service of the United States* (New York: Macmillan, 1964)

Beichman, Arnold, *The Other State Department: The United States Mission to the United Nations, its Role in the Making of Foreign Policy* (New York: Basic Books, 1967)

Beloff, Max, *New Dimensions in Foreign Policy: a Study in British Administrative Experience, 1947-59* (London: Allen and Unwin, 1961)

Benner, Jeffrey, *The Indian Foreign Policy Bureaucracy* (Boulder, Colo.: Westview, 1985)

_____, *Structure of Decision: The Indian Foreign Policy Bureaucracy* (New Delhi: South Asian Publishers, 1984)

Berkes, Ross N., Mohinder S. Bedi, *The Diplomacy of India: Indian Foreign Policy in the United Nations* (Stanford, Cal.: Stanford University Press, 1958)

Betts, R.K., "Analysis, War and Decision: Why Intelligence Failures are Inevitable," *World Politics* 31, 1978, pp. 61-89.

Bhambhri, C.P., *Bureaucracy and Politics in India* (New Delhi: Vikas, 1971)

_____, "The Indian Foreign Service," *Journal of Administration Overseas* 7, 1968, pp. 528-537.

Bishop, Donald Gordon, *The Administration of British Foreign Relations* (Westport: Greenwood, 1974)

Boardman, Robert, A.J.R. Groom, eds., *The Management of Britain's External Relations* (London: Macmillan, 1973)

Bobb, Dilip, "Operation Gangotri," *India Today*, March 31, 1982, pp. 82-93.

_____, "School for Scandal," *India Today*, May 15, 1982, p. 101.

Bobrow, Davis B., Steve Chan, John A. Kringen, *Understanding Foreign Policy Decisions* (New York: Free Press, 1979)

Bolaraman, K., "The Indian Press and Foreign Policy," *Journal of International Affairs* 10, 1956, pp. 178-184.

Brecher, Michael, *The Foreign Policy System of Israel* (New Haven: Yale University Press, 1972)

_____, B. Steinberg, J. Stein, "A Framework for Research on Foreign Policy Behavior," *Journal of Conflict Resolution* 13 (1), March 1969, pp. 75-101.

The Brookings Institution, International Studies Group, for the Bureau of the Budget, Executive Office of the President, *Administration of Foreign Affairs and*

Overseas Operations (Washington, D.C.: Government Printing Office, June 1951)

Brown, Newman and Martin, *Administration of United States Foreign Affairs: A Bibliography* (University Park, Penn.: Pennsylvania State University Libraries, n.d.)

Buck, Phillip Wallenstein, Martin Travis, eds., *Control of Foreign Relations in Modern Nations* (New York: W.W. Norton and Company, 1957)

Bundy, Harvey H., "The Organization of the Government for the Conduct of Foreign Affairs," in *U.S. Commission on the Organization of the Executive Branch of the Government* (New York: McGraw-Hill, 1949), pp. 71-72; also, (Westport, Conn.: Greenwood Press, 1970).

Caldwell, D., "Bureaucratic Foreign Policy-Making," *American Behavioral Scientist* 21, 1977, pp. 87-110.

Campbell, John Franklin, *The Foreign Affairs Fudge Factory* (New York: Basic Books, 1971)

_____, "What is to be Done?--Gigantism in Washington," *Foreign Affairs*, 49 (1), October 1970, pp. 81-99.

Campbell-Johnson, Alan, *Mission with Mountbatten* (London: R. Hale, 1951)

Cardozo, Michael H., *Diplomats in International Cooperation: Stepchildren of the Foreign Service* (Ithaca, N.Y.: Cornell University Press, 1962)

Casey, Baron Richard Gardiner, edited by T.B. Millar, *Australian Foreign Minister: the Diaries of R.G. Casey, 1951-60* (London: Collins, 1972)

Cecil, Algernon, *British Foreign Secretaries, 1807-1916: Studies in Personality and Policy* (London: G. Bell, 1927)

Chagla, M.C., *Roses in December* (Bombay: Bharatiya Vidya Bhavan, 1973)

Chandran, Ramesh, "A Formidable Choice," *India Today*, March 31, 1982, pp. 102-104.

Chase, E.P., "The War and the English Constitution," *American Political Science Review* 36 (1), 1942, 86-98.

Chawla, Sudershan, *The Foreign Relations of India* (Encino, Cal.: Dickenson Publishing, 1976)

Childs, James Rives, *American Foreign Service* (New York: Henry Holt and Co., 1948)

Clapham, C., *Foreign Policy Making in Developing States* (New York: Saxon House, Atheneum Publishers, 1978)

Clark, G., "The Australian Department of Foreign Affairs: What's Wrong with our Diplomats," *Australian Quarterly* 47 (2), pp. 21-35.

Clarke, Sir Richard William Barnes, *New Trends in Government* (London: H.M.S.O., 1971)

Cohen, Stephen P., "The Security Policymaking Process in India," in F.B. Horton, III, A.C. Rogerson, E.L. Warner, III, eds., *Comparative Defense Analysis* (Baltimore, Md.: Johns Hopkins University Press, 1974), pp. 156-168.

Collins, H., "The 'Coombs Report': Bureaucracy, Diplomacy and Australian Foreign Policy," *Australian Outlook* 30 (3), pp. 387-413.

Committee on Foreign Affairs Personnel, *Personnel for the New Diplomacy, Report* (New York: Carnegie Endowment for International Peace, 1962)

Craig, Gordon Alexander, Felix Gilbert, eds., *The Diplomats, 1919-39* (Princeton, N.J.: Princeton University Press, 1953)

Crocker, W.R., "Foreign Policy for Australia," *Institute of Public Administration Review* 25 (4), 1971, pp. 91-96.

Crossman, R.H.S., "Correspondence: Diplomatic Appointments," *New Statesman and Nation* 31, February 23, 1946, 137-138.

"Crying or Spying," *India Today*, August 16-30, 1980, p. 39.

"Cutting the 'Cab. Sec.' to Size," *India Today*, June 1-15, 1977, p. 16.

Cuttino, George Peddy, *English Diplomatic Administration, 1259-1339*, 2d edition (Oxford: Clarendon Press, 1971).

Das, Durga, *India from Curzon to Nehru and After* (New York: John Day, 1970)

Datt, Indra, *Diplomatic Service in Free India* (Lahore: Indian Book Company, 1947)

Davies, Ernest, "The Foreign and Commonwealth Services," *Political Quarterly* 25 (4), October-December 1954, pp. 347-360.

Davies, J.P., Jr., *Foreign and other Affairs* (New York: Norton, 1963)

Davis, D.H., *How the Bureaucracy makes Foreign Policy: An Exchange Analysis* (Lexington, Ky.: Lexington Books, 1972)

Dayal, H., "The Organization of Diplomatic and Consular Services, with Special Reference to India," *India Quarterly* 12 (3), July-September 1956, pp. 268-282.

DeConde, Alexander, *The American Secretary of State, An Interpretation* (New York: Praeger, 1962)

DeSantis, Hugh S., *The Diplomacy of Silence: The American Foreign Service, the Soviet Union, and the Cold War, 1933-1947* (Chicago: University of Chicago Press, 1983)

Destler, I.M., "Can One Man Do?", *Foreign Policy*, Winter 1971-72, pp. 28-40.

_____, *Presidents, Bureaucrats, and Foreign Policy: The Politics of Organizational Reform* (Princeton, N.J.: Princeton University Press, 1974)

_____, Leslie H. Gelb, Anthony Lake, *Our Own Worst Enemy: The Unmaking of American Foreign Policy* (New York: Simon and Schuster, 1984)

The Diplomatic Year Book (New York: Funk and Wagnall, 1950-   )

Dogan, Mattei, ed., *The Mandarins of Western Europe: The Political Role of Top Civil Servants* (New York: Halstead Press, 1975)

Dutt, Subimal, *With Nehru in the Foreign Office* (Calcutta: Minerva Publications, 1977)

East, Maurice A., "Coordinating Foreign Policy: The Changing Role of the Norwegian Foreign Ministry," paper presented to the 1983 International Studies Association meeting, photocopied.

_____, Lauri Karvonen, Bengt Sundelius, Jan Braathu, *Coordinating Foreign Policy in the Nordic Countries* (Oslo: Norwegian Institute of International Affairs, 1982)

Eayrs, James George, *The Art of the Possible: Government and Foreign Policy in Canada* (Toronto: University of Toronto Press, 1961)

_____, *Diplomacy and its Discontents* (Toronto: University of Toronto Press, 1971)

Edwards, P.G., *Prime Ministers and Diplomats: The Making of Australian Foreign Policy, 1901-1949* (Melbourne, New York: Oxford University Press in association with the Australian Institute of International Affairs, 1983)

Elder, Robert Ellsworth, *The Information Machine: The USIA and American Foreign Policy* (Syracuse, N.Y.: University of Syracuse Press, 1968)

_____, *The Policy Machine: The Department of State and American Foreign Policy* (Syracuse, N.Y.: Syracuse University Press, 1960)

Elliot, William Yandell, chairman, Woodrow Wilson Foundation, Study Group, 1950-1951, *United States Foreign Policy: Its Organization and Control* (New York: Columbia University Press, 1952)

Eran, Oded, *Mezhdunarodniki, An Assessment of Professional Expertise in the Making of Soviet Foreign Policy* (Ramat Gan, Israel: Turtledove, 1979)

Etzold, Thomas, *The Conduct of American Foreign Relations: The Other Side of Diplomacy* (New York: New Viewpoints, 1977)

Fisher, Glen H., *American Communication in a Global Society* (Norwood: Ablex Publishing Corp., 1979)

_____, "The Foreign Service Officer," *The Annals of the American Academy of Political and Social Science* 368, November 1966, pp. 71-82.

Forgac, Albert T., *New Diplomacy and the United Nations* (New York: Pageant Press, 1965)

Frankel, Charles, *High on Foggy Bottom*: *An Outsider's Inside View of the Government* (New York: Harper and Row, 1968)

Galbraith, John Kenneth, *Ambassador's Journal*: *A Personal Account of the Kennedy Years* (Boston: Houghton Mifflin, 1969)

Gamarekian, Barbara, "Homecoming for New Indian Envoy," *New York Times,* March 20, 1984, p. 12.

Gaur, Dharmendra, "Rs. 22 to Write a Letter," *Sunday,* October 2, 1977.

George, Alexander L., "American Policy-Making and the North Korean Aggression," *World Politics* 7 (2), January 1955, pp. 209-232.

_____, "The Case for Multiple Advocacy in Making Foreign Policy," *American Political Science Review* 66 (3), September 1972, pp. 751-795.

_____, *Presidential Decisionmaking in Foreign Policy*: *The Effective Use of Information and Advice* (Boulder, Colo.: Westview, 1980)

_____, et al., *Towards a More Soundly Based Foreign Policy*: *Making Better Use of Information,* vol. II, Appendix D (Washington, D.C.: U.S. Government Printing Office, 1975)

Ghosh, Partha S., Rajaram Panda, "Domestic Support for Mrs. Gandhi's Afghan Policy: The Soviet Factor in Indian Politics," *Asian Survey* 23 (3), March 1983, pp. 261-279.

Gillespie, John V., Dina A. Zinnes, eds., *Mathematical Systems in International Relations Research* (New York: Praeger, 1977)

Gold, H., "Foreign Policy Decision-Making and the Environment: The Claims of Snyder, Brecher and the Sprouts," *International Studies Quarterly* 22, 1978, pp. 545-568.

Gosses, Frans, *The Management of British Foreign Policy before the First World War, Especially During the Period 1880-1914* (Leiden: A.W. Sijthoffs, 1948)

Graebner, Norman A., ed., *An Uncertain Tradition*: *American Secretaries of State in the Twentieth Century* (New York: McGraw-Hill, 1961)

Greenwood, Gordon, Norman Harper, eds., *Australia in World Affairs 1961-65* (Melbourne: Cheshire, 1968)

Gudevia, Y.D., *War and Peace in Nagaland* (Dehra Dun: Palit and Palit, 1975)

Halperin, Morton H., *Bureaucratic Politics and Foreign Policy* (Washington, D.C.: The Brookings Institution, 1974)

_____, "The Decision to Deploy the ABM: Bureaucratic and Domestic Politics in the Johnson Administration," *World Politics* 25, 1972, pp. 62-95.

_____, "Why Bureaucrats Play Games," *Foreign Policy* (2), Spring 1971, pp. 70-113.

_____, Arnold Kanter, ed., *Readings in American Foreign Policy: A Bureaucratic Perspective* (Boston: Little, Brown and Co., 1973)

Hammond, Paul Y., "Foreign Policy-Making and Administrative Politics," *World Politics* 17, July, 1965, pp. 656-671.

_____, "A Functional Analysis of Defense Department Decision-Making in the McNamara Administration," *American Political Science Review* 62, 1968, pp. 57-69.

_____, "The National Security Council as a Device for Interdepartmental Coordination," *American Political Science Review* 54, 1960, pp. 899-910.

Hardgrave, Robert L., Jr., *India under Pressure* (Boulder, Colo.: Westview Press, 1984)

Harr, John Ensor, *The Anatomy of the Foreign Service: A Statistical Profile,* Foreign Affairs Personnel Study no. 4 (New York: Carnegie Endowment for International Peace, 1965)

_____, "Key Administrative Problems of the United States Information Agency," unpublished Master's Thesis (Chicago: Department of Political Science, The University of Chicago, 1961).

_____, *The Professional Diplomat* (Princeton, N.J.: Princeton University Press, 1969)

Havilan, Henry Field, ed., *The Formulation and Administration of United States Foreign Policy* (Washington, D.C.: The Brookings Institution, 1960)

Hawker, G., "The Coombs Report and Freedom of Information: Some Questions about Administration," *Rupert* 4, 1976, pp. 6-8.

Heimsath, C.H., Surjit Mansingh, *A Diplomatic History of Modern India* (Calcutta: Allied Publishers, 1971)

Higgins, Rosalyn, *The Administration of United Kingdom Foreign Policy through the United Nations* (New York: Maxwell School of Citizenship and Public Affairs, Syracuse University, 1966)

Hill, C., "Theories of Foreign Policy Making for the Developing Countries," in C. Clapham, ed., *Foreign Policy Making in Developing States* (New York: Saxon House, Atheneum Publishers, 1978)

Hilsman, Roger, "The Foreign Policy Consensus: Making an Interim Research Report," *Journal of Conflict Resolution,* 3 (4), December 1959, pp. 361-382.

_____, *The Politics of Policy Making in Defense and Foreign Affairs* (New York: Harper and Row, 1971)

Hoffmann, Stanley, *Gulliver's Troubles: or, the Setting of American Foreign Policy* (New York: McGraw Hill [for the Council on Foreign Relations], 1968)

Hogben, W. Murray, "An Imperial Dilemma: the Reluctant Indianization of the Indian Political Service," *Modern Asian Studies* 15 (4), 1981, pp. 751-769.

_____, "The Foreign and Political Department of India, 1876 to 1919; a Study in Imperial Careers and Attitudes," unpublished PhD. dissertation (Toronto: University of Toronto, 1973).

Holbrooke, Richard, "The Machine that Fails," *Foreign Policy* (1), Winter 1970-71, pp. 65-77.

Holsti, Ole R., "The 1914 Case," in John E. Mueller, ed., *Approaches to Measurement in International Relations: A Non-Evangelical Study* (New York: Appleton-Century-Crofts, 1969)

Hoopes, Townsend, "The Fight for the President's Mind," *Atlantic Monthly,* October 1969, pp. 97-114.

Horton, F.B., III, A.C. Rogerson, E.L. Warner, III, eds., *Comparative Defense Analysis* (Baltimore, Md.: Johns Hopkins University Press, 1974)

Howard, Nigel, "A Computer System for Foreign Policy Decision-Making," *Journal of Peace Science* 1 (1), Autumn 1973, pp. 61-68.

Huntington, Samuel P., "Interservice Competition and the Political Roles of the Armed Services," *American Political Science Review* 55, 1961, pp. 40-52.

_____, *The Common Defense: Strategic Programs in National Politics* (New York: Columbia University Press, 1961)

Ilchman, Warren Frederick, *Professional Diplomacy in the United States, 1779-1939: a Study in Administrative History* (Chicago: University of Chicago Press, 1961)

India, Government of, Standing Committee for Scientific and Technical Terminology, Ministry of Education, *Administrative Glossary: English-Hindi* (New Delhi: Government of India, 1965)

_____, Hindi Directorate, *List of Technical Terms in Hindi: Diplomacy*, two volumes (New Delhi: Government of India, 1962)

India, Government of, Ministry of External Affairs, *Annual Report* (New Delhi: Government of India, 1947-)

_____, External Publicity Division, *Economic and Technical Cooperation among Developing Countries: India's Views and Contributions* (New Delhi: Government of India, 1982)

_____, Protocol Division, *Protocol Handbook* (New Delhi: Government of India, 1972)

_____, *Supplement to the Protocol Handbook* (New Delhi: Government of India, 1974)

_____, *Supplement to the Protocol Handbook* (New Delhi: Government of India, 1976)

Indian Institute of Public Administration, *The Organization of the Government of India* (New Delhi: Somaiya Publications, 1971)

Ingram, Edward, "Family and Faction in the Great Game in Asia: The Struggle over the Persian Mission, 1828-1835," *Middle Eastern Studies*, July 1981, pp. 291-309.

_____, "Preview of the Great Game in Asia--IV: British Agents in the Near East in the War of the Second Coalition, 1798-1801," *Middle Eastern Studies,* January 1974, pp. 15-35.

Jan, George P., "The Ministry of Foreign Affairs in China since the Cultural Revolution," *Asian Survey* 17 (6), June 1977, pp. 513-529.

Johnson, Edgar Augustus Jerome, ed., *The Dimensions of Diplomacy* (Baltimore, Md.: The Johns Hopkins University Press, 1964)

Johnson, Richard Abraham, *The Administration of United States Foreign Policy* (Austin: University of Texas Press, 1971)

Jordan, Amos A., Jr., ed., *Issues of National Security in the 1970s* (New York: Praeger, 1967)

Joshi, Chand, "Out in the RAW," *India Today,* April 1-15, 1977, pp. 29-30.

Kapur, Ashok, *India's Nuclear Option: Atomic Diplomacy and Decision Making* (New York: Praeger Publishers, 1976)

Kato, Masakatsu, "A Model of U.S. Foreign Aid Allocation: An Application of a Decision-Making Scheme," in John E. Mueller, ed., *Approaches to Measurement in International Relations: A Non-Evangelical Study* (New York: Appleton-Century-Crofts, 1969)

Kaul, B.M., *Confrontation with Pakistan* (New Delhi: Vikas, 1971)

Kaul, Triloki Nath, *Diplomacy in Peace and War: Recollections and Reflections* (New Delhi: Vikas, 1979)

_____, *The Kissinger Years: Indo-American Relations* (New Delhi: Arnold-Heinemann, 1980)

_____, *Reminiscences, Discreet and Indiscreet* (New Delhi: Lancers Publishers, 1982)

Kegley, Charles W., Jr., Pat McGowan, *The Political Economy of Foreign Policy Behavior* (Beverly Hills: Sage Publications, 1981)

Kellerman, B., "Allison Redux: Three More Decision-Making Models," *Polity* 15, pp. 351-367.

Kennan, George F., "America's Administrative Response to its World Problems," *Daedalus* 87, Spring 1958

Kennedy, Aubrey L., "Reorganization of the Foreign Service," *Quarterly Review,* (566), October 1945, pp. 397-413.

Khanna, K.C., "Bugs that Bedevil the IB and RAW," *Illustrated Weekly of India,* May 23-29, 1982, pp. 23, 26, 29.

Krasner, Stephen D., "Are Bureaucracies Important? (Or Allison Wonderland)" *Foreign Policy* (7), Summer 1972, pp. 159-179.

Krishnamurty, G.V.G., *Modern Diplomacy: Dialectics and Dimensions* (New Delhi: Sagar Publications, 1980)

Langford, Richard V., *British Foreign Policy--its Formulation in Recent Years* (Washington, D.C.: Public Affairs Press, 1942)

Leacacos, John P., *Fires in the In-Basket: The ABC's of the State Department* (Westport, Conn.: Greenwood Press, 1977)

Levi, Werner, "Foreign Policy: the Shastri Era," in K.P. Misra, ed., *Studies in Indian Foreign Policy* (New Delhi: Vikas, 1969), pp. 185-194.

Lockhart, Sir Robert H. Bruce, *British Agent* (New York: G.P. Putnam's Sons, 1933)

London, Kurt, *How Foreign Policy is Made,* 2d edition (Princeton, N.J.: Van Nostrand Co., Inc., 1950)

_____, *The Making of Foreign Policy, East and West* (Philadelphia: Lippincott, 1965)

Louis and Chawla, "More Continuity than Change," *India Today,* January 16-31, 1979, p. 39.

Macmahon, Arthur Whittier, *Administration and Foreign Policy* (Urbana, IL: University of Illinois, Institute of Government and Public Affairs, 1956)

_____, *Administration in Foreign Affairs* (Tuscaloosa: University of Alabama Press, 1953)

Macomber, William B., Jr., *Diplomacy for the 70's: A Program of Management Reform for the Department of State* (Washington, D.C.: Government Printing Office, 1970)

Mann, Dean E., *The Assistant Secretaries* (Washington, D.C.: The Brookings Institution, 1965)

Marchetti, Victor, John D. Marks, *The CIA and the Cult of Intelligence* (New York: Dell, 1974)

Marett, Sir Robert Hugh Kirk, *Through the Back Door: an Inside View of Britain's Overseas Information Services* (Oxford: Pergamon Press, 1968)

Mathai, M.O., *My Days with Nehru* (New Delhi: Vikas, 1979)

_____, *Reminiscences of the Nehru Age* (New Delhi: Vikas, 1978)

Matthews, Russell L., ed., *Intergovernmental Relations in Australia* (Sydney: Angus and Robertson, 1974)

Maxwell, Neville, *India's China War* (New York: Doubleday and Company, 1972)

McAneny, George, *The Organization of the Modern Consular Service: How other Countries do it* (New York: The National Civil Service Reform League, 1899[?])

McCamy, James L., *The Administration of American Foreign Affairs* (New York: Alfred Knopf, 1950)

_____, *Conduct of the New Diplomacy* (New York: Harper and Row, 1964)

_____, Alessandro Corradini, "The People of the State Department and Foreign Service," *American Political Science Review* 48, December 1954, pp. 1067-1082.

McCarthy, G., ed., *Foreign Policy for Australia: Choices for the Seventies* (Sydney: Angus and Robertson, 1973)

McDermott, Geoffrey, *The New Diplomacy and its Apparatus* (London: Plume Press, 1973)

McGarvey, Patrick J., "The Culture of Bureaucracy: DIA Intelligence to Please," *Washington Monthly*, 2 (5), July 1970, pp. 68-75.

_____, "State Department Answers Fulbright: 'We Can Clean Our Own House,'" *Government Executive*, May, 1970.

McKittrick, Nathaniel, "Diplomatic Logjam: Esprit without a Corps at the Department of State," *New Republic,* March 27, 1965, pp. 8-11.

Mediansky, F.A., "New Challenges in Foreign Policy Administration: A Comment," *Australian Outlook* 28 (3), pp. 313-317.

Mehra, P.L., "The Institutions at Work During the 1962 Conflict," in *Foreign Policy Making in India and China,* Centre d'Etude du Sud-Est Asiatique et de l'Extreme-Orient, Proceedings, 3d Working Session (1968)

Mennis, Bernard, *American Foreign Policy Officials: Who They Are and What They Believe Regarding International Politics* (Columbus, Ohio: Ohio State University Press, 1971)

Menon, K.P.S., *Changing Patterns of Diplomacy* (Bombay: Bharatiya Vidya Bhavan, 1977)

_____, *The Flying Troika* (Oxford: Oxford University Press, 1963)

_____, *Many Worlds: An Autobiography* (Bombay: Oxford University Press, 1965)

Menon, Vapal Pangunni, *The Transfer of Power in India* (Princeton, N.J.: Princeton University Press, 1957)

Migdal, J.S., "Internal Structure and External Behavior: Explaining Foreign Policies of Third World States," *International Relations* 4, 1974, pp. 510-526.

Millar, Thomas Bruce, *Australia's Foreign Policy* (Sydney: Angus and Robertson, 1968)

_____, *Australia in Peace and War: External Relations 1788-1977* (New York: St. Martin's Press, 1978)

_____, *Foreign Policy: Some Australian Reflections* (Melbourne: Melbourne University Press, 1972)

Misra, K.P., *Foreign Policy and its Planning* (New Delhi: Asia Publishing, 1970)

_____, "Foreign Policy Planning Efforts in India," *Institute for Defence Studies and Analyses Journal,* April 1970, pp. 379-406.

_____, "Foreign Policy Planning: Some Suggestions," *International Studies* 17, 1978, pp. 827-833.

Modelski, G., "The World's Foreign Ministers: A Political Elite," *Journal of Conflict Resolution* 17, 1970, pp. 135-175.

Moe, Ronald C., *The Hoover Commissions Revisited* (Boulder, Colo.: Westview Press, 1982)

Mukherji, Girija Kanta, *Diplomacy: Theory and History,* updated multivolume set (New Delhi: Trimurti Publications, 1973-   )

Mukkerjee, Dilip, "Descision *(sic)* Making for Defence," *Institute for Defence Studies and Analyses Journal,* January 1969, pp. 103-109.

Mueller, John E., ed., *Approaches to Measurement in International Relations: A Non-Evangelical Study* (New York: Appleton-Century-Crofts, 1969)

Mullik, B.N., *My Years with Nehru: 1948-1964* New Delhi: Allied, 1972)

Murphy, Thomas P., Donald E. Nuechterlein, Ronald J. Stupak, *Inside the Bureaucracy: The View from the Assistant Secretary's Desk* (Boulder, Colo.: Westview Press, 1979)

Nair, N. Parameswaran, *The Administration of Foreign Affairs in India with Comparative Reference to Britain,* unpublished dissertation (New Delhi: School of International Studies, 1963)

Nanda, B.R., ed., *Indian Foreign Policy: The Nehru Years* (New Delhi: Vikas, 1976)

Nayar, Kuldip, *Between the Lines* (Bombay: Allied Publishers, 1969)

_____, *India: the Critical Years* (New Delhi: Vikas, 1973)

Nicolson, Honourable Harold George, *Diplomacy* (New York: Oxford University Press, 1968), 3d edition

Nightingale, R.T., *Personnel of the British Foreign Office and Diplomatic Service, 1851-1929* (London: Fabian Tract no. 232, n.d.)

Noorani, A.G., *Aspects of India's Foreign Policy* (Bombay: Jaico Publishing House, 1970)

Norton, Henry Kittredge, "Foreign Office Organization," *Annals of the American Academy of Political and Social Science* 143, Supplement, May 1929, pp. 1-83.

O'Leary, Michael K., William D. Coplin, *Quantitative Techniques in Foreign Policy Analysis and Forecasting* (New York: Praeger, 1975)

Ostrom, Charles W., Jr., "Evaluating Alternative Foreign Policy Decision Making Models: An Empirical Test Between an Arms Race Model and an Organizational Politics Model," *Journal of Conflict Resolution* 21, June 1977, pp. 235-266.

Oudes, Bruce J., "The Great Wind Machine," *Washington Monthly*, June 1970, pp. 30-39.

Panikkar, Kavalam Madhava, *An Autobiography* (Madras: Oxford University Press, 1977)

_____, *In Two Chinas: Memoirs of a Diplomat* (London: Allen and Unwin, 1955)

_____, *The Principles and Practice of Diplomacy* (Bombay: Asia Publishing, 1957)

Parks, Wallace Judson, *United States Administration of its International Economic Affairs* (Baltimore: The Johns Hopkins University Press, 1951)

"People of the Week: Panikkar, India's Ambassador to Peiping," *United States News* (New York) 30 (30), January 26, 1951.

Pillai, chairman, *Report of the Committee on the Indian Foreign Service* (New Delhi: Government of India, 1966)

Plischke, Elmer, *Conduct of American Diplomacy*, 3d edition (Princeton, N.J.: Princeton University Press, 1967)

_____, ed., *Modern Diplomacy: The Art and the Artisans* (Washington, D.C.: American Enterprise Institute, 1979)

Pradhan, Bishwa, *Foreign Policy and Diplomacy* (New Delhi: publisher unknown, 1964)

Price, Don Krasner, *The New Dimension of Diplomacy* (New York: Woodrow Wilson Foundation, 1951)

_____, ed., *The Secretary of State* (Englewood Cliffs, N.J.: Prentice-Hall, Inc., 1960)

Pruitt, Dean G., *Problem Solving in the Department of State*, The Social Science Foundation and Department of International Relations Monograph Series in World Affairs, No. 2 (Denver, Colo.: University of Denver, 1964-1965)

Putnam, Robert, "The Political Attitudes of Senior Civil Servants in Western Europe: A Preliminary Report," *British Journal of Political Science* 3 (3), July 1973, pp. 257-290.

Painter, Martin, Bernard Carey, *Politics Between Departments: The Fragmentation of Executive Control in Australian Government* (St. Lucia, Queensland: University of Queensland Press, 1979)

Raina, Asoka, *Inside RAW* (New Delhi: Vikas, 1981)

_____, "Return of the Veterans," *India Today*, September 1-15, 1981, p. 28.

_____, "Touching a RAW Nerve," *India Today*, June 16-30, 1980.

Ransom, Harry Howe, *The Intelligence Establishment* (Cambridge, Mass.: Harvard University Press, 1970)

Rao, P.V.R., "Government Machinery for the Evolution of National Defence Policy and the Higher Direction of War," *Institute for Defence Studies and Analyses Journal*, July 1968, pp. 1-11.

Rattinger, Hans, "Armaments, Detente, and Bureaucracy: The Case of the Arms Race in Europe," *Journal of Conflict Resolution* 19 (4), December 1975, pp. 571-595.

Regala, Roberto, *The Trends in Modern Diplomatic Practice* (Milan, New York: A. Giuffré, Oceana Publications, 1959)

_____, *World Order and Diplomacy* (Quezon City: Central Lawbook Pub. Co., 1969)

Reid, Escott, *Envoy to Nehru* (New Delhi: Oxford University Press, 1981)

Renouf, A.P., "New Challenges in Foreign Policy Administration," *Australian Outlook* 28 (2), 1974, pp. 109-117.

Rourke, Francis E., *Bureaucracy and Foreign Policy* (Baltimore, Md.: Johns Hopkins University Press, 1972)

Sapin, Burton M., *The Making of United States Foreign Policy* (New York: Praeger, 1966)

Satakopan, R., "The Indian Political Service," *The New Review* 13, 1941, p. 138.

Satow, Sir Ernest Mason, *Satow's Guide to Diplomatic Practice,* 5th edition (London: Longmans, Green, 1979)

Schlesinger, James R., "Quantitative Analysis and National Security," *World Politics* 15 (2), January, 1963, pp. 295-315.

Scott, Andrew MacKay, "The Department of State: Formal Organization and Informal Culture," *International Studies Quarterly* 13 (1), March 1969, pp. 1-18.

_____, "Environmental Change and Organizational Adaptation: The Problem of the State Department," *International Studies Quarterly* 14 (1), March 1970, pp. 85-94.

H. Dawson, eds., *Readings in the Making of American Foreign Policy* (New York: Macmillan, 1965)

Selby, Sir Walford, "The Foreign Office," *Nineteenth Century and After* 137 (821), July 1945, pp. 3-13.

Sen Gupta, Bhabani, Dilip Bobb, "In Danger of Isolation," *India Today,* December 16-30, p. 57.

Seton, M., *Panditji: A Portrait of Jawaharlal Nehru* (London: Dennis Dobson, 1967)

Sharma, Rajat, "Civil War in Intelligence Bureau," *Onlooker,* June 30, 1982, pp. 8-13.

Shlaim, Avi, Peter Jones, Keith Sainsbury, *British Foreign Secretaries since 1945* (North Pomfret, Vermont: David and Charles, 1977)

Simpson, Smith, *Anatomy of the State Department* (Boston: Houghton Mifflin, 1967)

_____, "The Rusk Enigma: Who Runs the State Department?" *The Nation,* March 6, 1967, pp. 294-298.

Singer, David J., ed., *Human Behavior and International Politics* (Chicago: Rand McNally, 1965)

Singh, Indu Prakash, *Diplometry* (Bombay: Somaiya Publications, 1970)

Singh, Sushil Chandra, *Rajanaya ke Siddhanta* (hindi) (New Delhi: Sagar, Sathi, 1965)

Smith, S., "Allison and the Cuban Missile Crisis: A Review of the Bureaucratic Politics Model of Foreign Policy Decision-Making," *Millenium* 9, 1980, pp. 21-40.

Smith, Terence, "Foreign Policy: Decision Power Ebbing at the State Department," *New York Times,* January 18, 1971, p. 1.

Snyder, Richard Carlton, Edgar S. Furniss, Jr., *American Foreign Policy: Formulation, Principles and Programs* (New York: Rinehart and Co., 1954)

Steiner, Zara S., *The Foreign Office and Foreign Policy, -16* (London: Cambridge University Press, 1969)

_____, *Present Problems of the Foreign Service* (Princeton, N.J.: Center for International Studies, 1961)

_____, *The State Department and the Foreign Service: The Wriston Report--Four Years Later,* Center for International Studies Policy Memorandum No. 16 (Princeton, N.J.: Center for International Studies, 1958)

Strang, Lord William, et al., *The Foreign Office* (London: George Allen and Unwin, Ltd., 1955)

Stuart, Graham Henry, *The Department of State: A History of its Organization, Procedure and Personnel* (New York: Macmillan, 1949)

Subrahamanyam, K., "Decision Making in Defence," *Institute for Defence Studies and Analyses Journal* 2, 1970, pp. 424-444.

_____, "Foreign Policy Planning in India," *Foreign Affairs Reports,* January 1975, pp. 1-12.

_____, "Nehru's Concept of Indian Defence," *Institute for Defence Studies and Analyses Journal*, October 1972, pp. 196-211.

_____, "Security and Elite Attitudes," *Niti*, October-December 1970, pp. 9-12.

Sundelius, Bengt, ed., *Foreign Policies of Northern Europe* (Boulder, Colo.: Westview Press, 1982)

Tanter, R., R. Ullman, eds., *Theory and Policy in International Relations* (Princeton, N.J.: Princeton University Press, 1972)

Tharoor, Shashi, *Reasons of State* (New Delhi: Vikas, 1982)

Thomson, Charles Alexander, Walter H.C. Laves, *Cultural Relations and U.S. Foreign Policy* (Bloomington, Ind.: Indiana University Press, 1963)

Tilley, Sir John Anthony Cecil, Stephen Gaselee, *The Foreign Office* (London: G.P. Putnam's Sons, 1933)

Truman, David B., ed., for the American Assembly, *The Congress and America's Future* (Englewood Cliffs, N.J.: Prentice-Hall, 1965)

Tyabji, Budrud-din, "Foreign Policy Set-Up: The Case for a Review Commission," *Statesman*, March 6, 1976.

U.S. Commission on the Organization of the Executive Branch of the Government (Westport, Conn.: Greenwood Press, 1970)

U.S. Commission on the Organization of the Government for the Conduct of Foreign Policy (Washington, D.C.: Government Printing Office, 1975) (Murphy Commission)

U.S. Department of State, *Towards a Stronger Foreign Service: Report of the Secretary of State's Committee on Personnel* Department of State Publication 5458 (Washington, D.C.: Government Printing Office, June, 1954)

U.S. Senate, Committee on Foreign Relations, Subcommittee on Foreign Service, *Establishment of a Single Foreign Affairs Personnel System and Nominations of USIA Officers as Foreign Service Officers* (Washington, D.C.: Government Printing Office, 1966)

U.S. Senate, Committee on Government Operations, Subcommittee on National Policy Machinery, *Organizing for National Security,* vol. 3 (Washington, D.C.: Government Printing Office, 1964)

Vagts, Alfred, *The Military Attaché* (Princeton, N.J.: Princeton University Press, 1967)

Van Doorn, Jacques, "The Officer Corps: A Fusion of Profession and Organization," *British Journal of Sociology* 6, 1965, pp. 262-282.

Venkatewaran, A.L., *Defence Organization in India* (New Delhi: Ministry of Information and Broadcasting, 1967)

Vertzberger, Yaacov, "Bureaucratic-Organizational Politics and Information Processing in a Developing State," *International Studies Quarterly* 28 (1), March 1984, pp. 69-95.

_____, "India's Border Crisis with China, 1962," *Jerusalem Journal of International Relations* 3, Winter-Spring 1978, pp. 117-142.

_____, *Misperceptions in Foreign Policymaking: The Sino-Indian Conflict 1949-1962* (Boulder, Colo.: Westview, 1984)

Villard, Henry Serrano, *Affairs at State* (New York: Thomas Y. Crowell, 1965)

Vital, David, *The Inequality of States: A Study of the Small Power in International Relations* (Oxford: Clarendon Press, 1967)

_____, *The Making of British Foreign Policy* (New York: Praeger, 1968)

Wakil, S. Pavez, ed., *South Asia: Perspectives and Dimensions* (CASAS, 1977)

Walker, Lannon, "Our Foreign Affairs Machinery: Time for an Overhaul," *Foreign Affairs,* 47 (2), January 1969

Wallace, William, *The Foreign Policy Process in Britain* (London: George Allen and Unwin, 1977)

Walther, Regis, *Orientations and Behavioral Styles of Foreign Service Officers,* Carnegie Endowment for International Peace, Foreign Affairs Personnel Study

No. 5 (New York: Carnegie Endowment for International Peace, 1965)

Warbey, William, "Correspondence: Diplomatic Appointments," *New Statesman and Nation* 31, February 23, 1946, p. 137.

Ward, Sir Adolphus W., G.P. Gooch, eds., *Cambridge History of British Foreign Policy*, three volumes (Cambridge: Cambridge University Press, 1922-1923)

Warden, David B., *On the Origin, Nature, Progress and Influence of Consular Establishments* (Paris:Smith,1813)

Warwick, Donald P., "Performance Appraisal and Promotions in the Foreign Service," *Foreign Service Journal*, 47 (7), July 1970, pp. 37-41, 45.

_____, *A Theory of Public Bureaucracy: Politics, Personality and Organization in the State Department* (Cambridge, Mass.: Harvard University Press, 1975)

Watt, Sir Alan Stewart, *Australian Diplomat: Memoirs of Sir Alan Watt* (Sydney: Angus and Robertson, 1972)

Watt, Donald Cameron, *Personalities and Powers: Studies in the Formulation of British Foreign Policy in the Twentieth Century* (London: Longmans, 1963)

Werking, Richard Hume, *The Master Architects: Building the United States Foreign Service, 1890-1913* (Lexington: University of Kentucky Press, 1977)

Williams, Murat W., "Life in the Diplomatic Service, 1939-62," *American Oxonian*, 49 (1), July 1962, pp. 189-193.

Willson, Francis Michael Glenn, *Administrators in Action* British Case Studies (Toronto: University of Toronto Press, 1961)

The World Diplomatic Directory and World Diplomatic Biography (London: 1950-   )

Wriston, Henry M., "Young Men and the Foreign Service," *Foreign Affairs* 33, October 1954, pp. 28-42.

Zinnes, Dina A., John Gillespie, eds., *Mathematical Models of International Relations* (New York: Praeger, 1976)

ORGANIZATIONAL THEORY

Albrow, M., *Bureaucracy* (London: Pall Mall, 1970)

Alexander, Christopher, *Notes on the Synthesis of Form* (Cambridge, Mass.: Harvard University Press, 1964)

Anderson, T.R., S. Warkov, "Organizational Size and Functional Complexity," *American Sociological Review* 26, 1961, pp. 23-28.

Argyris, Chris, *Interpersonal Competence and Organizational Effectiveness* (Homewood, Il.: Irwin, 1962)

Arora, S.K., Harold D. Lasswell, *Political Communication* (New York: Holt, Rinehart and Winston, 1969)

Ashby, W.R., *Design for a Brain*, 2d edition (New York: Wiley, 1960)

Athans, Michael, Peter Falb, *Optimal Control* (New York: McGraw-Hill, 1966)

Bales, R.F., *Interaction Process Analysis* (Cambridge: Addison-Wesley, 1951)

Barker, Ernest, *The Development of the Public Services in Europe* (New York: Oxford University Press, 1944)

Barnard, C.I., *Organization and Management: Selected Papers* (Cambridge, Mass.: Harvard University Press, 1948)

Barnlund, D.C., C. Harland, "Propinquity and Prestige as Determinants of Communication Networks," *Sociometry* 26, 1963, pp. 467-479.

Bavelas, A., "Communication Patterns in Task-Oriented Groups," *Journal of the Acoustical Society of America* 22, 1950, pp. 725-730.

Becker, S., Jean Carroll, "Ordinal Position and Conformity," *Journal of Abnormal Social Psychology* 65, 1962, pp. 129-131.

Bendix, R., "Bureaucracy," in D.L. Sills, ed., *International Encyclopedia of the Social Sciences*, (New York: Macmillan and Free Press, 1968)

Bennis, W.G., "Leadership Theory and Administrative Behavior," *Administrative Science Quarterly* 4, 1959, pp. 259-301.

Benson, C.S., "Internal Administrative Organization," *Public Administration Review* 1 (5), Autumn 1941, pp. 472-484.

Berelson, Bernard, *Content Analysis in Communications Research* (Glencoe, Ill.: Free Press, 1952)

Bishir, John W., Donald W. Drewes, *Mathematics in the Behavioral and Social Sciences* (New York: Harcourt, Brace and World, Inc., 1970)

Blau, P.M., "Formal Organization: Dimensions of Analysis," *American Journal of Sociology* 63, 1957, pp. 58-69.

_____, *The Dynamics of Bureaucracy*, revised edition (Chicago: University of Chicago Press, 1963)

_____, "The Hierarchy of Authority in Organizations," *American Journal of Sociology* 73, 1968, pp. 453-467.

_____, "Patterns of Interaction Among a Group of Officials in a Government Agency," *Human Relations* 7, 1954, pp. 337-348.

_____, "Structural Effects," *American Sociological Review* 25, 1960, pp. 178-193.

_____, R.A. Schoenherr, *The Structure of Organizations* (New York: Basic Books, 1971)

_____, W.R. Scott, *Formal Organizations: a Comparative Approach* (San Francisco: Chandler, 1962)

Blum, F.H., "Getting Individuals to give Information to the Outsider," *Journal of Social Issues* 8 (3), 1952, pp. 35-42.

Bonini, Charles P., *Simulation of Information and Decision Systems in the Firm* (Englewood Cliffs, N.J.: Prentice-Hall, 1964)

Braibanti, Ralph, et al., *Asian Bureaucratic Systems Emergent from the British Imperial Tradition* (Durham, N.C.: Duke University Press, 1966)

_____, "The Civil Service of Pakistan: A Theoretical Analysis," *The South Atlantic Quarterly* 58 (2), 1959, pp. 258-304.

Bremer, Stuart A., *Simulated Worlds: A Computer Model of National Decision-Making* (Princeton, N.J.: Princeton University Press, 1977)

Brock, H.W., "The Problem of the Active Coordination of Hierarchical Division Systems," Massachusetts Institute of Technology, Alfred P. Sloan School of Management, photocopy, 1971.

Burns, T., "The Directions of Activity and Communication in a Departmental Executive Group," *Human Relations* 7, 1954, pp. 73-97.

Campbell, D.T., "Systematic Error on the Part of Human Links in Communication Systems," *Information and Control* 1, 1958, pp. 334-369.

Caplow, T., "Organizational Size," *Administrative Science Quarterly* 1, 1957, pp. 484-505.

Cattell, R.B., "New Concepts for Measuring Leadership, in Terms of Group Syntality," *Human Relations* 4, 1951, pp. 161-184.

Chapin, F.S., "The Optimal Size of Institutions: A Theory of the Large Group," *American Journal of Sociology* 62, 1957, pp. 449-460.

Charlesworth, J.C., ed., *Mathematics and the Social Sciences* (Philadelphia: American Academy of Political and Social Science, 1963)

Chase, William, ed., *Visual Information Processing* (New York: Academic Press, 1973)

Cherry, C., "On the Mathematics of Social Communications," *International Social Science Bulletin* 6, 1954, pp. 609-622.

Christie, L.S., "Organization and Information Handling in Task Groups," *Journal of the Operations Research Society of America* 2, 1954, pp. 188-196.

Clark, Peter B., James Q. Wilson, "Incentive Systems: A Theory of Organizations," *Administrative Science Quarterly* 6 (2), September 1961, pp. 129-166.

Cohen, A.R., "Upward Communication in Experimentally Created Hierarchies," *Human Relations* 11, 1958, pp. 41-53.

Coleman, James S., *Introduction to Mathematical Sociology* (New York: Free Press, 1964)

_____, "Relational Analysis: The Study of Social Structure with Survey Methods," *Human Organization* 17 (4), 1958-1959, pp. 28-36.

Cooper, W.W., H.J. Leavitt, M.W. Shelly, II, eds., *New Perspectives in Organization Research* (New York: Wiley, 1964)

Crozier, Michel, *The Bureaucratic Phenomenon: An Examination of Bureaucracy in Modern Organization and its Cultural Setting in France* (Chicago: University of Chicago Press, 1964)

_____, "Human Relations at the Management Level in a Bureaucratic System of Organization," *Human Organization* 20, 1964, pp. 51-64.

Crum, W.L., *The Age Structure of the Corporate System* (Berkeley, Cal.: University of California Press, 1953)

Cyert, Richard M., James G. March, *A Behavioral Theory of the Firm* (Englewood Cliffs, N.J.: Prentice-Hall, 1963)

Dalton, M., *Men who Manage* (New York: Wiley, 1959)

Davis, K., "A Method of Studying Communication Patterns in Organizations," *Personnel Psychology* 6, 1953, 301-312.

Delany, W., "The Development and Decline of Patrimonial and Bureaucratic Administrations," *Administrative Science Quarterly* 7, 1963, pp. 458-501.

_____, "Some Field Notes on the Problem of Access in Organizational Research," *Administrative Science Quarterly* 5, 1960, pp. 448-457.

Deutsch, Karl W., "On Communication Models in the Social Sciences," *Public Opinion Quarterly* 16, 1952, pp. 357-380.

_____, *The Nerves of Government: Models of Political Communication and Control* (New York: Free Press, 1963)

Donald, Marjorie N., *Some Concomitants of Varying Patterns of Communication in a Large Organization,* unpublished dissertation (Ann Arbor, Mich.: University of Michigan)

Downs, Anthony, *Inside Bureaucracy* (Boston: Little, Brown and Company, 1967)

Dwyer, James H., *Statistical Models for the Social and Behavioral Sciences* (New York: Oxford University Press, 1983)

Encarnation, Dennis J., "The Indian Central Bureaucracy: Responsive to whom?", *Asian Survey* 19 (11), November 1979, pp. 1126-1145.

Entwisle, Doris R., J. Walton, "Observations on the Span of Control," *Administrative Science Quarterly* 5, 1961, pp. 522-533.

Etzioni, Amitai, "Authority Structures and Organizational Effectiveness," *Administrative Science Quarterly* 4, 1959, pp. 43-67.

_____, *A Comparative Analysis of Complex Organizations,* revised and enlarged edition (New York: Free Press, 1975)

_____, ed., *Complex Organizations* (New York: Holt, Rinehart and Winston, 1961)

_____, ed., *Readings on Modern Organizations* (Englewood Cliffs, N.J.: Prentice-Hall, 1969)

_____, "Two Approaches to Organizational Analysis: A Critique and a Suggestion," *Administrative Science Quarterly* 5, 1960, pp. 257-278.

Fagen, R.R., "Some Contributions of Mathematical Reasoning to the Study of Politics," *American Political Science Review* 55, 1961, pp. 888-900.

Feld, M.D., "Information and Authority: The Structure of Military Organization," *American Sociological Review* 24, 1959, pp. 15-22.

Festinger, L., "Informal Social Communication," *Psychology Review* 57, 1950, pp. 271-282.

_____, D. Katz, eds., *Research Methods in the Behavioral Sciences* (New York: Dryden, 1953)

Fiorina, Morris P., "Formal Models in Political Science," *American Journal of Political Science* 19 (1), February 1975, pp. 133-159.

Flament, C., *Aplications of Graph Theory to Group Structure* (Englewood Cliffs, N.J.: Prentice-Hall, 1963)

Freeman, John R., "Granger Causality and the Times Series Analysis of Political Relationships," *American Journal of Political Science* 27 (2), May 1983, pp. 327-358.

Fulton, Lord, Chairman, *The Civil Service, Report of the Committee, 1966-68* (London: H.M.S.O., 1968)

Gaus, J.M., L.D. White, M.E. Dimock, eds., *The Frontiers of Public Administration* (Chicago: University of Chicago Press, 1936)

Golembiewski, R., "Authority as a Problem in Overlays," *Administrative Science Quarterly* 9, 1964, pp. 22-49.

Gore, William J., *Administrative Decision-Making* (New York: John Wiley and Sons, 1964)

Gross, E., "Some Functional Consequences of Primary Controls in Formal Work Organizations," *American Sociological Review* 18, 1953, pp. 368-373.

Grusky, O., "Administrative Succession in Formal Organizations," *Social Forces* 39, 1960, pp. 105-115.

Guetzkow, H., *Simulation in the Social Sciences* (Englewood Cliffs, N.J.: Prentice-Hall, 1962)

_____, H.A. Simon, "The Impact of Certain Communication Nets upon Organization and Performance in Task-Oriented Groups," *Management Science* 1, 1955, pp. 233-250.

Gulick, Luther Halsey, L. Urwick, et al., eds., *Papers on the Science of Administration* (New York: Institute of Public Administration, Columbia University, 1937)

Gullahorn, J.T., "Distance and Friendship as Factors in the Gross Interaction Matrix," *Sociometry* 15, 1952, pp. 123-134.

Gusfield, J.R., "The Problem of Generations in an Organizational Structure," *Social Forces* 35, 1957, pp. 323-330.

Gyr, J., "Analysis of Committee Member Behavior in Four Cultures," *Human Relations* 4, 1951, pp. 193-202.

Haire, M., ed., *Modern Organization Theory* (New York: Wiley, 1959)

Harary, F., I.C. Ross, "The Number of Complete Cycles in a Communication Network," *Journal of Social Psychology* 40, 1954, pp. 329-332.

_____, R.Z. Norman, *Graph Theory as a Mathematical Model in Social Science* (Ann Arbor, Mich.: University of Michigan, Institute for Social Research, 1953)

Harrah, D., *Communication: a Logical Model* (Cambridge, Mass.: Massachusetts Institute of Technology Press, 1963)

Harris, D.R., "The Flow-Line of Information, Intelligence, and Policy Inputs to National Security Decision-Making," (Arlington, Va.: CACI, Inc., photocopy, 1974)

Healey, J.H., "Coordination and Control of Executive Functions," *Personnel* 33, 1956, pp. 106-117.

Herbst, P.G., "Measurement of Behavior Structures by Means of Input-Output Data," *Human Relations* 10, 1957, pp. 335-346.

Herson, L.J.R., "China's Imperial Bureaucracy: its Direction and Control," *Public Administration Review* 17, 1957, pp. 44-53.

Heydebrand, W.V., R.E. Stauffer, "The Structure of Small Bureaucracies," *American Sociological Review* 31, 1966, pp. 179-191.

Hibbs, Douglas A., Jr., "Communication," *American Political Science Review* 73, March 1979, pp. 185-190.

Holden, Matthew, Jr., "Imperialism in Bureaucracy," *American Political Science Review* 60, pp. 943-951.

Holsti, Ole R., "An Adaptation of the 'General Inquirer' for the Systematic Analysis of Political Documents," *Behavioral Science* 9, October 1964, pp. 382-388.

Hurwicz, Leonid, "Centralization and Decentralization in Economic Systems: On the Concept and Possibility of Informational Decentralization," *American Economic Review, Papers and Proceedings* 59 (2), 1969, pp. 513-525.

Hyman, H., *Survey Design and Analysis* (Glencoe, Ill.: Free Press, 1955)

"It's Hard to Keep a Leak Secret," *Economist,* March 31, 1984, p. 56.

Jackson, J.M., "Reference Group Processes in a Formal Organization," *Sociometry* 22, 1959, pp. 307-327.

Jacobson, E., R. Kahn, F.C. Mann, Nancy Morse, "Research in Functioning Organizations," *Journal of Social Issues* 7 (3), pp. 64-71.

Jacobson, E., S. Seashore, "Communication Practices in Complex Organizations," *Journal of Social Issues* 7, 1951, pp. 28-40.

Jacobson, E., W.W. Charters, Jr., S. Lieberman, "The Use of the Role Concept in the Study of Complex Organizations," *Journal of Social Issues* 7, 1951, pp. 19-27.

Jansen, B. Douglass, "A System for Content Analysis by Computer of International Communications for Selected Categories of Action," *American Behavioral Scientist* 9, March 1966, pp. 28-32.

Karlsson, G., *Social Mechanisms* (Glencoe, Ill.: Free Press, 1958)

Katz, E., "The Two-Step Flow of Communication: An Up-to-Date Report on a Hypothesis," *Public Opinion Quarterly* 21, 1957, pp. 61-78.

Kelley, H.H., "Communication in Experimentally Created Hierarchies," *Human Relations* 4, 1951, pp. 39-56.

Kemeny, J.G., J.L. Snell, *Mathematical Models in the Social Sciences* (Boston: Ginn, 1962)

Khanasch, Robert N., *The Institutional Imperative* (New York: Charterhouse Books, 1973)

Kim, W.H., R.T. Chien, *Topological Analysis and Synthesis of Communication Networks* (New York: Columbia: University Press, 1962)

Knight, Kenneth E., Reuben R. McDaniel, Jr., *Organizations: An Information Systems Perspectives* (Belmont, Cal.: Wadsworth Publishing, 1979)

Krippendorff, Klaus, *Content Analysis: An Introduction to its Methodology* (Beverly Hills, Cal.: Sage Publications, 1980)

Krupp, Sherman, *Pattern in Organization Analysis: A Critical Examination* (New York: Chilton Company, 1961)

Lancaster, Joan C., "The Scope and Uses of the India Office Library and Records with Particular Reference to the Period 1600-1947," *Asian Affairs*, February 1978, pp. 31-43.

Landsberger, Henry A., "The Horizontal Dimension in Bureaucracy," *Administrative Science Quarterly* 6, 1961, pp. 299-332.

_____, "Interaction Process Analysis of Professional Behavior," *American Sociological Review* 20, 1955, pp. 566-575.

Latane, Henry A., David Mechanic, George Strauss, George B. Strother, *The Social Science of Organizations* (Englewood Cliffs, N.J.: Prentice-Hall Inc., 1963)

Lazarsfeld, P.F., ed., *Mathematical Thinking in the Social Sciences* (Glencoe, Ill.: Free Press, 1954)

Leavitt, H.J., "Small Groups in Large Organizations," *Journal of Business* 28, 1955, pp. 8-17.

_____, R. Mueller, "Some Effects of Feedback on Communication," *Human Relations* 4, 1951, pp. 401-410.

Lindblom, Charles E., *The Intelligence of Democracy* (Glencoe, Ill.: Free Press, 1965)

Litwak, Eugene, "Models of Bureaucracy that Permit Conflict," *American Journal of Sociology* 67, 1961, pp. 177-184.

_____, L.F. Hylton, "Interorganizational Analysis," *Administrative Science Quarterly* 6, 1962, pp. 395-420.

Luce, R.D., R.R. Bush, E. Galanter, eds., *Handbook of Mathematical Psychology*, vol. two (New York: Wiley, 1963)

Maier, N., L. Hoffman, J. Hooven, W. Read, "Superior-Subordinate Communications in Management," *American Management Res. Studies* 52, 1961.

March, J.G., "Group Autonomy and Internal Group Control," *Social Forces* 33, 1955, pp. 322-326.

_____, ed., *Handbook of Organizations* (Chicago: Rand McNally, 1965)

_____, "An Introduction to the Theory and Measurement of Influence," *American Political Science Review* 49, 1955, pp. 431-451.

_____, Herbert A. Simon, *Organizations* (New York: John Wiley and Sons, 1958)

McCormack, William, "Problems of American Scholars in India," *Asian Survey* 16 (11), November 1976, pp. 1064-1080.

Meier, R.L., "Communications Overload: Proposals from the Study of a University Library," *Administrative Science Quarterly* 7, 1963, pp. 521-544.

Merton, Robert K., ed., *Reader in Bureaucracy* (Glencoe, Ill.: Free Press, 1952)

Mesarovic, M.D., D. Macko, Y. Takahara, *Theory of Hierarchical, Multilevel Systems* (New York: Academic Press, 1971)

Meyer, M.W., *Bureaucratic Structure and Authority* (New York: Harper and Row, 1972)

Miller, J.G., "The Individual as an Information Processing System," in David J. Singer, ed., *Human Behavior and International Politics* (Chicago: Rand McNally, 1965), pp. 202-212.

Mills, C.W., *The Power Elite* (New York: Oxford University Press, 1956)

Mitchell, Robert E., "The Use of Content Analysis for Explanatory Studies," *Public Opinion Quarterly* 31, Summer 1967, pp. 230-241.

Mulder, M., "Communication Structure, Decision Structure, and Group Performance," *Sociometry* 23, 1960, pp. 1-14.

Nie, N., D.H. Bent, C.H. Hull, *SPSS: Statistical Package for the Social Sciences* (New York: McGraw-Hill, 1970)

North, Robert C., Ole R. Holsti, M. George Zaninovitch, Dina A. Zinnes, *Content Analysis: A Handbook with Applications for the Study of International Crisis* (Evanston, Ill.: Northwestern University Press, 1963)

Oeser, O.A., F. Harary, "A Mathematical Model for Structural Role Theory, II," *Human Relations* 17, 1964, pp. 3-17.

Ore, O., *Theory of Graphs* (Providence: American Mathematics Society, 1962)

Parsons, T., "Suggestions for a Sociological Approach to the Theory of Organizations," *Administrative Science Quarterly* 1, 1956, pp. 63-85, 225-239.

Patterson, C.P., "The President as Chief Administrator," *Journal of Politics* 11, 1949, pp. 218-235.

Peabody, Robert L., "Perceptions of Organizational Authority," *Administrative Science Quarterly* 6, 1962, pp. 463-482.

Perrow, Charles, "Analysis of Goals in Complex Organizations," *American Sociological Review* 12, 1961, pp. 854-866.

Poe, Donald T., "Command and Control Changeless--Yet Changing," *U.S. Naval Institute Proceedings* 100 (9), October 1974, pp. 22-31.

Pool, Ithiel de Sola, ed., *Trends in Content Analysis* (Urbana, Ill.: University of Illinois, 1959)

Pressman, Jeffrey L., Aaron B. Wildavsky, *Implementation* (Berkeley, Cal.: University of California, 1973)

Presthus, R., "Social Bases of Bureaucratic Organization," *Social Forces* 38, 1959, pp. 103-109.

Pugh, D.S., ed., *Organization Theory* (New York: Penguin Books, 1983)

Reissman, L., "A Study in Role Conceptions in Bureaucracy," *Social Forces* 27, 1949, pp. 305-310.

Rosenblatt, D., *A Note on Communication in Organizations: Air Force Project in Intra-Firm Analysis* (Pittsburgh, Penn.: Carnegie Institute of Technology, Graduate School of Industrial Administration, 1951)

Rourke, Francis E., "The Politics of Administrative Organization: A Case History," *Journal of Politics* 19, 1957, pp. 461-478.

Runkel, P.J., "Cognitive Similarity in Facilitating Communication," *Sociometry* 19, 1956, pp. 178-191.

Scott, W.R., "Field Work in a Formal Organization," *Human Organization* 22 (3), 1963, pp. 162-168.

Seidman, Harold, *Politics, Position, and Power: The Dynamics of Federal Organization* (New York: Oxford University Press, 1970)

Selvin, H.C., *The Effects of Leadership* (Glencoe, Ill.: Free Press, 1970)

Selznick, Philip, "An Approach to the Theory of Bureaucracy," *American Sociological Review* 8, 1943, p. 49.

Shannon, Claude E., Warren Weaver, *The Mathematical Theory of Communication* (Urbana, Ill.: University of Illinois Press, 1949)

Shaw, M.E., "A Comparison of Two Types of Leadership in Various Communication Nets," *Journal of Abnormal Social Psychology* 50, 1955, pp. 127-134.

Siegel, Sidney, *Nonparametric Statistics for the Behavioral Sciences* (New York: McGraw Hill, 1956)

Sigal, Leon V., "Bureaucratic Objectives and Tactical Use of the Press: Why Bureaucrats Leak," paper presented at the sixty-seventh Annual Meeting of the American Political Science Association, 1971.

Simmel, Georg, *Conflict* (Glencoe, Ill.: Free Press, 1955)

Simon, Herbert A., *Administrative Behavior*, 2d edition (New York: Macmillan, 1957)

_____, "On the Concept of Organizational Goal," *Administrative Science Quarterly* 9 (1), June, pp. 1-22.

_____, Donald W. Smithburg, Victor L. Thompson, *Public Administration* (New York: Alfred A. Knopf, 1950)

Simpson, R.L., "Vertical and Horizontal Communication in Formal Organizations," *Administrative Science Quarterly* 4, 1959, pp. 188-196.

Slovic, P., S. Lichtenstein, "Comparison of Bayesian and Regression Approaches to the Study of Information Processing in Judgment," *Organizational Behavior and Human Performance* 6, 1971, pp. 649-744.

Smith, C.G., A.S. Tannenbaum, *Administrative Control Structure* (Ann Arbor: University of Michigan, Survey Research Center, 1962), photocopy.

Starbuck, W.H., ed., *Organizational Growth and Development* (New York: Penguin Books, 1971)

Stephan, F.F., "The Relative Rate of Communication between Members of Small Groups," *American Sociological Review* 17, 1952, pp. 482-486.

Stogdill, R.M., C.L. Shartle, *Methods in the Study of Administrative Leadership* (Columbus, Ohio: Bureau of Business Research, Ohio State University, 1955)

Stone, Philip J., Dexter C. Dunphy, Marshall L. Smith, Daniel M. Ogilvie, et al., *The General Inquirer: A Computer Approach to Content Analysis* (Cambridge, Mass.: Massachusetts Institute of Technology Press, 1966)

Suleiman, Ezra N., *Politics, Power and Bureaucracy in France: The Administrative Elite* (Princeton, N.J.: Princeton University Press, 1974)

Suojanen, W.W., "The Span of Control--Fact or Fable," *Advanced Management* 20 (11), 1955, pp. 5-13.

Tannenbaum, A.S., "The Concept of Organizational Control," *Journal of Social Issues* 12, 1956, pp. 50-60.

_____, "An Event-Structure Approach to Social Powers and to the Problem of Power Comparability," *Behavioral Science* 7, 1962, pp. 315-331.

_____, B.S. Georgopolous, "The Distribution of Control in Formal Organizations," *Social Forces* 36, 1957, pp. 44-50.

Tannenbaum, A.S., R.L. Kahn, "Organizational Control Structure," *Human Relations* 10, 1957, pp. 127-140.

Tarski, Alfred, "Contributions to the Theory of Models, I," *Indigationes Mathematicae* 16 (4), 1954, pp. 572-588.

_____, "Contributions to the Theory of Models, II, III," *Indigationes Mathematicae* 17 (1), 1955, pp. 56-64.

_____, *Introduction to Logic and Methodology of Deductive Sciences*, 3d edition, revised (New York: Oxford University Press, 1965)

Terrien, F.W., D.L. Mills, "The Effect of Changing Size upon the Internal Structure of Organizations," *American Sociological Review* 20, 1955, pp. 11-13.

Thompson, J.D., "Authority and Power in 'Identical' Organizations," *American Journal of Sociology* 62, 1956, pp. 290-301.

_____, W.J. McEwen, "Organizational Goals and Environment: Goal-Setting as an Interaction Process," *American Sociological Review* 23, 1958, pp. 23-31.

Thompson, Victor A., *Modern Organization: A General Theory* (New York: Alfred A. Knopf, 1961)

_____, *Organizations as Systems* (Morristown, N.J.: General Learning Press, 1973)

Tullock, Gordon, *The Politics of Bureaucracy* (Washington, D.C.: Public Affairs Press, 1965)

Udy, S.H., Jr., "The Structure of Authority in Non-Industrial Production Organizations," *American Journal of Sociology* 64, 1959, pp. 582-584.

Urwick, L., *Leadership in the Twentieth Century* (New York: Pitman, 1957)

_____, "The Span of Control--Some Facts about the Fables," *Advanced Management* 21, 1956, pp. 5-15.

Vroom, V.H., ed., *Methods of Organizational Research* (Pittsburgh, Penn.: University of Pittsburgh Press, 1967)

Wallace, Schuyler C., *Federal Departmentalization: A Critique of Theories of Organization* (New York: Columbia University Press, 1941)

Weiss, E.C., "Relation of Personnel Statistics to Organizational Structure," *Personnel Psychology* 10, 1957, pp. 27-42.

Weiss, R.S., "A Structure-Function Approach to Organization," *Journal of Social Issues* 12, 1956, pp. 61-67.

_____, E. Jacobson, "A Method for the Analysis of the Structure of Complex Organizations," *American Sociological Review* 20, 1955, pp. 661-668.

Whitin, T.M., "On the Span of Central Direction," *Naval Research Logistics Quarterly* 1, 1954, pp. 25-35.

Whyte, W.F., "Interviewing for Organizational Research," *Human Organization* 12 (2), 1953, pp. 15-22.

Wilensky, H.L., *Organizational Intelligence: Knowledge and Policy in Government and Industry* (New York: Basic Books, 1967)

Wilkinson, Rupert, *Gentlemanly Power: British Leadership and the Public School Tradition, A Comparative Study in the Making of Rulers* (New York: Oxford University Press, 1964)

Wilson, Woodrow, "The Study of Administration," June 1887; reprinted in *Political Science Quarterly*, December 1941, pp. 481-506.

Windeknecht, Thomas, *General Dynamical Processes* (New York: Academic Press, 1971)

Winkler, Robert L., William L. Hays, *Statistics: Probability, Inference, and Decision*, 2d edition (New York: Holt, Rinehart and Winston, 1975)

Wu, Silas H.L., *Communication and Imperial Control in China* (Cambridge, Mass.: Harvard University Press, 1970)

Yovits, M.C., G.T. Jacobi, G.D. Goldstein, eds., *Self-- Organizing Systems* (Washington, D.C.: Spartan, 1962)

Zajonc, R.B. "The Process of Cognitive Tuning in Communication," *Journal of Abnormal Social Psychology* 61, 1960, pp. 159-167.

_____, D.M. Wolfe, *Cognitive Consequences of a Person's Position in a Formal Organization*, Technical Report no. 23 (Ann Arbor, Mich.: University of Michigan, Institute for Social Research, Research Center for Group Dynamics, 1963)

Ziegler, Bernard, "A Conceptual Basis for Modeling and Simulation," *International Journal of General Systems* 1 (2), 1974, pp. 213-228.

Zipf, G.K., "Some Determinants of the Circulation of Information," *American Journal of Psychology* 59, 1946, pp. 401-421.

DECISION MAKING

Abel, Elie, *The Missile Crisis* (New York: Bantam, 1966)

Allan, Pierre, *Crisis Bargaining and the Arms Race* (Cambridge, Mass.: Ballinger, 1983)

Polsby, N.W., R.A. Deutler, P.A. Smith, eds., *Politics and Social Life* (Boston: Houghton Mifflin, 1963)

Schilling, Warner R., "The H-Bomb Decision: How to Decide without Actually Choosing," *Political Science Quarterly* 76 (1), March 1961, pp. 24-46.

Snyder, Glenn H., Paul Diesing, *Conflict among Nations: Bargaining, Decision-Making and System Structure in International Crises* (Princeton, N.J.: Princeton University Press, 1977)

Snyder, Richard C., H.W. Bruck, Burton Sapin, eds., *Foreign Policy Decision-Making* (New York: Free Press, 1962)

Snyder, Richard C., Glenn D. Paige, "The United States Decision to Resist Aggression in Korea: The Application of an Analytical Scheme," *Administrative Science Quarterly* 3 (3), December 1958, pp. 341-378.

Snyder, Richard C., James A. Robinson, *National and International Decision-Making* (New York: Institute for International Order, Program of Research no.4, 1961)

Steinbruner, John D., *The Cybernetic Theory of Decision: New Dimensions of Political Analysis* (Princeton, N.J.: Princeton University Press, 1974)

Thrall, R.M., C.H. Coombs, R.L. Davis, *Decision Processes* (Wiley: New York, 1954)

POLICY AND BUREAU STRUCTURE: METHODOLOGY

Bobrow, Davis P., Robert P. Stoker, "Evaluation of Foreign Policy," in P. Terrence Hopmann, Dina A. Zinnes, J. David Singer, eds., *Cumulation in International Relations Research*, Monograph Series in World Affairs (Denver, Colo.: Graduate School of International Studies, University of Denver, 1981)

D'Amato, Anthony A., "Psychological Constructs in Foreign Policy Prediction," *Journal of Conflict Resolution* 11, September 1967, pp. 294-311.

DeRivera, Joseph, *The Psychological Dimension of Foreign Policy* (Columbus, Ohio: Merrill Publishing Co., 1968)

Dunk, W.E., "The Role of the Public Servant in Policy Formulation," *Public Administration* (Sydney), 20 (2), 1961, pp. 99-113.

Fisher, Glen H., *Public Diplomacy and the Behavioral Sciences* (Bloomington, Ind.: Indiana University Press, 1972)

Frankel, J., "Towards a Decision-Making Model in Foreign Policy," *Political Studies* 7 (1), 1959, pp. 1-11.

Freedman, L., "Logic, Politics and Foreign Policy Processes: A Critique of the Bureaucratic Politics Model," *International Affairs* 52, 1976, pp. 434-449.

Greenstein, F.I., N.W. Polsby, eds., *Handbook of Political Science* (Reading, Mass.: Addison-Wesley, 1975)

Hanrieder, W., "Compatability and Consensus: A Proposal for the Conceptual Linkage of External and Internal Dimensions of Foreign Policy," *American Political Science Review* 61 (4), December 1967, pp. 971-982.

Hawker, G., "Behavioural Scientists: The Role of the Researcher," *Australian Journal of Public Administration* 25 (1), 1976, pp. 1-8.

Herring, Ronald J., *Land to the Tiller: The Political Economy of Agrarian Reform in South Asia* (New Haven, Conn.: Yale University Press, 1983)

Hopmann, P. Terrence, Dina A. Zinnes, J. David Singer, eds., *Cumulation in International Relations Research*, Monograph Series in World Affairs (Denver,

Colo.: Graduate School of International Studies, University of Denver, 1981)

Jervis, Robert, *Perception and Misperception in International Politics* (Princeton, N.J.: Princeton University Press, 1976)

Kelman, Herbert C., ed., *International Behavior: A Social-Psychological Analysis* (New York: Holt, Rinehart and Winston, 1965)

Lasswell, H.D., "Policy Sciences," in D.L. Sills, ed., *International Encyclopedia of the Social Sciences*, vol. 12 (New York: Macmillan and Free Press, 1968), pp. 181-189.

_____, "Research in Policy Analysis: The Intelligence and Appraisal Functions," in F.I. Greenstein, N.W. Polsby, eds., *Handbook of Political Science*, Vol. 6 (Reading, Mass.: Addison-Wesley, 1975)

Lerner, Daniel, Harold Lasswell, *The Policy Sciences* (Palo Alto: Stanford University Press, 1951)

Lindblom, Charles E., *The Policy-Making Process* (Englewood Cliffs, N.J.: Prentice-Hall, 1968)

McGowan, Patrick, ed., *Sage International Yearbook of Foreign Policy Studies*, vols. 1, 2 (Beverly Hills, Cal.: Sage, 1973-1974)

Modelski, George, *A Theory of Foreign Policy* (New York: Praeger, 1962)

Playfair, Sir Edward, "Who are the Policy-Makers? Minister or Civil Servant? II. Civil Servant," *Public Administration*, (London), 43, Autumn 1965, pp. 260-268.

Rose, R., *The Dynamics of Public Policy: A Comparative Analysis* (London: Sage, 1976)

Tanter, R., R.H. Ullman, eds., *Theory and Policy in International Relations* (Princeton, N.J.: Princeton University Press, 1972)

Zinnes, Dina A., "Three Puzzles in Search of a Researcher," *International Studies Quarterly* 24 (3), September 1980, pp. 315-342.

THE CENTRAL EXECUTIVE

Alsop, Stewart, *The Center* (New York: Harper and Row, 1968)

Barber, James David, *The Presidential Character: Predicting Performance in the White House* (Englewood Cliffs, N.J.: Prentice-Hall, 1972)

Barnard, C.I., *The Functions of the Executive* (Cambridge, Mass.: Harvard University Press, 1968)

Beck, Carl, et al., *Comparative Communist Political Leadership* (New York: David McKay, 1973)

Bernstein, Marver H., *The Job of the Federal Executive* (Washington, D.C.: Brookings Institution, 1958)

Brecher, Michael, "Elite Images and Foreign Policy Choices: Krishna Menon's View of the World," *Pacific Affairs* 40, Spring-Summer, pp. 60-92.

_____, *India and World Politics: Krishna Menon's View of the World* (New York: Praeger, 1968)

_____, *Nehru: A Political Biography* (Boston: Beacon Press, 1961)

_____, *Succession in India* (London: Oxford University Press, 1966)

Carlson, S., *Executive Behavior* (Stockholm: C.A. Strömberg Aktiebolag, 1951)

Carras, Mary C., *Indira Gandhi, in the Crucible of Leadership: A Political Biography* (Boston: Beacon Press, 1979)

Crocker, Walter R., *Nehru: A Contemporary's Estimate* (London: George Allen and Unwin, 1966)

Cutler, Robert, "The Development of the National Security Council," *Foreign Affairs* 34 (3), April 1956, pp. 441-458.

Devons, E., "Governing on the Inner Circle," *The Listener*, March 27, 1958, pp. 523-525.

Gawthrop, Louis C., *Bureaucratic Behavior in the Executive Branch* (New York: Free Press, 1969)

George, Alexander L., "The 'Operational Code': A Neglected Approach to the Study of Political Leaders and Decision-Making," *International Studies Quarterly* 13 (2), June 1969, pp. 190-222.

_____, *Presidential Decisionmaking in Foreign Policy: The Effective Use of Information and Advice* (Boulder, Colo.: Westview, 1980)

George, T.J.S., *Krishna Menon: A Biography* (London: Jonathan Cape, 1964)

Gopal, Sarvepalli, *Jawaharlal Nehru: A Biography, Volume Two, 1947-1956* (Cambridge, Mass.: Harvard University Press, 1979)

Graham, G.A., "The Presidency and the Executive Office of the President," *Journal of Politics* 12, 1950, pp. 599-621.

Granick, David, *The European Executive* (Garden City, N.Y.: Doubleday and Co., 1963)

_____, *The Red Executive* (Garden City, N.Y.: Doubleday and Co., 1961)

Hangen, W., *After Nehru, Who?* (London: Rupert Hart-David, 1963)

Hockin, T.A., *Apex of Power: The Prime Minister and Political Leadership in Canada* (Scarborough, Ont.: Prentice-Hall of Canada, 1971)

Jackson, Henry M., ed., *The National Security Council* (New York: Praeger, 1965)

Johnson, Robert H., "The National Security Council: The Relevance of its Past to its Future," *Orbis* 13 (3), Fall 1969, pp. 709-735.

Kirkpatrick, Sir Ivone, *The Inner Circle* (London: 1959)

Lasswell, Harold D., et al., *The Comparative Study of Elites* (Stanford, Cal.: Stanford University Press, 1952)

Mann, D.E., *Federal Political Executives* (Washington, D.C.: Brookings, 1964)

Marvic, D., ed., *Political Decision-Makers* (New York: Free Press, 1961)

Matthews, Donald R., *The Social Background of Political Decision-Makers* (New York: Random House, 1954)

Moraes, F., *Jawaharlal Nehru: A Biography* (New York: Macmillan, 1956)

Nehru, Jawaharlal, *Independence and After: a Collection of the more Important Speeches of Jawaharlal Nehru, from September 1946 to May 1949* (New Delhi: Publications Division, Ministry of Information and Broadcasting, 1949)

Neustadt, Richard E., "Approaches to Staffing the Presidency: Notes on FDR and JFK," *American Political Science Review* 57 (4), December 1963, pp. 855-863.

_____, *Presidential Power: The Politics of Leadership from FDR to Carter* (New York: John Wiley and Sons, 1980)

Pandey, B.N., ed., *Leadership in South Asia* (New Delhi: Vikas, 1977)

Panjabi, Kewal L., *The Indomitable Sardar* (Bombay: Bharatiya Vidya Bhavan, 1962)

Patel, Sardar Vallabhbhai Javerbhai, *Sardar Patel's Correspondence: 1945-50*, edited by Durga Das (Ahmedabad: Navajivan Publishing House, 1973)

_____, *Sardar's Letters--Mostly Unknown, Post-- Centenary Volume I, Part Two: Years 1947-'48* (Ahmedabad: Sardar Vallabhbhai Patel Smarak Bhavan, 1980)

Presthus, Robert, *Elites in the Policy Process* (Toronto: Cambridge University Press, 1974)

Rose, Richard, Ezra N. Suleiman, eds., *Presidents and Prime Ministers* (Washington, D.C.: American Enterprise Institute for Public Policy Research, 1981)

Shankar, V., *My Reminiscences of Sardar Patel*, two volumes (New Delhi: Macmillan, 1974)

Shils, E., "Influence and Withdrawal: The Intellectual in Indian Political Development," in D. Marvic, ed., *Political Decision-Makers* (New York: Free Press, 1961), pp. 29-56.

Sorensen, Theodore, *Decision-Making in the White House* (New York: Columbia University Press, 1963)

Stanley, David T., Dean E. Mann, Jameson W. Doig, *Men who Govern: A Biographical Profile of Federal Political Executives* (Washington, D.C.: Brookings Institution, 1967)

Stein, J.G., *Elite Images and Foreign Policy: Nehru, Menon and India's Policies,* unpublished PhD. dissertation (Montreal: McGill University, 1969)

Tahir-Kheli, S.R., *Pakistani Elites and Foreign Policy towards the Soviet Union, Iran, and Afghanistan,* unpublished PhD. dissertation (Philadelphia: University of Pennsylvania, 1972)

Warner, W. Lloyd,, Paul P. Van Riper, Norman H. Martin, Orvis F. Collins, *The American Federal Executive* (New Haven: Yale University Press, 1963)

Yarmolinsky, Adam, "Bureaucratic Structures and Political Outcomes," *Journal of International Affairs* 23 (2), 1969.

THE CAREER CYCLE: FROM RECRUITMENT TO RETIREMENT

Briggs, Ellis O., "The Case against a 'West Point' for Diplomats," *New York Times Magazine,* May 3, 1964, pp. 20ff.

Edinger, Lewis J., Donald D. Searing, "Social Background in Elite Analysis: A Methodological Inquiry," *American Political Science Review* 61, June 1967, pp. 428-445.

Fielder, Frances, Godfrey Harris, *The Quest for Foreign Affairs Officers--Their Recruitment and Promotion* (New York: Carnegie Endowment for International Peace, 1966)

Hickman, Martin B., Neil Hollander, "Undergraduate Origin as a Factor in Elite Recruitment and Mobility: The Foreign Service--A Case Study," *Western Political Quarterly* 19, June, 1966, pp. 337-353.

Hodge, Robert W., Paul M. Siegel, Peter H. Rossi, "Occupational Prestige in the United States, 1925-63," *American Journal of Sociology* 70 (3), November 1964, pp. 286-302.

Hyman, Herbert, *Political Socialization* (Glencoe, Ill.: Free Press, 1959)

McLean, Joseph E., ed., *The Public Service and University Selection* (Princeton, N.J.: Princeton University Press, 1949)

Potter, David, "Manpower Shortage and the End of Colonialization: The Case of the Indian Civil Service," *Modern Asian Studies* 7 (1), 1973, pp. 47-73.

Sayre, Wallace S., Clarence E. Thurber, *Training for Specialized Mission Personnel* (Chicago: Public Administration Service, 1952)

Searing, Donald D., "The Comparative Study of Elite Socialization," *Comparative Political Studies* 1, January, 1969, pp. 471-500.

Symington, Stuart, "Let's have a West Point for Diplomats," *This Week,* August 2, 1959, pp. 8-9.

Wilkinson, Rupert, ed., *Governing Elites: Studies in Training and Selection* (New York: Oxford University Press, 1969)

Willick, Daniel H., *The Recruitment and Promotion of Foreign Service Officers,* Working Paper no. 58 (Chicago: University of Chicago, Center for Social Organization Studies, February 1966)

RESOURCE ALLOCATION

Editorial staff, "Toward a Stronger Foreign Service," *Christian Science Monitor* 56, January 14, 1964, p. 16.

Harr, John E., *Program Budgeting Visits Foreign Affairs,* limited advance edition, Inter-University Case Program (Syracuse, N.Y.: Syracuse University, 1969)

Hurwicz, Leonid, "The Design of Mechanisms for Resource Allocation," *American Economic Review, Papers and Proceedings* 63 (2), 1973, pp. 1-30.

Jones, Arthur G., *The Evolution of Personnel Systems for U.S. Foreign Affairs* (New York: Carnegie Endowment for International Peace, 1965)

Kanter, Arnold, *Defense Politics: A Budgetary Perspective* (Chicago: University of Chicago Press, 1979)

Linehan, Patrick E., *The Foreign Service Personnel System: An Organizational Analysis* (New York: Westview Press, 1977)

Marrow, Alfred J., "Managerial Revolution in the State Department," *Personnel* 43 (6), November-December 1966, pp. 8-18.

McCamy, James L., "Rebuilding the Foreign Service," *Harpers* 219, November 1959, pp. 80-89.

Mosher, Frederick C., "Some Observations about Foreign Service Reform: 'Famous First Words,'" *Public Administration Review,* November-December 1969, pp. 600-610.

_____, "Personnel Management in American Foreign Affairs," *Public Personnel Review* 12, October 1951, pp. 175-186.

_____, John E. Harr, *Programming Systems and Foreign Affairs Leadership: An Attempted Innovation* (New York: Oxford University Press, 1970)

Myers, Dennis P., Charles F. Ransom, "Reorganization of the State Department," *American Journal of International Law* 31, October 1937, pp. 713-720.

Rowen, Henry S., Albert P. Williams, "Policy Analysis in International Affairs," in U.S. Congress, Joint

Economic Committee, Subcommittee on Economy in Government, *The Analysis and Evaluation of Public Expenditures: The PPB System* (Washington, D.C.: Government Printing Office, 1969), pp. 970-1002.

U.S. Congress, Joint Economic Committee, Subcommittee on Economy in Government, *The Analysis and Evaluation of Public Expenditures: The PPB System* (Washington, D.C.: Government Printing Office, 1969)

U.S. Senate Committee on Government Operations, Subcommittee on National Security and International Operations, *Planning-Programming-Budgeting* (Washington, D.C.: Government Printing Office, 1970)

White, Paul N., "Resources as Determinants of Organizational Behavior," *Administrative Science Quarterly* 19, 1974, pp. 366-379.

Young, Oran, *Resource Management at the International Level* (New York: Nichols Publishing Co., 1977)

Index

Abducted Persons
    Unit ... 184
Abstract sublevel-of-
    analysis ... 44
Academic
    community ... 122,
    139-140, 175
  and Historical
    Division ... 122
  and Indira Gandhi's
    foreign
    policy ... 140
  MEA cooperation
    with ... 139
  representation within
    MEA ... 140
Academy of Administration,
    Lal Bahadur
    Shastri ... 53
Act of 1858, government of
    India ... 17
Actual sublevel-of-
    analysis ... 44
Additional assistant
    secretary, assignment
    of ... 23
Additional
    secretary ... 85, 145
Additional secretary
    (Admin) ... 132
Additional secretary
    (PP) ... 133
Administration ... 108
  and leadership ... 108
  administration of ... 82
Administrative
    Division ... 81, 109
Administrative
    practices ... 12
  British ... 12
Advisors to Nehru ... 192
Afghanistan ... 1, 35, 133
  embassy to ... 133
  invasion of (1979) ... 1

Afghanistan, invasion of
    (1979) ... 182
Africa Division ... 81
Age of retirement ... 52
Agency for International
    Development (AID),
    United States ... 109
Agency-general ... 36-37,
    82
  to China, and Ram D.
    Sathe ... 37
Agency, the ... 21, 36
Aid programs,
    Indian ... 158
Air force, Indian ... 3
Air Intelligence,
    Directorate of
    (DAI) ... 145
Aiyar, Mani
    Shankar ... 170
Alexander,
    P.C. ... 209-210
  and G.
    Parthasarathi ... 210
Ali Khan, Mehdi ... 36
Allahabad
    University ... 53
Allegiance,
    perceived ... 39, 45
  of Indian IPS
    officers ... 39
  of seed cadre ... 45
Allegiance, service ... 83
Ambassador ... 48, 56, 77,
    84, 140
  academic as ... 140
  and secretary-
    general ... 77
  salary of ... 48
America (Amer)
    Division ... 102
America Division ... 218
  Europe Division ... 218
Anderson, Jack ... 167
Anjengo, treaty of ... 10

Apex groups ... 162
Appointment of academics to MEA ... 140
Appointment of ambassadors ... 213
  and Janata ... 213
Appointment, political ... 197
Area studies programs ... 175
Army staff, chief of ... 147
Assistant ... 12-13
Assistant secretary ... 12, 19, 35
Atomic Energy, Department of ... 115, 208
  and Tarapur nuclear fuel dispute ... 208
Attaché ... 93, 114, 159
  defense ... 159
Attached office ... 101
Autonomy, bureau ... 14
  British Indian ... 14
Aviation Research Centre (ARC) ... 149
Award for International Understanding, Jawaharlal Nehru Award for ... 179
Ayyangar, Gopalaswami ... 77
Ayyangar, N. Gopalaswami ... 66
Azad Memorial Lecture ... 179
Azad, Maulana ... 176, 193
  as Nehru's deputy ... 193

Bahadur Singh, I.J. ... 47, 116
Bajpai, Girija Shankar ... 46, 55-57, 82, 84, 187
  and Special Selection Board ... 57
Bajpai, Kayatyani Shankar ... 56, 82, 85
Bangladesh Division ... 102
Bangladesh intervention (1971) ... 80, 125, 131, 147, 159, 162
  and military intelligence ... 147
  and political-military coordination ... 162
  and PPRD ... 131
Bannerji, R.N. ... 141
Bannerji, S. ... 206
Batra, Brigadier M.N. ... 147
Benares Hindu University (BHU) ... 53, 138
Bhagat, B.R. ... 75
Bhagat, Usha ... 181
Bhalla, Manorama ... 177
Bhandari, Romesh ... 85, 156
Bhargawa, K.K. ... 118, 156
Bilateral economic relations ... 154
Biological weaponry ... 6
Board, review ... 113
Branch ... 94, 110
British influence, perpetuation of ... 33, 35, 45, 200
Budget, bureau ... 16
Bureaucracy ... 6
  definition of ... 6

Bureaucracy, foreign
    policy ... 20, 23, 25,
    28, 30, 92, 94, 96,
    100-102, 109, 199
  and the
    Commonwealth ... 28
  and Whitehall ... 25
  early procedures
    of ... 30
  functions of British
    Indian ... 20
  goals of ... 96
  Indian, compared with
    British ... 100
  infrastructure
    of ... 102
  of Communist
    states ... 101
  of early
    bureaucracy ... 30
  of United States ... 92
  Soviet ... 199
  systemic influences
    upon ... 23
  weaknesses of ... 94,
    109

Cabinet ... 4, 66, 71, 76,
    116-118, 123, 147,
    158, 162, 209
  and junior
    ministers ... 76
  Defence Committee
    of ... 162
  difference in British
    and Indian
    systems ... 66
  intelligence bodies
    of ... 147
  need for cabinet-level
    coordination ... 117
  planning efforts ... 123
  secretary ... 118
  transfer of JIC
    to ... 147
Cabinet Committee on
    Political Affairs
    (CCPA) ... 15, 145,
    158, 162
  creation of ... 162

Cabinet secretariat (Cab
    Sec) ... 34, 111, 118,
    146-147, 209, 212-213
  and introduction of
    RAW ... 147
  and Joint Intelligence
    Committee ... 146
  and the Office ... 213
  dismemberment during
    Janata ... 213
  operational code
    of ... 213
  reorganization
    of ... 213
Cancun, Mexico
    summit ... 118
Canning, Lord ... 18
Career leadership ... 194
  growth in power
    (1958-64) ... 194
Caroe, Olaf ... 26
Caste system ... 55
Central Bureau of
    Investigation
    (CBI) ... 213
Central Bureau of
    Investigations
    (CBI) ... 147
Central Cypher Bureau
    (CCB) ... 110
Central Passport and
    Emigration
    Organization ... 182
Central Passport
    Organization ... 183
Central Passport
    Organization
    (CPO) ... 183
Centralization ... 13-14
  domestic influences
    upon ... 14
  policy ... 14
Centre for Policy
    Research ... 138
Chagla, M.C. 45,
    68-70, 73, 113, 176
  and anti-Pakistani
    sentiments ... 70
  and Muslim lobby ... 69
  and Pillai committee
    report ... 113
  and seed cadre ... 45
  and the Syndicate ... 69

Chanda, Anil K. ... 75-76
Chandra, Satish ... 76
Charismatic leadership of Nehru ... 185
Charter Act of 1793 ... 18
Charter Act of 1833 ... 16
Chavan, Y.B. ... 71, 132
  as emergency foreign minister ... 71
Chief secretary ... 16
Chiefs of Staff Committee ... 162
China ... 84-85
  ambassadorship to ... 84
  1982 talks with ... 85
Chou En-lai ... 34
Cognitive dissonance theory ... 31
Cognitive maps ... 197
Colombo Plan ... 158
Combined Research Cadre ... 138, 140, 166
  and merger with IFS ... 138
Commerce and Industry, Ministry of ... 50, 153, 170, 211
  and backgrounds of PMPPS ... 211
Commercial Publicity Wing ... 170
Commerce, Department of ... 35
Commerce, Ministry of ... 158
  Department of Commerce ... 158
Commission, joint ... 114
Commissioner-general ... 153
Committee of Secretaries ... 4, 118, 127, 208
  and L.K. Jha ... 208
Committee on the Indian Foreign Service ... 59, 112
Commonwealth ... 85
  heads of mission conference ... 85
Commonwealth relations ... 28-29
Commonwealth Relations, Department of ... 29, 34-35, 81
Communal disturbances (1947-48) ... 184
Communications ... 13, 20-21, 110, 173, 211
  and XP Division ... 173
  international, and the Office ... 211
  speed of ... 13
  telegraphic ... 13, 20-21, 110
Communities, Indian overseas ... 26-27, 71-72, 133
  and Janata's A.B. Vajpayee ... 71
  and policy planning ... 133
  and Punjab crisis (1984) ... 72
Community, foreign policy ... 4, 29, 49, 72, 80, 92, 94, 111, 114, 116, 158, 165, 170
  and foreign minister ... 72.
  and interministerial role of secretaries ... 80
  and international economic policy ... 158
  and joint secretary ... 92
  and UN Division ... 165
  coordination of ... 114, 116
  factionalism within ... 4
  in the United States ... 72
Congress Party ... 189
  weakness of leadership ... 189
Congress split (1969) ... 71, 131, 147
  and cabinet control of RAW ... 147

Congress(I) ... 215
  party officials and international delegations ... 215
Congress(U) ... 214
Congress, Indian National ... 204
Constitutional structure, influence upon bureaucracy ... 31
Consular Division ... 182
  and Branch ... 182
Consular, Passport and Visa (CPV) Division ... 183
Control ... 5, 15, 17, 20, 24, 71, 91
  by the British after 1857 ... 17
  of bureau by central executive ... 5
  of bureaucracy before 1969 ... 71
  of information ... 91
  of policy after 1878 ... 20
  over Baroda, Sikkim and Bhutan ... 24
  superdepartmental ... 15
Coordination ... 23, 63, 115-117, 163
  as a group effort ... 116
  between London and Calcutta ... 23
  formal versus informal ... 117
  interministerial ... 63, 115
Coordination (Coord) Division ... 102
Coordination and Information Division ... 116-117
  Parliament Section of ... 117
Cornwallis, Lord ... 31
Corruption ... 60
Council of ministers ... 65

Council of Scientific and Industrial Research and G. Parthasarathi ... 210
Councils Act of 1861, Indian ... 18
Country director ... 92
Court of directors ... 15, 17
  chairman of ... 15
  deputy chairman of ... 15
  Secret Committee ... 17
  secret committee of ... 15
Cuban missile crisis (1962) ... 1, 3
  Navy blockade during ... 3
Cultural relations ... 167, 176
Current Research Division ... 124, 126
Curzon, Lord ... 23
Cypher Sub Cadre ... 111

Dalhousie, Lord ... 18
Defence Committee of the Cabinet ... 123
Defence Minister's Committee ... 162
Defence Studies and Analyses, Institute for (IDSA) ... 53
Defence, Ministry of ... 60-61, 147, 203
  and Krishna Menon ... 203
  and leaks of information ... 60
  and RAW ... 147
  intelligence efforts of ... 147
  manipulation of opinion by ... 61
Defense ... 123
  planning efforts ... 123
Delegation compositions, Janata and post-Janata ... 214
Delegation of authority ... 191

Department of Revenue
   Intelligence
   (DRI) ... 209
Department of
   State ... 175
   Bureau of Public
      Affairs ... 175
Deputy director ... 93,
   138
   and Combined Research
      Cadre ... 138
Deputy minister ... 70,
   75-76
   and British minister of
      state ... 75
Deputy permanent
   representative (DPR)
   to UN ... 164
Deputy secretary ... 19,
   23, 26, 35, 51, 63,
   91, 93, 172
   and the IFS(B) ... 51
Desai, M.J. ... 83, 85,
   159
Desai, Morarji ... 148,
   209, 214, 216
   and PMS name
      change ... 209
   and policy
      pluralism ... 216
   and the RAW ... 148, 214
Devaluation of rupee
   (1967) ... 157
Dhar, D.P. ... 80, 125,
   131-132, 162
   in Bangladesh
      intervention
      (1971) ... 80
Dhar, P.N. ... 209
Dhawan, R.K. ... 209
Diplomacy ... 10
   intra-
      subcontinent ... 10
Diplomacy, modular ... 212
Diplomats and intelligence
   officers ... 150
Director ... 90, 109, 148
   of Economic
      Division ... 109
   of RAW ... 148
Directorate-general of
   security
   (DG[S]) ... 149

Disarmament ... 120, 138,
   164
   Cell ... 120
   Unit ... 138
Discontinuities,
   theoretical ... 224
Dissent ... 60-61
Distrust of
   subordinates ... 196
Division ... 91, 93-94,
   101-102, 117
   administration of ... 91
   communication
      between ... 117
   deputy secretary control
      of ... 93
   development of ... 94
   subcategories of ... 102
Drafting ... 24, 207, 211
   and information
      advisor ... 211
   in the British Indian
      bureaucracy ... 24
   power of the PMS ... 207
Dual-cadre system ... 38
Dutt, Subimal ... 46

East Asia Research and
   Coordination
   Division ... 123
East India Company ... 10,
   17
   Board of control ... 17
   charter of ... 10
Eastern Division ... 95
Economic Affairs
   Division ... 153
Economic and Coordination
   Division ... 154
Economic Division ... 85,
   115, 153, 157
   communication with
      missions
      abroad ... 157
   specialization
      within ... 157

Economic Division
 (ED) ... 102, 154-156
 and central
  executive ... 156
 dichotomous structure
  of ... 154
 growth of ... 154
 responsibilities
  of ... 155
 structure of ... 155
Economic policy,
 international ... 154
Economy drives ... 109
Economy measures ... 13
Education, Health and
 Lands, Department
 of ... 26, 29, 82-84
 and N.R. Pillai ... 83
 Indian Overseas Section
  of ... 29
Education, Ministry
 of ... 170, 176
 Department of
  Culture ... 170, 176
Efficiency
 management ... 110-111
Ellenborough, Lord ... 16
Embassy ... 83-85, 101,
 153
 as attached
  office ... 101
 commercial section
  of ... 153
 to China ... 85
 to France ... 85
 to the Soviet
  Union ... 84
 to the United
  States ... 83
Emergency
 (1975-77) ... 131,
 209, 215
 similarity to Bangladesh
  intervention ... 215
Emergency
 Committee ... 123
Emergency Committee of the
 Cabinet ... 162
Emigration
 Organization ... 183
Enforcement, Department
 of ... 209
Europe Division ... 91

Executive council ... 18,
 82
 procedure of ... 18
Executive, central ... 2,
 7, 47
Expansion, British
 imperial ... 11-12
 scale of ... 12
Experimentation,
 administrative ... 63
External Affairs and
 Commonwealth
 Relations, Department
 of ... 34-35, 100
 criticism of ... 100
External Affairs,
 Department of ... 26,
 28, 32, 34-35, 167
 as independent
  bureau ... 28
 division with partition
  (1947) ... 32
 international outlook
  of ... 26
 merger with Department
  of Commonwealth
  Relations ... 34
 secretary of ... 26
External Intelligence
 Organization ... 147
External
 publicity ... 114,
 167, 170
 tensions within
  community ... 170

External Publicity (XP)
   Division ... 93, 102,
   168-173, 175, 177
 Administration ... 173
 and adaptation of
   material ... 171
 and the ICCR ... 177
 Audio-visual
   section ... 172
 budget of ... 169
 budgetary planning
   of ... 173
 Materials ... 172
 personnel strength
   of ... 172
 philosophy of ... 171
 review of ... 170
 Spokesmen ... 172
 structure of ... 168,
   171
 weaknesses of ... 169
External publicity
   division ... 4, 116
External Publicity
   Organization
   (EPO) ... 167

Filing system
   merger ... 17
Finance (Fin)
   Division ... 102
Finance, Ministry
   of ... 51, 111, 153,
   158, 209
 Department of Economic
   Affairs ... 158
 during the
   emergency ... 209
 Staff Inspection Unit
   of ... 111
First secretary ... 93
Follands company, and Gnat
   fighter ... 3
foreign ... 1, 10, 17
 definition of ... 17
 study of ... 1
Foreign Affairs
   Committee ... 123
Foreign Affairs
   Group ... 139

Foreign and Political
   Department ... 25,
   27-28, 84
 and Department of
   External
   Affairs ... 28
 X Section of ... 25, 84
Foreign Department ... 12,
   16-19, 21, 23-24
 and assumption of
   domestic
   responsibilities ... 21
 at time of portfolio
   reforms ... 19
 branches of ... 17
 establishment of ... 12
 growth in workload
   of ... 24
 new responsibilities
   of ... 21
 secretary to ... 23
Foreign
   minister ... 72-74,
   78, 118, 128
 and interdivisional
   coordination ... 118
 and operational
   involvement ... 73
 and policy ... 72
 and secretary-
   general ... 78
 as "rubber stamp" ... 73
 definition of tasks
   of ... 72
 in a system of checks
   and balances ... 74
 problems with
   independent ... 128
Foreign portfolio ... 188
 and international
   practice ... 188

Foreign
    secretary ... 25-27,
        37, 58, 78-81, 85,
        125, 150
    and position in policy-
        formulation ... 80
    and RAW director ... 150
    as head of PPRC ... 125
    as secretary-general's
        successor ... 79
    power of ... 27
    recent officers ... 85
    responsibilities
        of ... 26
Foreign Service
    Board ... 58
Foreign Service
    Inspectorate
    (FSI) ... 111
Foreign Service Institute
    proposal ... 54
Foreign Trade, Indian
    Institute of ... 53
Forward Policy ... 85, 160
    and M.J. Desai ... 85

Gandhi, Indira ... 70-71,
    80, 113, 118, 127,
    130, 165, 195,
    211-212, 215, 216, 219
    administrative style
        of ... 216
    and Bangladesh
        intervention
        (1971) ... 80
    and committee of
        secretaries ... 118
    and foreign
        minister ... 80
    and foreign
        secretary ... 80
    and initial shift toward
        left ... 70
    and MEA
        secretaries ... 211
    and Pillai committee
        report ... 113
    and the emergency ... 71
    and United
        Nations ... 165
    attempts to bypass
        foreign
        minister ... 127
    comparison with
        Nehru ... 80, 130
    distrust of
        careerists ... 215
    growth in power
        of ... 212
    lack of organizational
        initiatives ... 216
    Mauritius
        remarks ... 219
    organizational skill
        of ... 215
    travels abroad and
        Office ... 211
Gandhi, Mahatma ... 124
    and Nehru ... 124
Gangotri,
    Operation ... 118
Generalism ... 51, 140,
    157, 172
    in external
        publicity ... 172
    within the Economic
        Division ... 157
Geneva UN mission ... 164
Geographisation ... 154

Gnat fighter jet ... 3
Goa ... 203
  policy and Krishna
    Menon ... 203
Goa Research Unit ... 120
Goa takeover
    (1961) ... 192
  and Krishna
    Menon ... 192
Gonsalves, Eric ... 208
Government of India Act
    (1919) ... 28-29
Government of India Act
    (1935) ... 28
Governor-general ... 17-18
  and Foreign
    Department ... 18
  in viceroyal role ... 17
  policy veto of ... 18
Growth, bureau ... 51
  of IFS(B) ... 51
Growth,
    bureaucratic ... 5,
    16, 26, 47, 59, 100,
    189
  shortfalls in ... 59
Gupta, Sisir ... 80, 140
  in Bangladesh
    intervention
    (1971) ... 80

Haj cell ... 29, 182
Haksar, P.N. ... 128, 147,
    162, 209-210
  and cabinet control of
    RAW ... 147
Hierarchy,
    procedural ... 63, 92,
    95
  conventional and
    reorganized ... 95
  generalized ... 63
  of the 1950s ... 63
High Commission ... 35, 37
Himmatsinghji
    Committee ... 144
Hiremath ... 116

Historical Division
    (HD) ... 102, 120-121,
    129-130
  and PPRD ... 130
  comparison with
    PPRD ... 129
  legal duties of ... 121
Hoja, M.M.L. ... 141
Home Department ... 21
Home Ministry ... 111,
    147, 184, 206, 213
  Administrative Vigilance
    Division of
    the ... 111
  and Cab Sec
    reorganization ... 213
  and CPV Division ... 184
  and RAW ... 147
Hostel, External
    Affairs ... 102, 110
Housekeeping ... 110
Hungary, invasion of
    (1956) ... 83, 192
  and Krishna
    Menon ... 192
Hussain, Azim ... 69
Hussain, Zakir ... 207
Hyderabad House ... 102
Hyderabad state, and
    K.P.S. Menon ... 84

Implementation ... 94
Independence, Indian ... 9
India International
    Centre ... 139
Indian Administrative
    Service (IAS) ... 58
Indian Civil Service
    (ICS) ... 9, 32-33,
    38-39, 200
  and "ICS
    generation" ... 32
  and conflict with other
    services ... 33
  and Indianization ... 39
  their dominance within
    the Indian Political
    Service ... 38

Indian Council for
    Cultural Relations
    (ICCR) ... 116,
    176-179
  and IFS ... 177
  and XP Division ... 177
  budget of ... 179
  regional offices
    of ... 178
  reorganization
    within ... 178
  responsibilities
    of ... 178
  structure of ... 179
Indian Foreign Service
    (IFS) ... 40, 47-48,
    50, 58-59, 84, 93,
    140, 218
  {A,B} rivalry ... 59,
    140
  and differences with
    Indian Political
    Service ... 47
  and K.P.S. Menon ... 84
  and missions manpower
    shift ... 218
  and under-
    secretary ... 93
  B branch ... 50, 93
  exclusionist service
    attitudes ... 140
  initial cadre of ... 40
  Report of the Committee
    on the ... 58
  size of ... 48
Indian National Army
    (INA) ... 197
Indian Police
    Service ... 151
Indian Political Service
    (IPS) ... 31-32, 38-39
  age limitations in
    personnel
    selection ... 38
  and competition between
    ICS and Army ... 38
  and Indianization ... 39
  and 1911 reforms ... 38
  competitiveness
    within ... 38
  dual cognitive structure
    within ... 38

Indian Technical and
    Economic Cooperation
    (ITEC) ... 155, 204
Indianization ... 29, 36,
    39
  and the Political
    Agent ... 36
Indians Overseas,
    Department of ... 29
Indo-Iranian Cultural
    Committee ... 176
Indo-U.S. Friendship
    Society and
    Parthasarathi ... 210
Industry, Ministry
    of ... 50
Information ... 91, 122,
    130, 136, 167, 171
  and missions
    abroad ... 122
  and the PPRD ... 136
  as propaganda ... 167
  control of ... 91
  generation versus
    orientation ... 171
  processed versus
    raw ... 130
Information advisor to
    PM ... 211
Information and
    Broadcasting (I and
    B), Department
    of ... 168
Information and
    Broadcasting (I and
    B), Ministry of ... 4,
    76, 114, 168, 172-173
  Films Division ... 172
  Press Information Bureau
    (PIB) ... 173
  Press Information Bureau
    of ... 168
Information Service ... 49
Information Service of
    India (ISI) ... 168,
    170, 173
  induction into
    IFS ... 170
  Wings ... 173
Information theory ... 62
Information units ... 168,
    173
Inspector ... 111

Institute for Defence
    Studies and Analyses
    (IDSA) ... 138
Intelligence ... 15, 102,
    147, 159, 217
  and "Force 136" ... 147
  British ... 15
  bureaux of Home
    Ministry ... 102
  criticism of quality
    of ... 217
  military ... 159
Intelligence Bureau
    (IB) ... 15, 141, 144,
    149, 213
  and communist victory in
    Kerala ... 149
  and foreign
    intelligence ... 141
  and struggle between
    deputationists and
    direct
    recruits ... 149
  and tensions with
    Ministry of
    Defence ... 144
  present-day ... 149
Intelligence
    community ... 141,
    144, 149, 214, 216-217
  and Indira
    Gandhi ... 216
  and Janata ... 214
  and proposed American
    assistance ... 144
  and rumors of "watchdog
    committee" ... 149
  during Nehru
    period ... 141
  factionalism ... 217
  fragmentation
    within ... 149
Intelligence Unit ... 122
Interdepartmental
    group ... 118
Interdepartmental groups
    (IG) ... 211
  and the Office ... 211
Internal Work Study
    Unit ... 111
International Atomic
    Energy Commission
    (IAEC) ... 115

International Labor
    Organization
    (ILO) ... 114
International
    organizations ... 81,
    115
  and state
    governments ... 115
International Security
    Affairs, Bureau
    of ... 158
Interpreters' Cadre ... 49
Intuitive cognition in
    policy-making ... 124
Ismay, Lord ... 162

Jadavpur
    University ... 138
Jain, K.P. ... 138
Jaipur, state of ... 47
Janata ... 71, 75, 132,
    148, 170, 209, 213,
    215-216
  administration of
    foreign
    policy ... 215
  and external
    publicity ... 170
  and foreign minister
    A.B. Vajpayee ... 71
  and minister of
    state ... 75
  and policy
    planning ... 132
  and the Office ... 209
  and the RAW ... 148
  operational inertia
    during ... 216
Jawaharlal Nehru
    University
    (JNU) ... 53, 138
Jha, C.S. ... 46, 208
Jha, L.K. ... 204, 206
Joint
    commissions ... 154-155

Joint Intelligence
    Committee
    (JIC) ... 145-146,
    148, 162
  and Chiefs of Staff
    Committee ... 146
  and MEA
    participation ... 146
  and RAW ... 148
  comparison with
    PPRD ... 146
  responsibilities
    of ... 146
  Steering Committee
    of ... 145
  weaknesses of ... 146
Joint Intelligence
    Organization ... 147
Joint Planning
    Committee ... 123, 162
Joint secretariats,
  between governments of
    Bengal and
    India ... 16
Joint secretary ... 35,
    58, 63, 70, 90-92, 156
  and contacts with quasi-
    central
    executive ... 70
  and subordinates ... 92
  and the American country
    director ... 92
  comparison with
    secretary ... 91
  of Administration ... 58
Junior grades ... 48
Junior ministers ... 66,
    76-77
  and parliamentary
    work ... 77
  as bureau
    climbers ... 76
  prescriptions
    concerning ... 77
Junior officers ... 92,
    199, 216
  and Indira
    Gandhi ... 216
  Nehru's demands
    upon ... 199

Kalam Azad, Abul ... 83
Kamaraj ... 131

Kamaraj and M.C.
    Chagla ... 69
Kamaraj syndicate ... 204
Kao, Ram Nath ... 147-150
  as advisor-in-
    charge ... 149
Kapur, Yashpal ... 209
Kashmir ... 203
  policy and Krishna
    Menon ... 203
Kashmir Division ... 102
Kashmir Unit ... 120
Kashmiri Brahmans in
    government ... 196
Kaul, B.M. ... 80
Kaul, T.N. ... 150, 210
Kennedy, John F. ... 205
Keskar, B.V. ... 75-76
Khera, S.S. ... 118
Kosygin, Soviet deputy
    minister ... 207
Krishna Menon ... 193
  as ineffective
    deputy ... 193
Krishnamachari,
    T.T. ... 66, 83
Krishnan, N. ... 112
Kundu, Samarendra ... 75

Labor, Ministry
    of ... 133, 184
  and CPV Division ... 184
Lall, Ram ... 177
Language skill ... 49, 53
  in the Indian Foreign
    Service ... 49
  training facilities
    for ... 53
Lateral entry ... 59
Law of the Sea
    policy ... 158
Law, international ... 166
Leaks, journalistic ... 60
  and Indo-Soviet talks
    (1971) ... 60
Legal and Treaties (L and
    T) Division ... 158,
    166
Legal and Treaties
    Division ... 140

Levels-of-analysis ... 2, 44
  and three sublevels-of-analysis ... 44
Library, MEA ... 122
Locus of power ... 78, 204
Lok Dal ... 71, 215
London high commission ... 35
  and Department of Commerce ... 35
Lusaka Conference of the Non-aligned ... 215

MacCalfe House ... 53
Madhya Pradesh Social Forestry Project ... 109
Maharashtra, ruling family of ... 47
Mahmud, Dr. Syed ... 74
Mahmud, Syed ... 140
Malik, B.N. ... 141
Malik, H.S. ... 46
Management training ... 109
Manpower ... 102
  strength of ... 102
Manpower shift in missions abroad ... 217-218
  and Economic Division ... 218
  and IFS(B) opposition ... 218
  and UN Division ... 218
Manpower shortages ... 175
Marxism-Leninism ... 197
Mass Communications, Institute of ... 53
Media, hostility toward ... 167, 172
Mehta, Ashok ... 178
Mehta, J.S. ... 81
Mehta, Jagat Subha ... 77, 85, 126, 213, 215
  removal of ... 215
Member-in-charge of external affairs ... 35

Menon, Krishna ... 47, 66, 80, 159, 165, 191-193, 202-203
  and defence portfolio ... 203
  and dispute with Vijayalakshmi Pandit ... 202
  and quasi-central executive ... 66
  as scapegoat ... 193
  rise in power of ... 203
Menon, Kumar Padmanabha Sivasankara ... 25, 45-46, 56, 84
  and N.R. Pillai ... 84
  and seed cadre ... 45
  leaves MEA ... 84
Menon, Lakshmi N. ... 74-76
  as minister of state ... 74
  rise from parliamentary secretary to minister of state ... 76
Menon, P.A. ... 46
Middle East ... 85
  relations with ... 85
Military ... 31
  in the perpetuation of British influence ... 31
Military intelligence ... 144
Military Intelligence Organization ... 144
Military Intelligence, Directorate of (DMI) ... 145, 159
Minister of cabinet rank ... 74
Minister of state ... 74-75, 89, 114, 132
  and foreign secretary ... 75
  British ... 75
  for Tourism and Civil Aviation ... 114
  under Janata ... 75
Minister without portfolio ... 66

Ministry of
    Education ... 178
  Department of
    Culture ... 178
Ministry of External
    Affairs (MEA) ... 35,
    50, 76, 79, 94, 100,
    102, 148, 150, 173,
    176, 186, 189, 200,
    208, 213-214
  and Cab Sec ... 213
  and competition with
    RAW ... 214
  and formation of
    IFS(B) ... 50
  and friction with the
    PMS ... 208
  and RAW ... 148, 150
  and tension with I and B
    Ministry ... 173
  and the ICCR ... 176
  creation of ... 35
  development of internal
    structure ... 94
  library of ... 102
  responsibilities
    of ... 100
  two early departmental
    divisions ... 79
  weaknesses of ... 186,
    189, 200
Mishra, S.N. ... 71, 76
Misra, K.P. ... 138
Missionaries, as
    diplomats ... 9
Monopoly, policy ... 187,
    189
  bureaucratic effects
    of ... 189
Monthly Intelligence
    Summary ... 122
Moscow
    ambassadorship ... 32
Mountbatten, Lord ... 31,
    33
  post-1947 influence
    of ... 33
Mukerjee, N.K. ... 148
Multifunctional officer,
    the ... 51
Muslim League ... 32

Muslim officers ... 32, 69
  as source of bureau
    friction ... 69
  perceived allegiance
    of ... 32

Naga Unit ... 102
Nair, K. Sankaran ... 148
Nanda, home
    minister ... 206
Narasimha Rao,
    P.V. ... 71, 177
Narayan, J.P. ... 80
  in Bangladesh
    intervention
    (1971) ... 80
National Defence
    College ... 158
National security
    advisor ... 202
National Security Council
    (NSC) ... 212
  and the Office ... 212
National Security Study
    Memoranda
    (NSSM) ... 130
Naval Intelligence,
    Directorate of
    (DNI) ... 145
Navy, United States ... 3
Nehru, B.K. ... 83, 195

Nehru, Jawaharlal ... 3, 19, 32, 34, 47, 56, 66-67, 74, 76-78, 80, 82-83, 102, 116, 120-123, 128, 161, 165, 171, 174, 185-189, 192, 193, 195-197, 199, 203, 207
  administrative drive of ... 199
  advisors to ... 192
  and "old men" ... 189
  and caste influence ... 197
  and contact with secretaries ... 128
  and division structure ... 102
  and Dr. Syed Mahmud ... 74
  and drafting duties ... 187
  and early Historical Division ... 121
  and family ... 67
  and family appointments ... 196
  and foreign policy administration ... 66
  and foreign portfolio ... 67, 203
  and Historical Division ... 122
  and Indira Gandhi ... 80
  and Mahatma Gandhi ... 185
  and operations ... 188
  and overseas communities ... 174
  and perceived Muslim officer allegiance ... 32
  and portfolio control ... 187
  and realpolitik ... 161
  and research bodies ... 120
  and secretaries of MEA ... 78
  and secretary-general ... 78
  and senior officers ... 189
  and subordinates ... 187
  and survival of British influence ... 34
  and the junior minister ... 76
  and the role of women in bureaucracy ... 56
  and United Nations ... 165
  and 1956-58 crisis period ... 83
  as administrator ... 186
  decline of ... 193
  external publicity under ... 171
  foreign policy administration of ... 67
  intuition and personnel selection ... 197
  pattern of preference for subordinates ... 195
  policy-monopolization of ... 19, 47, 116
  research and analysis priorities of ... 123
  staffing pluralism of ... 207
Nehru, R.K. ... 46, 78, 83, 195, 202
  and dispute with N.R. Pillai ... 202
Neo-reductionism ... 2
Nepal ... 16, 23, 25, 95, 138
  Centre for the Study of ... 138
  unit of Eastern Division ... 95
Nepotism ... 196
Non-aligned Conference (1983) ... 182
North (N) Division ... 102
North-East Frontier Agency (NEFA) ... 10
North-South international relations ... 154
  and Economic Division ... 154

North-West Frontier
   Province
   (NWFP) ... 10, 25

Office of the Prime
   Minister
   (Office) ... 112, 118,
   132, 204, 209, 211
 and interdepartmental
   groups ... 211
 and MEA ... 211
 and the MEA ... 211
 creation of ... 209
 radicalism of ... 209
 structure of ... 211
 triphasal evolution
   of ... 211
Openness,
   bureaucratic ... 214
 under Janata ... 214
Operations
   research ... 111
Opposition, the ... 211
Organization and Method (O
   and M) Section ... 111
Organization,
   international ... 114
Organizational sublevel-
   of-analysis ... 44
Organizations,
   international ... 27
 and the power of the
   foreign
   secretary ... 27
Outer Space Treaty, United
   Nations ... 115
Overage
   recruitment ... 47,
   57-58
Overseas Communication
   Service (OCS) ... 173
Overseas Indian
   communities ... 174,
   183-184, 217
 and external
   publicity ... 174
 in Middle East ... 184
 Janata policy
   toward ... 217
Overseas Indians
   Cell ... 133
Oxford University ... 45
 and seed cadre ... 45

PakIraf Division ... 85,
   90
Pakistan ... 32, 69-70,
   80, 86
 ambassador to ... 86
 as policy-area ... 69
 war with (1965) ... 70
 war with (1971) ... 80
Pakistan Division ... 91
Palam International
   Airport ... 182
Pandit,
   Vijayalakshmi ... 32,
   67, 165, 192, 195,
   202-203
 and foreign
   ministership ... 203
 and foreign
   portfolio ... 67
Panikkar, Sardar Kavalani
   Madhava ... 47,
   192-193
Paris Conference
   (1976) ... 154
Paris peace
   conference ... 163
Parliament ... 76, 172,
   175
 Consultative
   Committees ... 172
Parthasarathi, G. ... 118,
   125, 132, 210
 background and policy
   role ... 210
Partition of
   India ... 32-33
 and Mountbatten ... 33
Passport and Emigration
   Division ... 182
Passport officer,
   chief ... 183
Passport, Emigration and
   Consular (PVC)
   Division ... 133
Patel, Sardar Vallabhbhai
   Jhaverbhai ... 32
Pathiala House ... 102
Patnaik, Biju ... 159
Permanent representative
   (PR) to UN ... 164,
   210
 G. Parthasarathi
   as ... 210

Persian Gulf states ... 89
  relations with ... 89
Personnel and Administrative Reforms, Department of ... 51, 111
Pillai Committee ... 112
Pillai, N.R. ... 46, 83-84, 112, 202-203
  and undercutting by Krishna Menon ... 203
Pillai, Sanjivi ... 141
Pitt's India Act ... 15
Planning and Coordination Staff (S/PC) ... 117, 128
Planning minister ... 132
Pluralism ... 115, 126
  and Shastri ... 126
Policy ... 1-2, 18-19, 24, 66, 72, 80, 175, 191, 194, 210
  advisory triangle of Parthasarathi, Haksar and Kaul ... 210
  agreed ... 18
  and foreign minister ... 72
  and the Indian public ... 175
  foreign ... 2
  foreign policy as political symbol ... 80, 194
  formulation of ... 18
  formulation/implementation distinction ... 66
  interpretation of ... 191
  liberalization, and organizational process ... 24
  monopoly ... 19
  role of secretary in formulation of ... 80
  static approach ... 2
Policy Assessment and Review Staff ... 134
Policy influence of ... 82

Policy planning ... 138
  academic debate surrounding ... 138
Policy Planning and Review Committee (PPRC) ... 125, 127-128, 131-132, 214
  and D.P. Dhar ... 131
  and Janata ... 214
  and PPRD ... 128
  structure of ... 128
  termination of ... 132
Policy Planning and Review Division (PPRD) ... 89, 102, 117, 125-126, 129-132, 134, 136, 140, 209
  and diplomatic communications ... 129
  and information ... 136
  and merger with Historical Division ... 134
  and the cabinet secretariat (Cab Sec) ... 209
  as career assist ... 132
  creation of ... 126
  growth in influence of ... 129
  modern prominence of research within ... 132
  peak of influence ... 131
  structure of ... 134
  suggestions for the improvement of ... 130
  weaknesses of ... 125
Policy planning process ... 125
  weaknesses of ... 125
Political ... 10, 13, 17, 22, 27
  and distinction from foreign ... 22
  as distinct from foreign ... 27
  definition of ... 17
  relations ... 13
Political Affairs Committee ... 162

Political agent ... 36
  as Indian
    national ... 36
Political agent,
  the ... 36
Political
  Department ... 28
Political involvement in
  bureaucracy ... 214-215
Political secretary ... 25
Political-military
  policy ... 47, 54, 80,
    85, 145, 158, 160-162
  and MEA ... 162
  and realpolitik ... 161
  dichotomy ... 47
  prescribed permanent
    bureau for ... 161
  prescription for a
    bureau to
    formulate ... 160
  role of
    secretaries ... 80
  training ... 54
Politico-Military Affairs,
  Bureau of ... 158
Portfolio system ... 18
  beginnings of ... 18
  of Lord Canning ... 18
Portfolio, foreign ... 67
Portfolios and
  Nehru ... 187
Prasad, Nirmala ... 214
Press Relations
  section ... 168
Press Trust of India
  (PTI) ... 173
Press, British, and
  British Indian
  administration ... 14
Prime minister ... 66, 78,
  209, 212
  and secretary-
    general ... 78
  augmentation of power
    of ... 212
  principal private
    secretary (PMPPS)
    to ... 209

Prime Minister's
  Secretariat
  (PMS) ... 206-207, 209
  and economic
    policy ... 206, 209
  and ICS
    influence ... 206
  and Indira
    Gandhi ... 209
  growth of ... 207, 209
  original
    proposal ... 206
Private assistant
  (P.A.) ... 116
Promotion ... 58, 151, 190
  and MEA-RAW competition
    within
    missions ... 151
  and Nehru ... 190
  and the Foreign Service
    Board ... 58
Propaganda ... 26, 80,
  167, 171
  in Bangladesh
    intervention
    (1971) ... 80
  of Department of
    External
    Affairs ... 26
Protest, institutionalized
  versus
  personalized ... 175
Protocol ... 100, 181
  and gifts ... 181
Protocol
  Division ... 181-182
  Ceremonial ... 181
  Facilities ... 181
  Hospitality ... 182
  manpower
    variance ... 182
  Privileges and
    Immunities ... 181
  structure of ... 182
Public
  Department ... 12-13,
  16
Public opinion
  surveys ... 122
Public relations
  officers ... 168

Public,
    international ... 171
    and external
        publicity ... 171
Punjab crisis ... 72
    and P.V. Narasimha
        Rao ... 72

Railways, in the
    perpetuation of
    British
    influence ... 31
Rajagopalachari, C. ... 66
Ram, Lala Shri ... 57
Ranks, structure of
    career ... 35
Rann of Kutch ... 70
Rao, V.K.R.V. ... 176
Rasgotre, M.K. ... 85, 211
Rashtriapati Bhavan ... 34
Recording and Indexing (R
    and I) Unit ... 110
Recruitment ... 32, 53,
    57, 59
    and academic
        requirements ... 53
    and societal
        prestige ... 59
    early problems of ... 32
Regional passport
    offices ... 184
Reorganization
    Unit ... 111

Representation,
    diplomatic ... 9, 13,
        35-37, 47, 51, 73,
        108, 111, 114, 153,
        156, 163, 174, 217
    and Economic
        Division ... 156
    and foreign policy
        community ... 114
    and ISI Wings ... 174
    and the embassy ... 13
    British Indian ... 9, 36
    change from British to
        Indian (1947) ... 37
    distribution of ... 217
    efficiency management in
        missions
        abroad ... 111
    growth in ... 47
    in the United
        States ... 73
    manpower strength
        of ... 108
    of economic
        ministries ... 153
    power of ... 13
    shift in manpower ... 51
    strength before
        1947 ... 35
    UN, in New York ... 163
Research and Analysis Wing
    (RAW) ... 131,
    147-149, 214, 216-217
    after Janata ... 149
    and employee
        strikes ... 149
    and Janata ... 214
    budget of ... 148
    post-Janata
        purges ... 217
    purge and downgrading of
        leadership ... 148
Research and Intelligence
    Section ... 122
Research and
    Reference ... 122
Research bodies ... 120
    ad hoc ... 120
Research Cadre ... 49-50,
    121, 130
    strength of ... 130
Research Cadre,
    Combined ... 138

Research officer ... 93, 125
Research Wing ... 134
Resignation ... 60
Resource shortfalls ... 94
Responsiveness ... 94
Revenue Department ... 12
Revenue Intelligence ... 147
Reviews, cadre ... 51
Rivalry,
　interservice ... 49
　horizontal rather than temporal ... 49
Roe, Sir Thomas ... 10

Sahib, Rao ... 209
Salaries ... 12, 17, 33, 38, 40, 48, 100
　of Public and Secret secretary ... 12
　scale of ... 48
　within the Indian Political Service ... 38
Sansad ... 76, 175
Sarkar, Chanchal ... 170
Sathe, Ram D. ... 37, 85, 118
Scheduled Castes-Scheduled Tribes (SCST) ... 55
　guidelines ... 55
　representation in MEA ... 55
School of International Studies ... 53, 138
Second secretary ... 93
Secondment (deputation) of officers ... 119
Secrecy ... 39
　and the Indianization process ... 39
Secret Department ... 12-13, 15
　branches of ... 15
　secretary to ... 12-13
Secret, definition of ... 17

Secretaries ... 80, 190, 202
　and relationship with Nehru ... 190
　as communicatively open ... 80
　in Bangladesh intervention (1971) ... 80
　weakness of (1950-55) ... 202
Secretary ... 12-13, 16-18, 27, 35, 48, 58, 63, 77, 81, 83, 85, 91, 102, 109, 128
　and prime minister ... 128
　as secondary path around cabinet ... 81
　comparison with joint secretary ... 91
　East ... 58
　growth of influence of ... 83
　in procedural hierarchy ... 63
　junior ... 81
　of Administrative Division ... 109
　of Secret, Political, Revenue and Judicial Departments ... 16
　of the Foreign Department ... 18
　of the Secret Department ... 12
　of the Secret, Political and Foreign Department ... 16
　power of ... 27
　salary of ... 48
　to External Affairs ... 35
　to the Foreign and Political Department ... 27
　West ... 58
Secretary (Commonwealth) ... 78
Secretary of Defense, United States ... 6
Secretary of state, American ... 72, 202

Secretary of state,
    British ... 17-18
    authority of ... 17
    bureau role of ... 18
Secretary(commonwealth) ... 8
Secretary(EA-I) ... 81
Secretary(EA-II) ... 81
Secretary(east) ... 81,
    165, 171
Secretary(economic
    relations) ... 155
Secretary(ED) ... 155
Secretary(special) ... 81,
    109, 163, 206
Secretary(west) ... 81
Secretary-general ... 75,
    77-79, 82-83, 109,
    116, 187, 203
    abolition of ... 78
    and community
        coordination ... 116
    and minister of
        state ... 75
    and suggestions to name
        him advisor ... 78
    creation of ... 78
    end of ... 83
    recommendations
        concerning revival
        of ... 79
Secretary, foreign ... 118
Section ... 94, 102
Section officer ... 93
Security of
    communications ... 110
Seed cadre ... 45-46
    cognitive structure
        of ... 45
    with international
        relations
        experience ... 46
Selection of
    personnel ... 33, 38
    and fears of impaired
        Muslim
        allegiance ... 33
    based upon linguistic
        skill ... 38
Sen Gupta, Arjun ... 211
Sen, T. ... 176
Senior ministers ... 66
Senior scale ... 48

Services, multiplicity
    of ... 48-49
Sethna, H.N. ... 208
Shankar, V. ... 209
Sharada Prashad,
    H.Y. ... 211
Sharma, Naurekha ... 181
Shastri Bhavan ... 102
Shastri, Lal
    Bahadur ... 4, 67, 78,
    112, 126, 190, 204,
    206
    and foreign policy
        administration ... 67
    and Nehru ... 190
    and Pillai
        Committee ... 112
    and policy
        planning ... 126
    and secretaries ... 78
    low valuation of foreign
        policy ... 206
    personalistic-
        institutional
        style ... 206
Shrivastava (of
    PMS) ... 206
Simla talks (1972) ... 131
Singh, Avtar ... 155
Singh, Charan ... 209
    and Office ... 209
Singh, Dinesh ... 69-70,
    73, 75, 118, 176
    and new left
        policy ... 70
    as deputy minister to
        Nehru ... 70
    as institutional foreign
        minister ... 69
Singh, L.P. ... 206
Singh, Natwar ... 85
Singh, S.K. ... 89
Single-country
    divisions ... 93

Sino-Indian border
    conflict
    (1962) ... 34, 74, 85,
    121, 123, 144-145,
    159, 188, 195
  and end of Historical
    Division's research
    dominance ... 123
  and Historical
    Division ... 121
  and intelligence
    community ... 144
  and Lakshmi N. Menon as
    minister of
    state ... 74
  and MEA ... 159
Socialization
    process ... 55-56, 84
  and cognitive
    structure ... 56
  and families ... 56
Soni, U.C. ... 117
South (S) Division ... 102
South African high
    commission ... 35
South Block ... 34, 102
South-South international
    policy ... 218
  and manpower shift in
    missions
    abroad ... 218
South-South international
    relations ... 155
  and Economic
    Division ... 155
Soviet Union ... 14, 115
  administration of ... 14
  treaties with ... 115
Space, Department
    of ... 115
Special assistant
    secretary ... 23
Special Bureaux ... 149
Special Frontier
    Force ... 149
Special Selection Board,
    of the Federal Public
    Service Commission
    (FPSC) ... 57
Specialist officers ... 35

Specialization ... 172,
    205
  and staffs ... 205
  in external
    publicity ... 172
Spokesman,
    government ... 116
Sri Lanka ... 188
  prime minister and
    foreign
    policy ... 188
Staffs ... 116-117, 135,
    205, 207, 212
  American development
    of ... 212
  in the United
    States ... 207
  need for
    coordinative ... 117
  role of ... 116
  versus line
    bureaucrats ... 207
Stalin, Josef ... 199
State government ... 115
State, Department
    of ... 73, 92
States, Indian ... 10,
    15-16, 36
  British representation
    to ... 36
  international relations
    of ... 16
Static models ... 44
Structuralism ... 6
Style, political and
    administrative ... 186
Sub-methodologies ... 2
  bureaucratic ... 2
Sub-secretary ... 12-13,
    16
Subordinate
    office ... 101-102
Suez crisis ... 83, 192,
    203
  and Krishna
    Menon ... 192, 203
Suntook, N.F. ... 214
Superintendent ... 35
Swaran Singh,
    Sardar ... 67-68, 70
  policy influence
    of ... 68

Symbols, use of
  political ... 34
Syndicate ... 131
Syndicate and M.C.
  Chagla ... 69

Technology ... 13-14, 20,
  115, 172
  and XP Division ... 172
  influence of ... 13-14,
  20
  nuclear ... 115
Teheran, envoy to
  (1798) ... 15, 36
Teja, J.S. ... 89, 116,
  133, 140
Telegraphy ... 173
Territorial
  divisions ... 92, 95,
  117, 122, 153-154,
  156, 182, 218
  and bilateral economic
  policy/relations ... 56
  and Historical
  Division ... 122
  and international
  economic
  policy ... 153-154
  and protocol ... 182
  opposition to mission
  manpower
  shift ... 218
  reorganization of ... 95
Territories, non-
  regulation ... 21
  to the United
  States ... 82
Toshakkhana ... 110
Trade relations ... 158
Training ... 52-54
  administration of ... 54
  and Bharat
  Dharshan ... 54
  and language
  skill ... 53
  critiques of ... 54
  Directorate of ... 54
  Gandhian
  influences ... 54
  in the U.S., Great
  Britain ... 53
  on-the-job ... 54

Transfer, of
  personnel ... 23
Transition, from British
  to Indian
  control ... 30-32
Transmissions ... 173
Travancore, Raja of ... 10
Treaties ... 10
Tribals ... 15, 26, 35
  administration of ... 35
Trivedi, V.C. ... 81

Under-secretary ... 35,
  51, 63, 93
  and the IFS(B) ... 51
Undersea cable ... 13, 20
  Red Sea ... 20
Union Public Service
  Commission
  (UPSC) ... 55, 57
United Nations
  (UN) ... 81, 84,
  163-165, 203
  and MEA ... 81
  and MEA budgetary
  support ... 165
  Economic Committee
  of ... 164
  Indian conception of
  diplomacy within
  the ... 164
  Korea commission
  of ... 84
  policy and Krishna
  Menon ... 203
  Security Council and
  committees ... 163
United Nations (UN)
  Division ... 158
United Nations and
  Conference (UN)
  Division ... 93, 95,
  163-165
  and IFS ... 164
  structure of ... 165
United Nations mission
  (New York) ... 174
  and ISI Wings ... 174
United News of India
  (UNI) ... 173
United States foreign
  service ... 55
  minorities in ... 55

Urs, Devraj ... 214

Vajpayee, A.B. ... 71, 73, 85, 171, 174, 177, 213, 216-217
  and Indian overseas communities ... 217
  and Morarji Desai ... 216
Vellodi, defence minister ... 3
Verghese, George ... 211
Verma, S.P. ... 141
Vienna Convention ... 181, 188
Vietnam ... 158
  U.S. involvement in ... 158
Vigilance Unit ... 111
Vira, Dharam ... 204

Washington embassy ... 171
Welfare Unit ... 110
West Asia and North Africa (WANA) Division ... 81, 102
Western Division ... 120
Westphalia, treaty of ... 62
Whitehall ... 14
Women, role of ... 56
Work Study Unit ... 111
Work, pattern of ... 94
World Press Review ... 172

Xenophilia, Indian ... 194

Zachariah, director(HD) ... 121
Zafrullah Khan ... 84

Augsburg College
George Sverdrup Library
Minneapolis, MN 55454